CRASH!
From Senna To Earnhardt
How the *hans* Helped Save Racing

BY **Jonathan Ingram**
WITH **Dr. Robert Hubbard** AND **Jim Downing**

For Bob Hubbard
(1943–2019)

CRASH! is published by:
RJP Books
Atlanta, GA
USA

Copyright © RJP Books and Jonathan Ingram 2019

No part of this publication may be reproduced, stored in a retrieval system or transmitted, in any form or by any means, electronic, mechanical, photocopying, recording or otherwise, without prior permission in writing from RJP Books and Jonathan Ingram.

ISBN: 978-1-7923-1299-1

Printed and bound in the UK by:
Gomer Press Ltd
Llandysul Enterprise Park
Llandysul, Ceredigion
Wales, SA44 4JL
www.gomerprinting.co.uk

Design and production by:
Damion Chew Design Ltd
Tel: +44 (0)1723 871500
Email: info@damionchewdesign.com
www.damionchewdesign.com

Front cover photography: Gary Milgrom

hans
hans
EXHIBITOR
Jim Downing
HANS PERFORMANCE
PRODUCTS
Atlanta GA
Exhibitor
hans
hans

Contents

	Foreword	viii
1	The Intimidator	1
2	Downing's Awakening	4
3	The Family Connection	12
4	Creating the Device	17
5	Building the HANS	25
6	Fame, Wealth, Tragedy	31
7	The Fire Next Time	42
8	Death of Senna	50
9	Safety Gone Awry	54
10	The Black Sport	59
11	Hubert and HANS	63
12	German Engineering	69
13	CART's Black Autumn	76
14	Crucible of Opportunity	82
15	'Testy' Testing Brings First Mandate	87
16	World's Fastest Track Slow	93
17	Deadly Year 2000	99
18	Idling at Daytona	105
19	Earnhardt and HANS	109
20	The Fateful 500	114
21	Earnhardt Was Racing	120
22	No. 3 Car Investigation	126
23	NASCAR Mandates HANS	134
24	SAFER Barrier Arrives	139
25	F1 Mandates HANS	143
26	Weekend Warriors: Living Dangerously	152
27	HANS Performance Products	161
28	Saving the Day	169
	Awards	171
	Acknowledgements	172
	Bibliography	173
	Scientific Papers	174
	Index	175
	HANS Safety Timeline	180

Crash! How the HANS Helped Save Racing

Foreword

DID AUTO RACING'S FIRST HEAD AND NECK restraint, the HANS Device, save an entire sport?

The short answer is no. When auto racing's major series undertook a safety revolution at the turn of the 21st Century, hundreds of technical experts, race team members and sanctioning body professionals helped make the unprecedented movement a success. Yet, there was a critical distinction to the HANS reminiscent of an ancient rhyme. For want of a nail a kingdom might have been lost.

Between 1994 and 2001, the world's major series—Formula 1, the Indy Racing League (IRL), Championship Auto Racing Teams (CART), and NASCAR—had to confront a safety crisis resulting from a sudden jump in the number of driver fatalities. The crisis began with the stunning death of three-time World Champion Ayrton Senna in 1994 and reached another major turning point with the death of seven-time NASCAR champion Dale Earnhardt in 2001. In between, Indy 500 pole winner Scott Brayton and rising CART superstar Greg Moore were killed in Indy-type cars. In total, nine drivers lost their lives in these major series during this seven-year span.

The cause behind the sudden rise in fatalities was the same in all series. Higher cornering speeds greatly increased the chances of a crash with enough G-force to overwhelm the existing standards of safety for cars, cockpits, driver equipment, and barriers. Suddenly, some of the world's best drivers, competing for the finest teams, were being killed in crashes.

These crashes often appeared on live television, the cornucopia of financial clout that threatened to become the source of motor racing's demise if the deaths continued. Could the sport thrive if its heroes were being killed behind the wheel as millions of viewers looked on?

The safety crisis shook each of the major sanctioning bodies to their very foundation. The specter of ongoing fatalities threatened to unravel crucial business relationships with manufacturers, sponsors and media partners. Unwelcome external intervention from governments was a serious concern for race organizers as well. It had happened before. American manufacturers pulled out of racing in the early 1970s due to pressure from the U.S. Congress about the lack of safety in highway cars. Switzerland outlawed auto racing in 1955 after the tragedy at Le Mans.

The major sanctioning bodies responded to the crisis with an array of safety initiatives. Regardless of series or the type of car, it became obvious that any safety improvements had to address the problem of basal skull fractures. Absent the HANS Device—

designed to prevent this usually fatal injury—the safety revolution might have failed.

Dale Earnhardt's fatal meeting with the wall at the Daytona International Speedway in 2001 became the final turning point for acceptance of the HANS Device. His death launched much controversy and there was no shortage of mystery concerning an incident watched by an estimated 17 million viewers. But an analysis of all the available facts confirms that a HANS Device would have saved his life.

Once the HANS was mandated by the major sanctioning bodies, a rising tide of basal skull fractures came to an end. Of the nine deaths in the major series starting with Roland Ratzenberger, killed at Imola the day before Senna, seven resulted from basal skull fractures. "If you set out to solve a problem and the problem disappears," said HANS inventor Dr. Robert Hubbard, "then you have succeeded in reaching your goal."

It was a long, complicated process for Hubbard and his business partner, Jim Downing, to gain acceptance for their device. Without their perseverance, head and neck restraints would not have played a crucial role in a new generation of auto racing safety.

Crash! tells the back story of Hubbard, Downing and racing's first head and neck restraint, a tale that provides an insider view of the safety revolution that helped auto racing embrace a new century. Unlimited access to these two gentlemen, plus many other key participants in the safety revolution who contributed their time and expertise, greatly enhanced the book's detail and scope.

The author also owes a great debt to *On Track* and *Autosport* magazines for the facts, figures and real time quotes provided by their detailed coverage of auto racing. In addition, I drew from my own experience over a period of 30 years as a contributor to those two magazines as well as other publications where my stories appeared such as *Autoweek* and *Sports Illustrated*.

It was my goal to remember with respect and admiration those who died when safety—and let's face it, driver judgement—did not account for possibilities that turned out to be deadly.

The book is dedicated to the courage and that special quality in all race car drivers that enable them to challenge the laws of physics in extraordinary ways, bringing satisfaction and joy to fans as well as the participants themselves.

Jonathan Ingram
July, 2019
www.jingrambooks.com

1

The Intimidator

IT TAKES SOME LOOKING TO FIND THE statue of Dale Earnhardt at the Daytona International Speedway. Standing in front of administrative buildings, it's far off the main pathways leading to the massive array of grandstands.

For a man who made his mark in the thundering cauldron of stock car racing, by location and composition the memorial is deceptively quiet. Reminiscent of the works by the great sculptor Rodin, the bronze Earnhardt holds the massive Harley Earl trophy with one arm and the other has a fist raised high in the air, celebrating after a long-sought win in the Daytona 500 in 1998. The eyes slyly smiling above a wide grin and bristly mustache aren't directed toward the sky or the horizon in a typical winner's pose. An all-seeing gaze looks where his fans would be, taking them in as much as they might be looking up at him, all reveling in the moment of triumph.

That was Earnhardt, a big man who stood out but appreciated his fans as much as they admired his unalloyed commitment to prevailing against the odds. For all of Earnhardt's outsized image as "The Intimidator" and his wealth minted from success and fame, he retained his roots. He understood the physically and psychologically demanding work behind the wheel symbolized the struggles faced by stock car racing fans, most of them work-a-day Americans, the same as Earnhardt's family. He also understood the sport he loved had always needed champions willing to help grow its popularity by being accessible.

What brings the statue to life is the tension created by the one arm cradling the heavy trophy to his side and the other lifted in exultation high above his head. The stance has his upper body, shoulders and neck slightly bowed—Rodin-like—as if to exemplify the strength and combative persistence needed by a 20th Century racing hero, standing his ground, testing himself against the resistance, propelled by an almost super-human inner drive to rise to the challenges posed by the sport and its inherent risks.

There is a universal humbleness to the slightly stooped posture, which is also a reminder of the sad ending. The odds finally won at the Daytona 500 in 2001, when a typically aggressive Earnhardt was killed on the final lap by what seemed to be an uneventful meeting with the wall during a battle for third place. A few degrees in either direction in the angle of impact and the No. 3 car's inertia would have been absorbed by an ongoing series of spins instead of one deadly thud at 160 mph.

As the statue testifies, due to the tragic and sensational nature of his demise, Earnhardt will remain transcendent in the sport of stock car racing. But just as significantly, the legacy from Earnhardt's death is better racing safety. When it comes to the physical risks of a dangerous sport, his death changed the odds dramatically.

The man who so often dared to cheat destiny and dared his fellow competitors to do likewise stands forever at the intersection of two racing worlds. What followed Earnhardt's death was an unprecedented safety initiative by sanctioning body NASCAR. In the ten

The Intimidator

DALE EARNHARDT The bronze version at Daytona helps keep him alloyed to his fans.
(Photo by Chuck Kleinschmidt)

years before Earnhardt's death, six drivers had been killed in NASCAR's three major series. In the 18 years since his car hit the Turn 3 wall at Daytona, no driver had been killed or critically injured in these series due to the safety initiatives undertaken as a result of the sport's greatest star dying behind the wheel.

One of NASCAR's key safety initiatives was becoming the first major series in the world to mandate head restraints for all races in its premier series. As a result, NASCAR drivers subsequently walked away from high-speed crashes similar to the one that claimed the life of Earnhardt, who died from a basal skull fracture injury that the HANS was designed to prevent.

Beyond NASCAR, Earnhardt's death inspired many other race car drivers to begin using the HANS and NASCAR's initiative led to other sanctioning bodies mandating the device.

Nobody in motor racing became more familiar with Earnhardt's twin legacy than Jim Downing, the man who quietly started a revolution in safety 20 years before Earnhardt died. After one of his fellow drivers was killed by a basal skull fracture in 1981, Downing asked a significant question—why can't something be done about crippling or fatal head injuries in motor racing? Robert Hubbard, Ph.D., an accomplished professor of biomechanical engineering who got to know Downing as a result of marrying his sister and later buying a Porsche 911 from him, eventually answered that question by creating motor racing's first head and neck restraint.

Earnhardt certainly had a chance to consider using the HANS Device which, in the opinion of racing safety experts, would have saved his life. But this was the same driver who had resisted full-face helmets while riding in an idiosyncratic and slightly reclined position, helmeted head cocked low to the left. The sightlines enabled him to get a unique view of the all-important left front of the car while cornering on ovals. His open-face helmet allowed Earnhardt to "feel the air" of the high-speed drafts—where he enjoyed an almost god-like status for his ability to maneuver. The full-face helmets were safer and used by 95 percent of the drivers, but Earnhardt wasn't about to change a winning combination.

The seven-time champion made his reputation in part by walking away from big crashes. In the 1997 Daytona 500, for one of many examples, Earnhardt's black Chevy had ended up on its roof due to an aggressive effort to block Jeff Gordon during the closing laps. The black No. 3 slid down the back straight in a fiery sea of red sparks. The driver emerged unrepentant and went on to win the 500 the following year. "Was I scared?" he said. "No, I ain't never been scared in a race car."

The year before, a multi-car crash at Talladega, where straight-line speeds were even faster than Daytona, left Earnhardt with a snapped collar bone and a fractured sternum. Before getting any treatment, he had the ambulance driver stop at his Richard Childress Racing team's pits so he could tell his crew he was OK. Two weeks later, Earnhardt won the pole at the Watkins Glen, N.Y., road circuit and nearly won the race despite his painful injuries.

It was the stuff of a Bunyan-esque legend—except

all so real and there for the fans to witness and appraise. Half the fans hated and booed the supremely talented Earnhardt, because of the braggadocio of his nickname and what was perceived as deliberate efforts to wreck other drivers. T-shirts reading "Anybody but Earnhardt" abounded. The other half of the crowds stood and roared their approval, gloating with arms uplifted any time the man in black came out on top.

Earnhardt wasn't averse to safety. As the owner of the Dale Earnhardt Inc. team, he had private discussions with NASCAR's Gary Nelson, the director of the Winston Cup Series, about how to improve the safety of cars. Through Nelson, he followed progress on the so-called "soft walls" under development at the University of Nebraska in a joint venture with the Indianapolis Motor Speedway. He had once flown to the GM Motorsports headquarters from North Carolina in his private plane to look at a new seat under development and considered to be safer before declining to use it. Earnhardt had suggested painting the yellow "out of bounds" line between the apron and racing surface of the tracks at Daytona and Talladega to improve both competition and safety, a rule that eventually became integral to the running of the races at those two high-speed tracks.

Only Earnhardt knew if his response to the HANS resulted from a desire to retain a competitive advantage—like the open-face helmet. Maybe he considered an element of danger to be in his favor. Perhaps he simply didn't believe in the strange-looking device with its high collar and yoke, a response received from many star drivers around the world by Downing and Hubbard. It's possible he thought this unfamiliar device in the cockpit might create injuries in a crash. Long before the 2001 Daytona 500, it was clear that Earnhardt would not be wearing the HANS Device on board the black No. 3, a decision that would cost him his life—and help save hundreds of others.

In the week after Earnhardt's death, HANS Performance Products took more orders for its safety device than in the previous 10 years.

2

Downing's Awakening

A FIVE-TIME ROAD RACING CHAMPION, JIM Downing first met Dale Earnhardt in the NASCAR hauler at the Indianapolis Motor Speedway in 2000, where he was talking about the HANS Device to a longtime acquaintance, Mike Helton, soon to be named the NASCAR president.

After the deaths of Adam Petty and Kenny Irwin from basal skull fractures earlier that year during two separate NASCAR events at the New Hampshire International Speedway, Helton was very interested in talking with Downing about motor racing's first head and neck restraint. Since NASCAR closely controlled all aspects of its racing series, any safety device used by drivers had to have the sanctioning body's approval.

Downing had met the future NASCAR president in the early 1980s while building Mazda RX-7 pace cars at his Downing/Atlanta race shop for the Atlanta International Raceway, where Helton was the general manager and in charge of securing the cars to fulfill a sponsorship deal financed by Mazda. Not long after that deal with Downing, Helton left his post at the Atlanta track to take a similar job at the giant oval in Talladega, Alabama, before moving to Daytona Beach as an employee at NASCAR's Florida headquarters. Tall and broad with imposing eyes beneath a thick mane of dark hair, Helton had gradually worked his way up the NASCAR hierarchy.

"I knew Jim Downing from his racing days when he was the Mazda driver, when he was up in the wine country of Georgia and I was down in the moonshine country," recalled Helton. "I knew Jim Downing as a racer. Atlanta Raceway had a deal one year with Mazda. We had Mazda RX-7 pace cars and they were souped-up by Downing. Bob Hubbard came along with that process of knowing Jim and in that time (after the driver deaths) we were getting more aggressive in talking with folks like that."

Earnhardt wanted nothing to do with the HANS Device at the Indy test. "Dale came through the door of the NASCAR hauler, just walked right in while I was talking to Mike about the HANS," said Downing of his first meeting with the driver known as "The Intimidator." "They had a little desk in there and he threw his leg over the corner of it and kind of sat down. He looked at us with that bristly mustache and a grin as if to say, 'What are you guys talking about?' The message was pretty clear he didn't want to have anything to do with the HANS and didn't want Mike listening to what I had to say. Earnhardt sitting there pretty much brought the discussion with Mike to an end."

Twenty years prior to meeting Earnhardt, Downing's own experience with a head injury resulted in a fortunate outcome—given the dangerous nature of his crash on a track in Canada in 1980. On a sweltering August day at the Mosport Park track near Toronto, Downing was sweating profusely while competing in the Molson 1000. On board a Mazda RX-7 entered by the Racing Beat factory team, the tall, slender Downing was running first in the GTU class with the other Racing Beat Mazda immediately behind him in second place. Its driver, John Morton, was looking for a way past.

The HANS quest for Downing, here at Road Atlanta in 1989, was a solitary endeavor for many years. (Photo by David Allio)

The 10-turn Mosport track undulates around glacially carved hills. Because of the almost non-stop high speeds, it's a thrilling place to watch drivers race. On this summer day, fans, many of them camping overnight in tents on the various overlooks, had come out to see the World Championship of Makes race sanctioned by the Fédération Internationale de l'Automobile (FIA). The race also paid points for the International Motor Sports Association (IMSA). The entry list featured some of the world's best sports cars and drivers.

This included numerous Porsche 935 Turbos, relatively crude silhouette cars. These ill-handling tube-frame machines were wicked fast due to turbocharged engines producing gobs of torque that hit the drive train like a thunderstorm. They were driven by sports car stars such as Brian Redman and John Fitzpatrick and by moonlighting Indy car drivers Rick Mears, Danny Ongais and Johnny Rutherford. Twenty-year-old future star John Paul, Jr. was another of those behind the wheel of the Porsches. The fearless and fast German, Walter Rohrl, co-drove a Lancia Turbo in search of FIA points, and renowned team owner Bob Tullius of Group 44 competed in a Triumph TR-8 for British Leyland.

In IMSA's standard endurance racing formula, the GTU class for cars with smaller engines consisted of Mazdas, Datsun 240Z's and Porsche 911 Carreras. While they relied more on momentum and less on horsepower, the GTUs were scary to drive at Mosport, too, because of their nimble cornering speeds—and the constant swarm of faster Porsche Turbos.

The winners on this day—Fitzpatrick and Redman—would average 100.354 mph during the 1,000 kilometers, including pit stops for driver exchanges and a trip on each lap through the second gear Moss Curve. The track's many high-gear corners helped sustain speeds, but could have their price. The circuit was already infamous for the number of fatal accidents due to literally wide-open corners when it came to the layout of the asphalt. There was little to prevent a driver from collecting the nearby barriers in a high-speed departure from the track.

Situated in the relatively isolated, thickly wooded expanses north of Lake Ontario, the track was about 30 miles east of the last, dwindling outskirts of Toronto's sprawl. The location was a testimony to the old joke about Canada having too much geography. As Redman had once learned after a crash in Canada when the ambulance carrying him blew a tire—it was a long way to the nearest hospital.

During this particular summer, the heat and humidity were not unusual for August. But to find more speed,

Downing's Awakening

the engineer at the Racing Beat factory team had closed off most of the airflow into the cockpit. Downing had worked his way into the graces of Mazda's racing management due to his quickness, reliability and a low-key confidence that fit in well with the Japanese. He intended to sustain his career momentum and decided not to protest the lack of air coming through the cockpit.

Already a championship contender aboard Mazda RX-3s in the RS series of IMSA for compact cars running on radial street tires, he was looking to advance to the big leagues of American sports car racing and into the GTU category where Mazda was a major player. But he lost so much perspiration during the race's first hour in the muggy cockpit that he passed out behind the wheel while heading into Turn Two—a fast, sweeping, left-hand corner.

For the first and only time in his career, the crash briefly knocked Downing unconscious. Events became fuzzy as he was taken to the track medical center. It was like a dream—tumult and noise all around him, but everything distant and one step removed, the roar of the cars on the nearby track now a distant hum. The memory lingered after an overnight stay in the hospital.

"I just got lucky and the car turned backwards," recalled Downing. "It was a concrete wall with a hill behind it. The impact cracked and broke the wall. The car was so bad, they left it in Canada after stripping a few pieces off of it."

Downing realized a head-on crash could have been deadly. (Five years later, Manfred Winkelhock was killed by a head-on meeting with the wall in Turn 2 on board a Porsche 962C during a World Endurance Championship race.)

Downing began to think about the number of head and neck injuries happening in racing at the time. Like so many racers, he shrugged off his crash as part of the business. Then the following spring, Downing learned that a frontal impact by fellow GTU racer Patrick Jacquemart at the end of the back straight of the Mid-Ohio Sports Car Course during a test was indeed fatal. The cause of death was a basal skull fracture.

Slight in build and relatively tall, Frenchman Jacquemart was not imposing physically, but he was very engaging and had a broad, white-toothed smile. Passionate and good-humored, Jacquemart worked as the manager of competition at Renault USA in the four years prior to his death. An executive at Renault, he earned his fellow drivers' respect by carefully crafting a racing career while promoting his company's brand. He was a clean driver who steadily indexed himself up to the next level, starting with club racing and then the IMSA RS series. The crash that claimed his life might have happened to any driver who ran into an unexpected technical problem like brake failure, resulting in a head-on collision with a barrier.

"He was smart to figure out how to get that Renault Le Car to run well in a pretty competitive series," said Downing. "At one time, I looked up his finishing positions. He worked himself up. That's what a good guy does. He figures out what it takes and then does it."

At the time of the Mid-Ohio crash, Jacquemart was testing in preparation for a move by Renault into the GTU class with a turbocharged Le Car. "He didn't have any of the attitude that Americans think the French have," said Downing. "We weren't bosom buddies. He was just a friendly guy. You felt like when you met him, he was a friend. I think that's why there were so many people at his funeral."

Funerals were part of the racing landscape in the 1980s as were head injuries that left drivers temporarily on the sidelines, crippled or, in a fate worse than death, laying in nursing homes in persistent vegetative states before gradually succumbing.

Downing's first reaction to his own near miss typified the ambitious racer's point of view, whether it was Formula 1, Indy cars, sports cars, stock cars or rallying. 'It won't happen to me again,' he thought. But when Jacquemart's crash occurred, the realization sunk in with Downing that it might have been his funeral. He then asked himself once again: 'Why can't something be done about head injuries?'

From his earliest interest in racing, Downing had considered safety a significant factor in racing. As a teenager too young to drive, in 1957 he took a bus from his home town of Atlanta to Indianapolis to see the Indy 500, where Sam Hanks was the winner. He had already raced in the Soap Box Derby and been to the Sebring 12-hour to see driving greats like Juan Manuel Fangio, Sterling Moss and future American F1 champion Phil Hill. He was anxious to go racing himself.

But the young Downing was slightly nonplused with the Indy cars—so much speed, yet so near the walls. The fact the imperious and fast "Mad Russian" Bill Vukovich had been killed while seeking an unprecedented third straight victory at Indy in a violent multi-car crash during the 1955 race was still fresh in Downing's mind when he visited the famed oval.

Yet, there was never any doubt that he wanted to go racing from the time he first learned about it. "Everybody in racing has their early experience with the sport," said Downing. "Mine was listening to the radio when I was nine years old at my father's used car lot. The mechanics had the radio on, listening to the Indy 500. I was down there doing things a 9-year-old could do. I was putting black stuff on the tires so they'd look newer."

James C. Downing, his father, had put himself through college at the University of Kentucky during the latter days of the Depression by buying and selling cars, invariably swanky convertibles or imports. Tall and broad-shouldered, he stood out when he drove convertibles around the University of Wisconsin campus while pursuing a doctorate in business. It was at Wisconsin that he met Jean Jacobsen who later became his wife and the mother of James R. Downing, not a junior because his middle name was taken from his uncle Russell.

Leaving his pursuit of a doctorate behind, James C. Downing took a job at the U.S. Department of Agriculture, which eventually landed him in Atlanta, where he helped promote the planting of kudzu throughout the Southeast in support of the war effort in the early 1940s.

The kudzu project was a success in terms of getting farmers in the Southeast to accept the leafy plant for combating soil erosion and to provide fodder for cattle. Farmers were paid by the acre for planting kudzu. But when the boll weevil and cotton crop failures sent many family farmers looking for urban work in the 1950s, the unattended kudzu continued to grow unchecked and by 1970 the agriculture department had declared it a noxious weed.

By then, James C. Downing had changed careers. "When I was younger, we lived on Techwood Drive, catty-corner to Bobby Dodd Stadium on the Georgia Tech campus," said Downing. "My dad had a garage in the back where he could fix up cars and sell them from there. After a while, he realized he could make a better salary if he did that."

The Southeastern Sports Car Center, which sold all manner of new imports and mostly British sports cars, was eventually established on Atlanta's famous Peachtree Street. "The cars my father liked were interesting cars," said Downing. "They weren't Fords and Chevys, but Cords and Hudsons." Next door stood Downing Motors for used car sales, a three-story building that became famous to nearby Georgia Tech students for its exotic foreign cars that were rare in the South. Working in the basement with the mechanics for 50 cents an hour, Downing received a hands-on education about cars and the car business, eventually progressing to a sales position.

In the post-war years, Atlanta became a breeding ground for various kinds of racing—from drag racing and speed record attempts on the beach in Daytona to stock cars and road racing—a perfect location for a young man with his eye on competing behind the wheel.

The city was rife with bootleggers, who caterwauled down the mountain roads into Atlanta from the foothills of the Appalachians. In their spare time, they caterwauled around the city's 1.0-mile Lakewood Speedway or the quarter-mile Peach Bowl, a short track located in the city's old livestock yards. Starting in the 1930s, barnstorming Indy cars, followed soon by what

Downing's Awakening

became known as stock cars, raced around the city's reservoir at Lakewood. At the Peach Bowl's bullring, stock cars and the open-wheel quarter midgets, essentially small-sized Indy cars that came into vogue during the 1930s, drew regular weekly crowds.

The garages and the neighborhood around the Georgia Tech campus, cheek-by-jowl to the city's business district, were rife with bootleggers and their swaggering reputations. Engine builders like Gober Sosebee, a winning driver on the old Beach and Road Course at Daytona as well as short tracks around the Southeast, thrived while earning ready cash from bootleggers for installing aftermarket parts so their Fords, Chevys and Dodges were fast enough to outrun the Revenuers, who were shooting wads of buckshot. The ample pay for bootleggers attracted all manner of whiskey trippers to Atlanta such as the Flock brothers. Bob, Fonty and Tim Flock moved to Atlanta from Alabama to drive the whiskey cars of Peachtree Williams before they became famous for their NASCAR driving and antics. Fonty liked to wear "Bermooda" shorts during races and two-time NASCAR champion Tim briefly carried a monkey named Jocko Flocko in his car.

The city's biggest bootlegger, Raymond Parks, kept his cars at the garage of Red Vogt on Spring St., where the brilliant mechanic built the Olds that shrapnel-scarred war veteran Red Byron drove to NASCAR's first strictly stock championship in 1949, using a special clutch pedal for his injured leg. Vogt's garage, located not far from the Southeastern Sports Car Center, had two bays. He built bootlegger cars on

1995 Downing jumps into his Kudzu DG-3 at Le Mans, a race he won onboard a Kudzu LM the following year. (Photo courtesy of MazdaSpeed)

8   *Crash!* How the HANS Helped Save Racing

one side and the cars for the Revenuers who pursued the bootleggers on the other. "The whiskey cars were always faster," Vogt would say, "because the government cars had too many rules about what you could do to them." The bootleggers also paid large sums of cash.

Racing cars were a fact of life on the city streets in Atlanta. Bob Flock became famous for driving through the fence—which also doubled as a gate—at the Lakewood track to get away from an outstanding warrant after police had recognized him on the starting grid, despite a bandana covering his face, and chased him around the track. After busting through the fence, he then drove his Ford Modified race car through the streets of downtown to escape the motorcycle cops.

"I once drove a V-8 midget race car down Spring Street all the way out to the governor's mansion," said Downing. "You could do that in those days. You could effectively drive your race car on the street as long as you didn't do it stupidly. You didn't go to a race track to test. You went out in the streets to shake your car down."

Downing saw his first local sports car race on an airport circuit in nearby Gainesville, where races were held annually from 1957 to 1960. Because his father's dealership sold sports cars, tickets were readily available. "It had all the big sports cars of the day like the D-Type Jaguars," said Downing. "It's what pushed me to try to get a racing license. Actually, it was a little scary at that point. I was in high school and those cars were scary fast on skinny tires. It was a pretty exciting thing. You sat on the side of the hill and you were pretty close to the cars, safety not being what it is today. Hay bales were the only protection."

He started by competing in slaloms, which required only a driver's license, but had to wait until he turned 21 to get a racing license from the Sports Car Club of America (SCCA). By then, he was a student at Georgia Tech—where he could hear the engines calling like sirens from the nearby Peach Bowl while studying at night for an industrial management degree. He simultaneously operated a British car repair business in a shop adjacent to the campus. It became a *modus operandi* Downing would maintain throughout his racing career: running car and racing-related businesses to help sustain his pursuit of racing.

Downing bought his first race car for $200, a totaled Elva Courier which he tested on the streets of the Garden Hills neighborhood after rebuilding it over the course of 18 months. He took it to an SCCA driving school in Walterborough, S.C., near Columbia the same month he turned 21. "I borrowed a Chrysler Imperial that had a tow hitch on it and used an old nasty trailer to get over there to this small airport where they held the school. There was no interstate at the time. You had to go cross country. I would have gone around the world to go to my first driver's school."

From the beginning, Downing, who had played high school sports mostly out of peer pressure, recognized he had a knack for getting through the corners better than those around him. "My first race was the Chimney Rock Hill Climb, an SCCA Regional race. My second race was at Daytona and I placed third in my E-production Elva. I waited around to get my trophy and just never got one. They weren't giving out trophies and I didn't realize it for a while."

By the 1960s, a high-banked stock car superspeedway had been built on the south side of Atlanta, replacing the Lakewood track as the home of stock car racing. The one thing missing from the Atlanta racing scene was a bona fide road racing circuit. Downing and college friend Alan Wilcox bought land in the city's eastern outskirts and proceeded to build a circuit using not much more than a small bulldozer and their own noodling for a track layout. But another pair, Dave Sloyer and Earl Walker, beat them to it with help from Atlanta Coca-Cola Bottling Company executive Arthur Montgomery, opening Road Atlanta near Gainesville in the fall of 1970.

Downing's life revolved around racing and sustaining businesses that enabled him to keep pursuing it. His single-minded confidence in his own passion and vision would remain hallmarks of his daily approach to racing and business for five decades. Shortly after graduation

Downing's Awakening

from Georgia Tech, he and Wilcox created a machine shop behind a house Downing purchased on Standard Drive in Northeast Atlanta. It would become the home of Downing Racing and the shop from which Downing would win all five of his IMSA driving championships. Downing also ran a used car business called Autosport that specialized in sports cars.

One person who fit well into this circle of activity was Downing's brother-in-law Bob Hubbard, who had met Jim's sister JoAnn while in college at Duke. They were married in Atlanta on the same day in 1966 that Jim graduated from Georgia Tech.

Downing, who had three brothers, was close to his only sister, a year younger. "Once both of us were old enough to talk, we talked to each other all the time and never stopped," recalled JoAnn. "Jim helped me with my math and I helped him with his reading. He played string bass and I played violin. Summers, our family would go up to Wisconsin and stay there for a month. Part of the time they had a small cabin on the lake. Once Jim and I found a racing rowboat that was buried, dug it up, tarred it and built a sail boat with two sets of oars."

Hubbard, who majored in mechanical engineering, and Downing shared an interest in cars and road racing, which brought them closer than just brother-in-law status. "Jim and Bob grew up at the time cars were such a big deal to teenagers," said JoAnn, who had helped Jim paint the lettering on his Soap Box Derby entry. "The fifties and sixties were really a big deal for cars."

Downing and Hubbard often spent time together when Bob visited Atlanta. Hubbard enthusiastically joined the intense but informal dirt bike races Downing and Wilcox competed in on the rough-cut layout of their planned road racing circuit in the woods east of Atlanta. When Hubbard decided he wanted to buy a Porsche 911, he bought one from Downing's Autosport lot. Soon enough, they would have an opportunity to work together in a major new professional road racing series.

Just as the rising tide of interest in sports car racing had created Road Atlanta, a new professional racing series came to life in the early 1970s. The International Motor Sports Association was founded by former SCCA president John Bishop and NASCAR founder "Big Bill" France. It would replace the SCCA, where members were more interested in amateur events, as the premier sanctioning body for professional road racing in the U.S.

Established in 1969, IMSA soon gained a promotional budget from the R.J. Reynolds Tobacco Company, which title-sponsored the Camel GT. It featured sports cars that fit the same international rules specifications as those running in the FIA's international races and at the 24 Hours of Le Mans, the epicenter of sports car endurance racing. In 1974, a new entry level series for compacts created by Bishop featured cars racing on shaved street radials—which held down costs—and was promoted by the BF Goodrich tire company, which helped increase the purse money.

Before moving up to the GTU class, Downing owned every record in the RS series worth having—most victories, most poles and most money won. A driver could win as much as $5,000 for a victory at a major track like Daytona, a tidy sum for relatively short 75-mile races. And the year-end bonuses for a champion could total nearly $20,000. Factory support, a key element, amounted to $50,000 a year from Mazda.

Downing's expertise in running a racing shop became fundamental to his success. He became infamous for scrimping on money by such tactics as using an old Greyhound bus as his hauler. An exemplary son of a Depression-era father when it came to saving money and relying on personal enterprise instead, in the early years Downing's team used a "North South" truck. A flatbed, the "North South" truck had enough room to also haul the crew, because two truck cabs had been welded together—facing opposite directions.

No one could doubt Downing spent his money wisely when it came to racing and building cars. In 1981, the same year he won the RS title, he received funding to the tune of $100,000 from BF Goodrich to build a Mazda RX-7 to run IMSA's longer endurance races on street tires in the GTU class. The next season, he converted the car to compete on race tires for his first full season of competition in the GTU class, where he again won a championship.

With Downing having clinched back-to-back championships, it was a no-brainer for Mazda's manager of racing in North America, Damon Barnett, to call on Downing when the company decided to step up to the new prototype class. The new class had been created by IMSA leader Bishop and would replace the production-based Camel GT cars such as the Porsche 935 Turbos as the premier category in IMSA. Manufacturers like Jaguar, Ford and Porsche were embracing the new GTP category and Barnett thought a lighter prototype might have a chance to win one of the longer endurance races due to the consistency and endurance of Mazda's rotary engines. This time, the budget would be $350,000.

Thus, Downing's career began as a prototype driver—the ultimate ride in sports car racing. Working out of his Standard Drive shops, which had been extensively expanded by the construction of a larger building between the house and the nearby railroad tracks, Downing began campaigning an Argo chassis mated to a Mazda rotary. When Bishop decided, at the suggestion of Downing, to create a separate class for the lighter weight prototypes with smaller engines, the Atlanta driver and his team rose to the occasion. (Steve Conover, a smoker and Downing's crew chief, came up with the name of Camel Lights for the series.) With consistent driving, engine durability and expert preparation of the cars, Downing won three straight Camel Lights championships, starting with the 1985 season.

As the status of IMSA continued to grow, Downing became a popular champion. The Grand Touring Prototypes were among the fastest and most technically sophisticated cars in the world. Corvette, Nissan and Toyota had all joined the fray against the likes of Porsche, Jaguar and Ford in the GTP class for bigger engines, while Pontiac and Buick took up the cudgel in Camel Lights versus Mazda.

In 1988, Downing moved his shop to a brick building on the other side of the railroad tracks in Chamblee, just across the Atlanta city limits, that had been used for light industry. A year later, he married Connie Goudinoff, whom he met when she worked as a public relations representative for the Kelly American Challenge Series of IMSA. (This also precipitated a change of residence for Downing, whose first marriage was scuttled in part because of the living arrangement on Standard Drive, which included the racing shop out back.)

In the expanses of the new Downing/Atlanta headquarters, Downing began to build his own prototypes instead of buying chassis made in England. With an eye on a promotional angle concerning the noxious weed his father had introduced to the Southeast—which happened to be a plant native to Japan—he named his chassis Kudzu. With Rick Engman-built Mazda engines supplying the power, he would eventually drive a Kudzu to the LMP2 class victory at Le Mans in 1996 and to a class victory at Daytona's 24-hour in 2001. In all, 11 Kudzu chassis were built and they won more races than Downing could keep track of.

Fame as a champion race driver and car builder was not to be the final accomplishment for Downing. Ultimately, he would become far better known for the significant question he asked after Patrick Jacquemart's crash in 1981.

By creating the HANS Device, brother-in-law Hubbard, who had become a professor of biomechanical engineering at Michigan State, answered Downing's question about head injuries. After clinching the 1986 Camel Light championship, Downing wore the HANS Model I in the season finale at Daytona. A little like the Wright brothers lifting off at Kitty Hawk on the Outer Banks, few took much notice, some mocked him and most didn't see the need. For Downing, bringing this new life-saving device to the marketplace along with his brother-in-law Hubbard would prove far more difficult than any racing championship.

3

The Family Connection

BOB HUBBARD ENCOUNTERED DALE EARNhardt for the first time while working in the garage at the Daytona International Speedway. Hubbard could see that Earnhardt was taking notice as he answered questions about the HANS Device for two other NASCAR champions. During the days leading up to the Daytona 500 in 2001, Hubbard was helping Dale Jarrett and Bill Elliott get comfortable in their racing seats in order to use his safety invention.

"I was walking back and forth between the cars of Jarrett and Elliott and halfway between the two was Earnhardt," said Hubbard. "I was within a few feet of Earnhardt and he just didn't want to hear about the HANS. He wasn't interested. You don't go where you're not invited at high levels. I was in the garage at the invitation of these teams and I knew who was going to listen to me and I knew who wasn't going to listen."

It wasn't personal with Earnhardt. In the previous month of January during the annual testing at Daytona, John Melvin, a longtime colleague of Hubbard and an advocate for his safety invention, had been invited by NASCAR to give a presentation on the HANS Device to assembled drivers during the annual test days. Chevrolet officials supposedly made attendance mandatory, but Earnhardt was conspicuous by his absence during Melvin's presentation to the Chevy drivers.

Once Speed Weeks began, Hubbard followed up to help those drivers who were interested in wearing a HANS. "We were cooperating closely with Steve Peterson, the technical director at NASCAR, and the car companies to educate the drivers," he said. "The car companies were buying devices from us and giving them to the drivers. The drivers didn't have to pay for them. They were pushing the drivers to wear the HANS Device basically in response to the fatal crashes the previous summer. At that point, I don't think it was any secret that NASCAR was managing its risk by having it be a driver and team decision. Wearing a head and neck restraint wasn't something NASCAR was going to mandate before the race. I never second-guessed that. They were responsible for running the racing business and it was up to us to work according to how they ran things."

Encouraged by the response of some of the drivers at Daytona after more than a decade of trying to persuade NASCAR stars to upgrade their safety, Hubbard left the track early on Friday to catch a plane to join his family in Michigan on a cross-country skiing jaunt. There would be five drivers, including Jarrett, Kyle Petty, Matt Kenseth, Brett Bodine and Andy Houston, who would be wearing the HANS in the 500. Others, such as Elliott, needed modifications to their seats and cockpits to allow the device to fit and postponed using it.

Two days later, by the time Earnhardt's Chevy met the Turn 4 wall on the 200th lap of the race, Hubbard was schussing through white powder. An accomplished hurdler in his college days at Duke University, he was enjoying the effort and the crisp winter air in northern Michigan after the stressful days in Daytona. Without a cell phone, he did not learn of the fatal crash until he returned to his house in East Lansing late Sunday evening. He called Jim Downing to get information about the crash, and then responded to two calls for interviews, including one with ESPN, before going to bed. The next morning, he awoke early and spent the entire day and evening responding to calls from media representatives from around the country.

After 20 years of largely unheralded work, Bob Hubbard had become an overnight sensation.

"I was shocked by the media response. I recorded about 80 entries in my telephone log the first day. And I didn't even write them all down. I was on national television ten times that Monday."

Hubbard became the most talked about racing person in Lansing since Ransom E. Olds, but for not necessarily the right reasons—the reflected fame of a great champion who had been lost, bandwagon reporting by the media and after-the-fact interest in his "new" device.

At the turn of the 20th Century, Ransom Olds had raced his Pirate—a race car built in Lansing—on the hard-packed shores of Daytona and Ormand Beach. The races against Alexander Winton's Bullet in 1903 were destined to become the initial grain of sand through the hour glass leading to stock car racing on the beach; the creation of NASCAR; the building of the Daytona International Speedway; and the Daytona 500. A century later, the world of American racing had come full circle back to Lansing and another significant invention from within its confines, one that would help save not only lives, but help save professional racing. In this case, the invention started on the dining room table of the Hubbard household with a manila envelope and pieces of cardboard. Tape and glue were used to hold together the first HANS prototype.

The son of a professor of physical education at the University of Illinois in Champaign-Urbana, Hubbard was among the promising young students coming out of the Midwest when he arrived in Durham, N.C. and Duke University in the fall of 1961, determined to excel and make his mark at a school already well known for its dedication to high academic standards. Some characterized the school's ambitions as trying to become the "Harvard of the South." In fact, Duke's aggressive agenda made it tougher than many Ivy League schools in terms of expectations and workloads.

Those workloads in pursuit of a mechanical engineering degree would eventually influence Hubbard's passion for athletics. With strong shoulders, a deep chest and narrow waist, Hubbard had the perfect build for a hurdler. But once he discovered he could not excel at

The automotive and racing safety careers of Hubbard and Melvin ran on parallel paths for several decades.
(Photo by Tom Gideon)

The Family Connection

both the intermediate hurdles and in the classroom, he cut back on his track training to be sure he graduated near the top of his class, which would bring the best options for post-graduate studies. He trained in between meets, running the precipitously steep steps at Wallace Wade Stadium as part of his regimen. But he felt he couldn't give it the time needed to be an Atlantic Coast Conference champion.

"I made it to the finals at the ACC track meet that year, but I knew I wasn't prepared enough to beat the other guys," said Hubbard of his last shot at winning the conference hurdles title. "I think I could have beaten them if I had been able to do the training. In the finals, I decided I would go out at a very aggressive pace. You can't just run an event like that at full speed from start to finish because it's too grueling. But I wanted to see if I could spook the contenders and maybe get them to change their race strategies. It was the only chance I had. I was in the outside lane where they could all see me and I started very fast, so fast that my timing was off because I had fewer steps to get to the hurdles. It didn't work; I ran out of gas; and I remember feeling very bad physically once the race was over."

The sacrifice paid off on the academic side. Having started with a 3.2 grade average in his freshman year, Hubbard maintained nearly a 4.0 average his senior year in pursuit of his degree despite his 20 hours per semester class schedule.

His strong physical build also had served Hubbard well back home in Urbana when it came to singing baritone in his church choir. Shortly after arriving at Duke, he went to the Duke Chapel to try out for the Chapel Choir. Hubbard noticed a tall blonde among the sopranos gathered on the opposite side of the chancel. It was his future wife, JoAnn Downing.

"The sunlight was coming in through the stained glass windows. When I looked across at the freshmen women who were trying out, JoAnn with her blonde hair really stood out," said Hubbard. But like his studies, the romance with JoAnn took a while before gaining momentum. "She didn't express much interest in me

When instructing drivers like World Champion Schumacher, Hubbard's teaching experience came in handy.
(Photo by James Penrose)

initially. It wasn't until after about a year or so that we finally had a date."

The courting of Hubbard and JoAnn Downing became a significant development as events played out over time. It would bring the future inventor together with his future business partner Jim Downing, her older brother.

JoAnn had attended Grady High School in Atlanta, one of the city's best due to drawing many bright students from some of the nearby upper middleclass neighborhoods. This included the Sherwood Forest home of the Downings. In addition to both being good students and their shared interest in music and mathematics, Bob and JoAnn had other things in common. They each had mothers from Wisconsin and liked the same food they were fed such as macaroni and cheese, and red Jello. "I was a Girl Scout and he was a Boy Scout," said JoAnn. "We both liked camping. We didn't get into trouble and didn't spend our weekends getting drunk."

The romance resulted in marriage and fraternal twin children—each of whom eventually pursued careers in music. "JoAnn didn't go to college to get married," recalled Jim Downing of his younger sister. "But I remember her saying something like, 'How am I going to do any better than this guy? He's a good athlete, he does almost everything right.'" The clincher? All four of her brothers liked Bob.

Jim, the oldest of the four boys, skipped his graduation ceremony at Georgia Tech to participate in the wedding of Bob and JoAnn at Peachtree Christian Church at the corner of Peachtree and Spring Streets in June of 1966.

Hubbard had first become interested in racing through his own family. His older brother Bill was a car enthusiast, which meant lots of car talk and racing magazines in the house. Bill had a 1950 Ford convertible and installed a rebuilt 1954 Ford engine. The boys' uncle, Joe Pike, worked in marketing for General Motors. During summers while visiting their grandmother's house in Wisconsin, the teenagers went to races at Elkhart Lake as a guest of GM, courtesy of Uncle Joe.

At a time when sports car racing enjoyed rather exalted status in the U.S. due to the sophisticated import cars like Ferrari, Jaguar and Maserati and an appeal to the upper crust, Hubbard got to meet Texan Carroll Shelby—destined for the cover of *Sports Illustrated* and a Le Mans 24-hour victory for Aston Martin—and Englishman Ken Miles, *en route* to becoming one of the great endurance drivers of the 1950s and 1960s.

Sadly, Miles' death when his brakes failed while testing Ford's J-car at the Riverside, California, track in August of 1966 would become part of the litany of racing's dangers.

Hubbard liked racing and sports cars, but unlike his brother-in-law in Atlanta, who spent every spare minute trying to organize a racing career, engineering remained the primary focus of Hubbard's professional aspirations once he graduated from Duke, but not in association with cars. As the saying goes, biomechanical engineering had been around since the first pirate made a peg leg. A rapidly developing field, that's where Hubbard eventually focused the knowledge and skills first acquired at Duke and then in post-graduate studies.

After earning his master's degree in Theoretical and Applied Mechanics at the University of Illinois, the next step became a Ph.D. in the same field. Hubbard chose to write his doctoral thesis on the properties of the skull bone, a pathway into biomechanical engineering, but not one offered at Illinois. In order to finish his dissertation, Hubbard took a job as a research assistant at the Highway Safety Research Institute (HSRI) at the University of Michigan, staffed by researchers who also taught classes at the university. Looking to excel, whether in academics, athletics, in music, or at his church, and as a family man, Hubbard sought the position at HSRI because it was on the cutting edge of biomechanical research.

HSRI's research mission focused on better safety for car occupants, which necessarily meant the human body and engineering. One of those working at the HSRI was John Melvin, a Ph.D. who accepted Hubbard as a research assistant and sponsored the final stages of his doctoral thesis on skull bone properties. Once awarded his doctorate by the University of Illinois, it became a logical step for Hubbard to move from research at the Michigan campus in Ann Arbor and take a position as a research engineer at the General Motors Research Laboratories. Here he led the specification, design, and validation of the head for the Hybrid III dummies used by GM for car occupant crash testing. His thesis on the

The Family Connection

properties of skull bone meant Hubbard could design a dummy head that would mimic real life properties of a human head in order to gain accurate data that could help improve safety.

"I worked with a group that studied the biomechanics of injury and the measurements of crash injury, mechanical ways to assess injury," Hubbard said. "I chose to work in the dummy development area. There weren't any truly successful crash injury computer models. Computer models weren't used very much for car design at that point."

Having earned his spurs in biomechanical engineering, the next stop for Hubbard was an academic appointment at Michigan State in 1977, the beginning of his 30-year career at the College of Engineering, a tenure which included the Withrow Excellence in Teaching Award and being honored with the designation as Distinguished Professor.

After a little less than a decade at Michigan State, one of the classes Hubbard introduced for engineering students focused on new products. The class, which became widely popular and continues to be taught at MSU in cooperation with the marketing department, started with just 12 students and grew out of Hubbard's own interest in "designing products that function mechanically with the body."

The course covered quantitative steps needed for invention, starting with identifying an unmet need. The second step required defining the benefits of a product and identifying the attributes that provided the benefits. The final steps were building a functional prototype and then testing it with users to guide the development of the prototype. In effect, Hubbard made a college class out of his own efforts to design better automobile seats, office chairs, and a head and neck restraint for motor racing.

By this time, Hubbard had been an occasional member of Downing's racing team for almost 20 years. During this span, Downing and his team became a full-fledged factory representative of Mazda. The team always needed volunteer weekend warriors at the races, an opportunity for Hubbard to participate. "I remember one year seeing Jim's RX-7 come down the pit road at Daytona during the 24-hour with a torn front fender," recalled Hubbard. "My job as a Ph.D. in engineering was to go find somebody on Jim's team who could fix the bodywork and suspension."

In addition to their love and appreciation of JoAnn as a wife and sister as well as a shared interest in cars, racing and engineering, Hubbard and Downing were close in the way that blood brothers or fraternity brothers become close through shared experiences. The two men shared Downing's racing pursuits as a matter of competitive passion and camaraderie, but not always in formal racing settings. They raced dirt bikes together on the make-shift circuit built by Downing just outside of Atlanta, for instance, where Downing literally once ran over an overturned Hubbard accidentally in the heat of battle.

Another more serious close call came in one of the IMSA races where Hubbard was working as the fueler. A malfunctioning vent resulted in a shower of gas that sent him to the track's medical center. It also sent the Downing team members into temporary shock over the close call with racing's most feared incident—fire.

On the day in 1980 that Downing had his first life-threatening crash at the Mosport Park circuit, Hubbard was not present. Neither man was present when one of their fellow racers, the well-liked Renault executive Patrick Jacquemart, died from a basal skull fracture at the Mid-Ohio Sports Car Circuit. Once Downing shook off the denial about his own near miss at Mosport, he asked Hubbard what the professor described as the significant question about head injuries in racing. Hubbard's response would eventually change motor racing safety.

Crash! How the HANS Helped Save Racing

4

Creating the Device

DECADES BEFORE 3-D PRINTING AND PLAStic prototyping, the first HANS Device took shape on a dining room table at a modest three-bedroom home in a leafy neighborhood near the Michigan State University campus in East Lansing. Starting with manila envelopes and masking tape, then later cardboard and duct tape, Bob Hubbard taught himself how to make a three-dimensional prototype. "I developed a method where I cut out pleats and put the pieces together to make pieces with compound curvatures," he said.

Long before cobbling together his first prototype, Hubbard faced a far bigger challenge in responding to Jim Downing's significant question—developing an abstract model for understanding the violent and complex events in a racing car crash. If lives were at stake, a head and neck restraint had to prevent head injuries in a way that could be verified scientifically and not cause unintended consequences.

The assumption of scientific development alone was radical idea when it came to motor racing safety. Throughout the 20th Century, safety had invariably come into the sport through generally understood recognitions—cars with increased weight were stronger and slower and therefore safer. Or safety improvements arrived through specific inventions that had worked in aeronautics such as seatbelts, helmets, fuel cells and fire suits.

Confident about finding the verifiable answers needed to create an entirely new safety device, Hubbard thought that he could perhaps reverse the previous methodology. Maybe he could create a device used in aeronautics as a result of first being successful in motor racing. His extensive knowledge gained from the study of car crashes while working for General Motors gave him a fundamental grasp of how head injuries occurred. He had a network of academic and automotive industry colleagues to consult as a sounding board for his process. Biomechanical engineering was his specialty and inventing a product was already a passion expressed by work on new ideas for office chairs and auto seats.

"Jim Downing asked the good question, but at the time we didn't understand exactly how good it was," said Hubbard in a conversation around the dining room table at his house in East Lansing nearly 30 years after he cobbled together the initial prototype. "Why were people dying like Patrick Jacquemart did, when his torso was restrained and his head was unrestrained? We didn't know. We didn't really understand how important the question was because we didn't know at that time a basal skull fracture was a common way for drivers to be killed. People weren't keeping track. Racers were thinking things were meant to be as if they had no control over them. I didn't feel that way."

Hubbard had the typical outlook for an engineer. But oddly, engineers were not a prevalent species in motor racing in the 1970s and 1980s. When they were present, engineers usually worked for factory teams and were focused primarily on the goal of winning, like everyone else in the sport. How ironic that Jacquemart himself was an engineer developing a new race car for Renault USA when he suffered his fatal injury.

For the most part, motor racing continued to be

Creating the Device

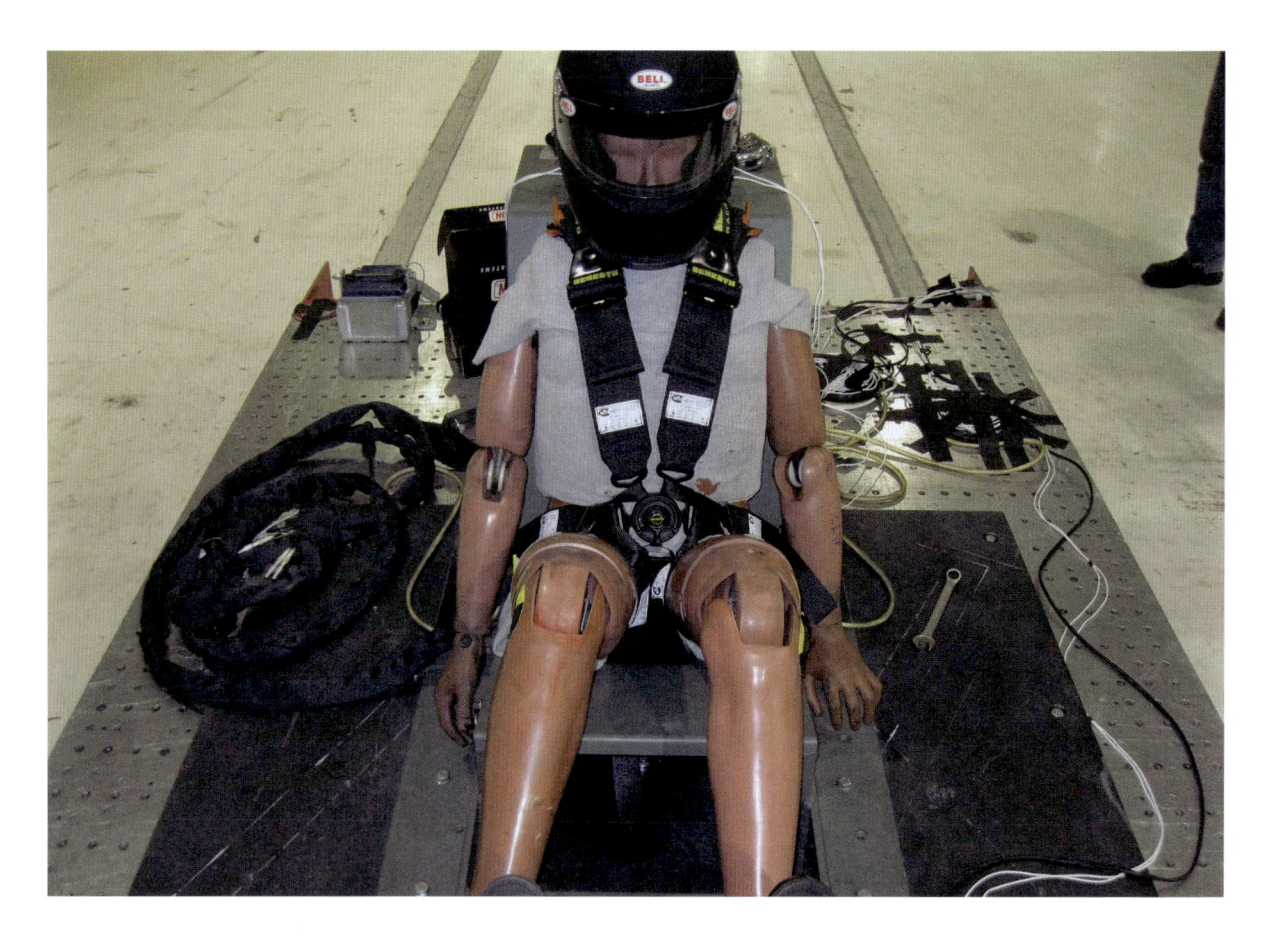

The original design drawn up by Hubbard for the head of anthropomorphic crash test dummies remained state-of-the-art for several decades. (Photo by of Center for Advanced Product Evaluation)

made up of self-taught mechanics with on-the-job training. The shrewdest and smartest autodidacts rose to the top of the racing heap. The only prerequisites were a love of the sport and the acceptance of relatively brutal working hours and conditions—including losing far more often than winning and low job security. Other than those on factory teams, engineers were often actively disdained by established mechanics. This sort of prejudice led Bob Riley, a brilliant car designer and the man behind A.J. Foyt's record fourth Indy 500 victory in 1977, to keep quiet about his degrees in mechanical engineering and aeronautics from Louisiana State University. "I thought it was better," he said, "if nobody knew."

Although Hubbard participated selectively in racing through his brother-in-law Downing's competitive efforts, he drew his point of view from the classic school of engineering, an attitude perhaps best exemplified by an old engineering school story. It's about a golfing threesome composed of a priest, a doctor and an engineer who were being delayed by three blind golfers on the course ahead of them. When they learned the blind golfers had been given a lifetime pass after losing their sight while fighting to save the clubhouse from a fire, there were different reactions.

The priest said he'd pray for them. The doctor said

Creating the Device

he'd contact his friends in ophthalmology. The engineer asked why couldn't the blind firemen play at night?

Engineers, said Hubbard, are less likely to look at things in a social context and instead think of a solution. "Engineers look at the world and they respond by defining and solving problems," he said. "So, there's potential solutions to things that are happening in the world that include the understanding that one person might have."

In the case of motor racing and head injuries in the 1970s and 1980s, the context combined fatalism and a false sense of security once seat belts, fire suits, helmets and fuel safety cells had markedly improved drivers' chances in crashes despite the inevitable increase in speeds. Racing continued to be a dangerous sport that would occasionally suffer the loss of participants simply because it was dangerous, went this thinking. The underlying premise: it wouldn't be racing without that risk occasionally being measured in fatalities.

In 1973, one season after he became NASCAR's first rookie of the year, the handsome Larry Smith hit a glancing blow to the wall at the Talladega track after a tire blew. He was dead before safety crews reached him. Photos of the car after the crash show heavy impact on the right front corner of his Mercury, but an official cause of death remains unknown due to no record in the Talladega County coroner's office, which was primarily a funeral home. Veteran racing reporter Gene Granger was covering the event and wrote for the *Spartanburg Herald* that Smith died of "massive head wounds." The fatal crash was the first at the 2.66-mile behemoth of speed after four years of operation and one of the first indications that higher speeds in NASCAR could result in head injuries despite all the safety equipment available to drivers.

Tellingly, those in the press box that day initially thought an injury unlikely and in Granger's account many reporters praised the driver for "holding the car against the wall" to avoid getting hit by other drivers, not realizing he had been killed. Eventually, participants shrugged off the accident as the first of many mysterious events at the high-speed Alabama track. A seat that broke loose, a failed mounting bracket on the safety harness or a basal skull fracture, any one of several events could have been the source of a gruesome head injury. But clearly, those familiar with the sport didn't expect ordinary contact with the wall to be potentially fatal.

Because of his background and experience and out of respect for Downing's desire to avoid a bad outcome from a severe head injury, Hubbard didn't see fatal crashes as part of the sport.

As the son of a University of Illinois professor of physical education, Hubbard grew up with the idea that researching the human body comprised a beneficial and worthy pursuit. His father had researched ballistic motion and how muscles work, devising an experiment to establish the limits of muscle force during elongation, a key element in physical training. "It was early biomechanics," said Hubbard.

While writing his master's thesis on stress risers—hairline fractures in metal resulting from pressure during the operation of machines such as airplanes, cars and ships—Hubbard's adviser received a unique inquiry. "He got a case where an orthopedic company had some cracks in its devices made to replace human bones," said Hubbard. "That's where I got interested in bones and their mechanical properties."

Once the study of skull bone became his thesis, the pursuit of Hubbard's doctorate led him to the Transportation Research Institute at the University of Michigan and later to General Motors' crash testing program for passenger cars. In 1965 the U.S. Congress had made automobile manufacturing a regulated industry by passing the National Highway Traffic and Safety Act. With a specific focus on occupant restraints and already using anthropomorphic test devices—crash test dummies—GM made a push to improve these testing devices, leading to the creation of the Hybrid III.

Formally known as the Hybrid III 50th Percentile Male Crash Test Dummy, the Hybrid III was introduced to the world in 1976 and destined to be the standard for evaluating frontal crash restraints for the following

Creating the Device

40 years. Built by Denton ATD of Rochester Hills, Mich., the height of the male dummy was five feet, nine inches and it weighed 173 pounds, the average size of a U.S. male. Assigned the task of designing the test dummy's head, Hubbard began work on it in 1973. An aluminum structure, the head had vinyl skin and the shape was based on human geometry data to achieve an average size. The neck supporting this head, made with rubber and aluminum with a center cable, accurately simulated dynamic movements, including rotation and extension responses.

The methods for recording the results from tests using the Hybrid III initially were relatively crude. "They collected data on light-sensitive paper with instrumentation that caused traces to be drawn on reams of this special paper," said Hubbard. "Then you measured the data off the paper with a ruler, basically. The level of instrumentation and analysis were quite limited relative to what we have today. We were in a different time in terms of what we could do."

But if this data collection helped determine what happened in a passenger car accident, it fell short of pinpointing when injurious forces became fatal. The task for researching these questions often fell to Wayne State University in Detroit, where testing with cadavers started in the late 1930s. According to an issue of *Michigan Technic* in 1960, Lawrence M. Patrick eventually pioneered experiments such as fitting a cadaver with accelerators on the head, then dropping it down an elevator shaft to determine "the accident threshold for fractures" to bones under acceleration. At the dawn of space flight, this "threshold" also interested engineers at the National Aeronautics and Space Administration (NASA).

When it came to automotive testing, there were specific questions that needed to be answered, many of which were taken up by Patrick's successors at Wayne State. Due to the rather indelicate matter of using cadavers, the automotive industry preferred to farm out such questions to university research facilities. At what speed would a human head, which weighs about 10 pounds on average, break a windshield in a frontal crash? How much deflection of the rib cage could be tolerated before internal organs were injured? According to Mary Roach's book about cadavers titled *Stiff*, the automotive industry wanted to know,

For Hubbard's purposes, he needed to know the point where tension and shear forces in the neck at the base of the skull led to a basal skull fracture. The cadaver experiments at Wayne St., plus sled testing by the U.S. Air Force using crash test dummies, and in some cases chimpanzees, plus the work of the Transportation Safety Institute as well as the General Motors Hybrid III program all contributed to a recognition of the force involved in head and neck injuries. Particular attention was paid to incidents resulting from the acceleration, flailing or whipping of the head.

The Society of Automotive Engineers (SAE) regularly reported on and updated research in this area of head whip. As part of its testing program with the Hybrid III test dummy, GM representatives corresponded with the SAE's Human Biomechanics and Safety Subcommittee to determine guidelines in 1984 for "the limits of neck forces... at the head-neck junction." The criteria were drawn from an SAE research report first published in 1964 titled "Human Tolerance to Impact Conditions as Related to Motor Vehicle Design," which was regularly reviewed as new research became available. The SAE also led research on "Human Mechanical Response Characteristics" in a report first published in 1976, also reviewed regularly to establish criteria for testing with human surrogates, i.e., test dummies.

Research eventually determined that a forward or rear shearing force of 3,100 Newtons (or about 700 pounds) as measured by test dummies was sufficient for injury to occur in the neck. Along with limits for neck flexion, extension (or stretching), tension and compression, this standard for injury from shear forces at the head-neck junction, recognized by GM in 1984, was eventually adopted by the National Highway Traffic Safety Administration in 1998.

Hubbard knew how head and neck injuries were being measured as a result of his experience at GM in the 1970s and had an ongoing relationship with the Transportation Research Institute's John Melvin, who participated on SAE task forces with research committees and corresponded with GM to help create its guidelines. Hubbard developed a strategy for evaluating how fatal basal skull fractures occurred in racing. "It was useful technology that was fairly mature," he said. "Patrick Jacquemart died in 1981 and it wasn't too long after that I came up with the idea or understood that if I could restrain the head relative to the torso in ways that wouldn't cause injury, that would be a big step in solving the basal skull fracture problem in racing."

He knew what forces were at work. "I had experience with specifying, then developing the head for the crash test dummy," said Hubbard. "What is it you measure that is relatable to injury? I had intimate knowledge and experience with the way to measure injury indicators. It's important to realize that if you're going to develop something that you hope performs in a meaningful way to prevent injury, you have to understand how what you're measuring relates to injury."

Injuries to the base of the skull that are fatal usually result from loss of blood from a broken basal artery, not necessarily due to a fracture of the skull. The head is attached to the cervical spine, or neck, at the C1 vertebra and is held in place by ligaments and tendons, anchored at the base of the skull. The left and right vertebral arteries flow up the neck along the cervical spine and then meet to form the basal artery. It enters the skull at the top of the cervical spine and joins a network of arteries the provide blood to the brain.

NASCAR driver Ernie Irvan suffered a life-threatening basal skull fracture at the Michigan International Speedway in the summer of 1994 after hitting the wall in practice, but he survived and eventually returned to racing. That's because his basal skull fracture did not result in a fatal compromise of the basal artery and an emergency, on-the-scene tracheotomy prevented him from drowning in his own blood. When basal skull fractures are fatal, those arriving on the scene usually find blood pouring from the nose, mouth and ears of a driver who has died within a few seconds from the loss of blood flowing to the brain after the basal artery is severed.

Scientists were also aware that the vertebra in the cervical spine could separate and stretch by as much as one inch under severe neck tension, or lift. Given the number of cervical vertebra and one inch for each one, that could result in quite a lengthy head excursion. For many years, drivers, race teams and sanctioning bodies also had been aware of just how far the neck might stretch under the forces of an accident when a driver was strapped into a racing seat. Before in-car cameras came along, marks on the helmet and corresponding marks in the cockpit became a telltale sign of just how far a driver's neck might extend. Oftentimes, a driver would walk away with merely a headache after the steering wheel or part of the roll cage stopped an accelerating head.

For years, Indy car drivers, who raced in a partially reclined position were often saved from head injuries because their helmets tended to hit the steering wheel or the surrounding high sides of the cockpit (initially installed to keep wheel and tire assemblies out of the cockpit in crashes). Excursion of the helmeted head stopped before enough tension and shear force could create a basal skull fracture. When driver Scott Brayton was killed at Indianapolis in 1996 during practice for the Indy 500, he drove a shorter teammate's car. That meant he was sitting too high to benefit from the protection of the cockpit surround during his side impact. He died of a basal skull fracture.

A driver's physical toughness certainly had much to do with whether he walked away or not. In 1987, A.J. Foyt hit the wall in Turn 4 at the Charlotte Motor Speedway on board his NASCAR chassis. When a scuffed spot showed up on his orange helmet and an orange spot on part of the tube frame in his car, it indicated the four-time Indy winner's head had traveled more than a foot. The incident left Foyt's crew

Creating the Device

chief, Tex Powell, shaking his own head in disbelief. NASCAR quietly grandfathered out any cars with roll cages that included the offending bar, which ran from the overhead roll cage to the center of the floor pan on the nominal passenger's side of the cockpit. Yet, in retrospect, that bar may have saved Foyt from something worse than a concussion.

Hubbard took an engineer's approach to what happened with Jacquemart, who was in an upright seat. "In terms of the mechanics of head and neck injury, I was very aware of the state of the art," he said. "I was able to figure out what caused Jacquemart's death in ways that were measurable with the current injury assessment technology."

In addition to making sure his solution could be verified in a way that was measurable, Hubbard recognized he had to narrow the scope to a specific task. It wasn't just a matter of stopping the head. Rather, he had to decide how to transfer the forces in a way that maintained the relative posture of the head, neck and torso. "What did this device need to do?" recalled Hubbard. "It needed to restrain the head relative to the torso. That came from the understanding that motion of the head relative to the torso was directly related to the injury-causing mechanism.

"The neck is attached at the torso and at the base of the skull," continued Hubbard. "If you can keep those from moving relative to one another, the neck loads can be controlled. The movement of the neck is related to how the top and bottom of the neck are moving. If you reduce one, you must reduce the other." Hubbard decided to control the head with something connected to the torso rather than trying to control the motion of the head or torso relative to the chassis of the car.

Cars deform under the loads of a crash, so no reliable method of attachment could be obtained that would either guarantee a good outcome—or prevent a bad outcome by unintended movement of the head and neck due to deformation of the car.

Assuming a properly installed and secure racing seat and safety harness, Hubbard arrived at the conclusion that a device strapped to the body by a driver's harness and attached to the helmet by tethers would be the most efficient way to keep the head, neck and torso in relative alignment under the loads created by a sudden stop in a crash. Because of the dynamic of huge loads in a short period of time—milliseconds—the loads would have to be transferred from an accelerating head to defuse the excessive tension on the neck. The tethers were the key element—how they attached to the helmet and how they attached to a device to transfer the load to the torso.

"I wanted to figure out how to handle the forces to transfer them to the tethers in a non-injurious way," said Hubbard. How much compression (the opposite of tension) would be introduced to the cervical and thoracic spine if the head were restrained? Could a device that extended to the chest area cause enough deflection of the rib cage to create a hazard to internal organs? These criteria would also have to be mathematically modeled and tested.

Getting the tether attachments right became paramount. Tethers mounted in the wrong way might facilitate the head continuing to move in a manner that would increase the tension or compression between the head and neck.

The Hybrid III's crash test dummy head had three uniaxial accelerometers inside the skull at its center of gravity. In engineering terms, they measured the head's accelerations in the rearward to forward direction (x), downward to upward direction (y), and left to right directions (z). In a racing crash, Hubbard needed to restrain a driver's head, transfer energy and not allow movement in any of the directions that might introduce injurious forces.

In addition to an accelerometer, the Hybrid III dummy heads carried a load cell. "There was a load cell that measured the x and y and z axis and the loads around those axes," said Hubbard. "I had defined the geometry of the head for the test dummy and I knew where the head was attached to the neck by doing the work at GM. I knew the geometry, how much the head

How the HANS Device Works
Frontal crash into a barrier or another car

(Original illustration by David Downing, adapted by Damion Chew)

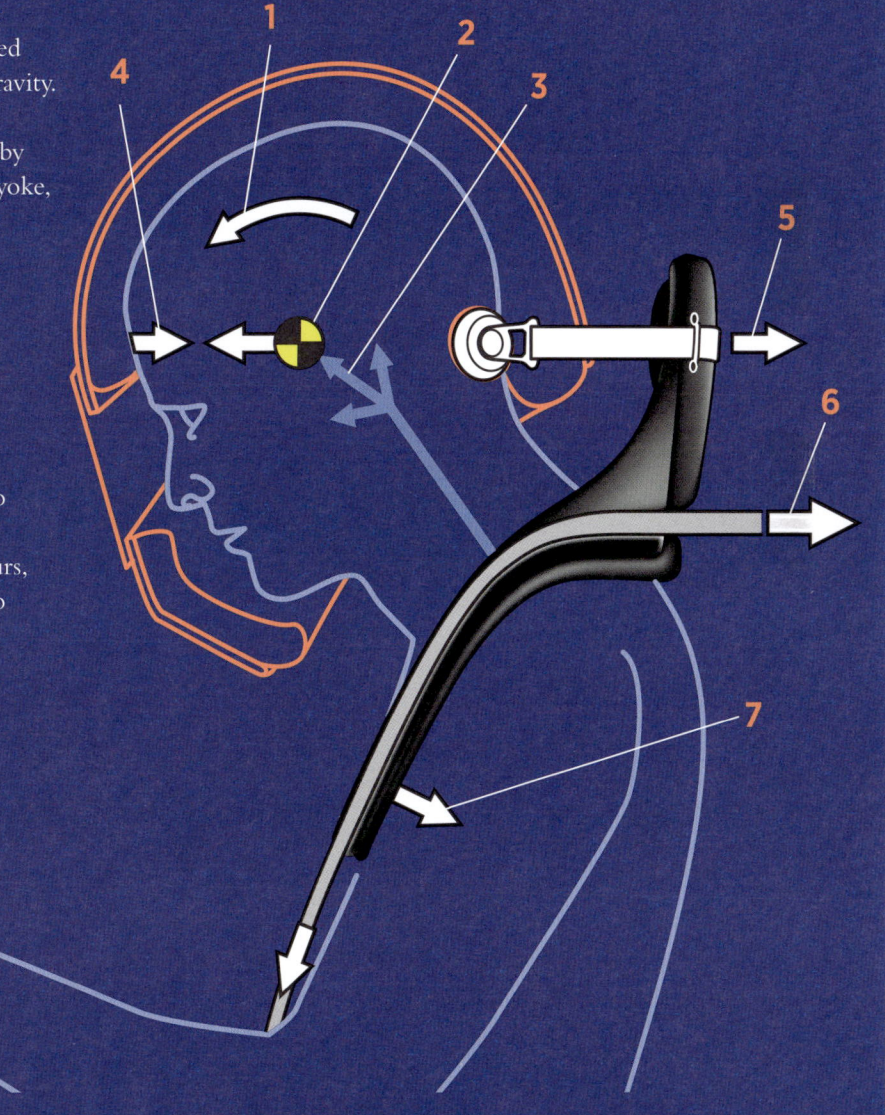

1. Head excursion occurs as driver's head continues at speed of Delta V.

2. Forces act according to head's center of gravity.

3. Neck tension and shear forces build as a result of head excursion.

4. Tethers hold helmet in place at forehead. Tethers are located relative to head's center of gravity.

5. Excursion forces transferred by tethers to carbon collar and yoke, then shoulders and torso.

6. HANS initially slides under harness towards rear before friction rubber on top of legs holds it in place.

7. Chest compression occurs, but not substantial enough to cause critical or fatal injury. Spinal compression also occurs, but not substantial enough to cause critical or fatal injury.

Creating the Device

weighed and how that weight was distributed, which was the center of gravity. I also knew how stiff the head was when it was loaded in injurious ways."

His state-of-the-art information told Hubbard the head and neck could accept a relative amount of forces that were below the threshold of injury, which led him to find a way to catch the head in order to transfer the energy from its acceleration.

He paid careful attention to tolerances for injury. Race car drivers and many on the engineering side of the sport, for example, believed a fully tightened shoulder harness could induce enough G-force in the chest to be fatal in a high-speed crash. Onboard data recorders and accelerometers introduced in the 1990s would eventually show that premise to be false, because the rib cage under a racing harness continued to resist fatal deflection even at high G-forces. In 2002, Richie Hearn sustained 130 Gs in a testing crash in an Indy car at the Kentucky Speedway, according to the data recorder, without any chest injuries—or any neck injury while wearing a HANS Device.

Since Hubbard's method for loading, then transferring the forces to the torso relied on tethers, the tethers had to be attached to the helmet in a manner that could take advantage of where the center of gravity is located in a human head. "I put the attachments of the tethers to the helmet just below and behind the center of gravity," he said.

In a crash where the driver's torso is strapped to the seat and the head begins to accelerate, the tethers in this location would always adapt to the motion of the helmet. The helmet rotates around the center of gravity in part due to its slippage on the head, an established observation about drivers wearing helmets during a crash. This slippage and tethers in the proper location could produce the desired result. "The top of the helmet would rotate forward and load the brow or forehead," said Hubbard. "That would hold the helmet relative to the head. Once the forces began to build up and the tethers tightened, the helmet would be effectively restrained relative to the head." With the helmet in a fixed position, the load could then be transferred from the forehead through the head's center of gravity to the tethers. The forces would be transferred to the device holding the tethers and to the torso where the device rested.

The elegant beauty of this approach concerned its universal application. "If you think of having a ball that's going to be restrained and this business of the ball going forward and being restrained by tethers, it's self-evident that the forces will go through the center of gravity," said Hubbard. "In this case, it meant the forces always going through the tethers because of the mounting locations on the helmet behind and below the head's center of gravity."

For a device to work in motor racing, it had to produce results, no matter what the size of a driver's head, neck and shoulders. The device also had to weather the usual problems of misapplication in the field. The fact the tethers were relatively insensitive to the variability of driver's neck and the length of the tethers themselves within a small range became another benefit of this tether system. "The concept of transferring the load, the way the device aligned itself and the way the loads developed were insensitive to the variations," said Hubbard.

If the forces were always going to find and go through the center of gravity, once the head was "captured" in the helmet, what was the most efficient and safest way to transfer those forces? It followed logically that the tethers needed to connect directly to a holding device at a similar height as the mounting point on the helmet. If the device was to fit under a driver's shoulder harness and rest on the shoulders, the concept of a yoke with a weight-bearing high collar became the next step of development.

5
Building the HANS

ONCE HE DECIDED TO BUILD A DEVICE, with tethers mounted on a tall collar, it would be six years before Hubbard was able to actually test it. When tests were finally run at Wayne State University in 1989, it constituted a landmark event in motor racing safety. The sled tests conducted by Hubbard and Dr. Paul Begeman were the first scientific study of forces at work on the head and neck in a motor racing crash. More significantly, the tests evaluated a device that could keep those forces below the injury threshold.

Long before the first sled test, Hubbard sought an informal peer review in 1983. Having worked with some of the leading experts in car crash safety, Hubbard arranged a meeting with four colleagues to vet his idea for a head and neck restraint. The meeting at Wayne State University included John Melvin, then working at the University of Michigan, Albert King, Ph.D., from Wayne State, Harold Mertz, Ph.D., who directed the development of the Hybrid III test dummy at GM, and Dr. John States, a physician from Rochester, N.Y. and a pioneer in car and racing safety.

"In confidence, I disclosed my ideas for a head restraint," said Hubbard. "After extensive discussion, they all agreed that my understanding of the problem was correct and that my approach should counteract the injurious head motions and neck forces without any foreseeable negative outcomes. They urged me to continue."

Once Hubbard had confirmed the concept of tethers mounted on a high collar, creating a device became his next challenge. Again, his experience at GM's safety research operations proved useful, if only because the creation of crash test dummies required a lot of data on the variety of sizes and shapes people came in. At first, he viewed a resolution as impossible, but then came to a revelation.

"I understood the extent of diversity in terms of people's shape and size," he said. "My original design thinking for HANS was that the part of the device on the torso should fit down over the front and back of the ribcage. To shape a device that fit people's diverse body sizes seemed to be impossible. It was apparent that the part on the back of the torso would interfere with the seat and not be comfortable. So, while my concept for restraining the head without adding injurious forces had merit, the problems with the device fitting between the driver's back and the seat made the concept unfeasible."

"After some further thinking and analysis of the forces and motions," he continued, "I realized that in a frontal crash, the device would be loaded on the front. It would be pulled rearward by the shoulder belts into the front part of the upper torso. At the same time, if a part of the device covered the backside of the torso, it would move rearward and come away from the torso, serving no purpose. So, I did not need the device to fit over the back of the driver's torso."

Under the influence of this revelation, Hubbard attacked the remaining fit problems: shoulder shape, width, and collar angle, which were significant design challenges. Once Hubbard realized those challenges could be overcome, he had a conversion experience. "I suspected these problems could be solved. Coming

Building the HANS

to this realization was a turning point. Before then, I did not believe there was a practical possibility. I had a change in belief, a conversion experience. After that, I felt morally obligated to continue because I knew that if I was successful, HANS could become broadly used and would reduce the risk of racers from dying from a basal skull fracture."

To produce the first devices, Hubbard visited the long-familiar shops of Downing Racing in Atlanta on Standard Drive and the team where he had worked as a part-time crew member. Using "test dummy" Downing while seated upright in one of his race cars with his helmet on, Hubbard created a plaster mold. Prior to flying to Atlanta, Hubbard had worked with a local prosthesis device maker in Michigan to create a soft rubber version of the HANS. Hubbard draped it over Downing's torso in order to make the plaster of Paris cast. A one-inch piece of foam was put between Downing and his helmet to be sure there was a gap to accommodate the helmet inside the future device. "I put the cast in my carryon luggage and brought it with me on the plane back to Michigan," said Hubbard.

The professor had an academic year appointment at Michigan State, which meant he could pursue his own interest for ten weeks in the summer. During the summer of 1985, he set out to make the first HANS Devices, working in the shop of a large Lansing-based company, the Demmer Corporation, which had diverse activities and was a supplier of metal parts to the automotive and defense industries. The company owners, John and Bill Demmer, joined many who helped the Michigan State professor find out if he could make a significant difference in motor racing safety.

"John Demmer and his son Bill were big Michigan State fans and they took me in under their wing," said Hubbard. "My main purpose that summer was to make a mold to lay up composite HANS prototypes. From the cast made in Downing/Atlanta, we made a positive shape, which was scanned with a digital inspection machine. This digital data was massaged to make the shape smooth and symmetrical. Then a laminated wood

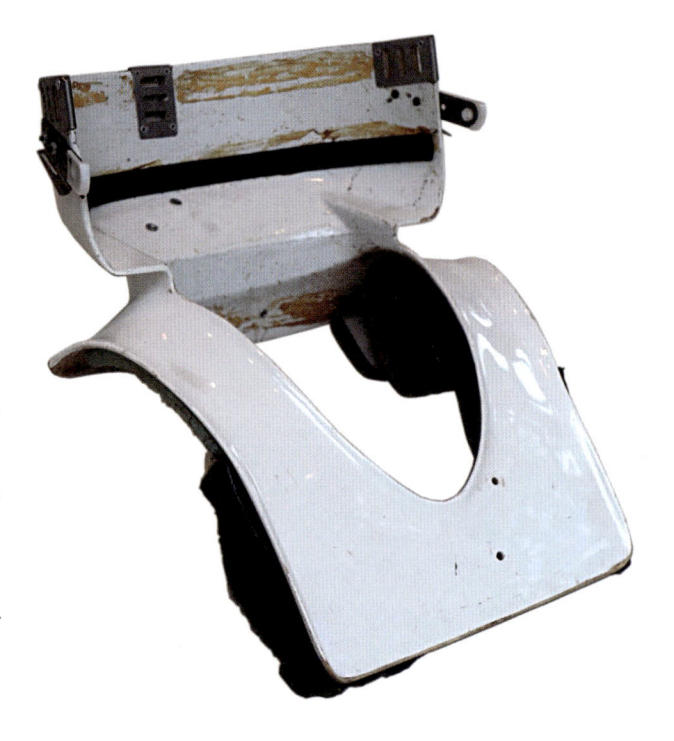

The "breast plate" HANS had issues. (Robert Hubbard Collection)

block was machined as the basis for a mold. Most of this mold making was done by the technicians at Demmer at no charge to me."

The first device, made from fiberglass, had a simple curve between the yoke and collar. The high collar wrapped around the helmet and held one tether on each side with one in the back. These three tethers extending from the collar were attached by vertical slots cut in the helmet and secured by a three-way weave. With a tether on each side and one attached to the helmet at the back, the HANS Model I could catch and retain the helmet, head and neck relative to the torso in side or frontal impacts.

The wraparound collar introduced bulk that didn't fit in all cockpits, an obvious drawback. It did, on the other hand, provide a method for support of the neck to reduce fatigue from G-forces in corners due to a tether on each side. This was an important consideration for Downing's own racing and one he thought would help sell the device. Most importantly, this approach could help prevent injuries to drivers in various types of crashes.

The yoke was connected across the chest with a "breastplate." The continuous strip across the chest was to prevent the device from cocking sideways in the course of an accident. But the cross section could perhaps hit the driver in the larynx if the HANS moved up and back, causing a possible fatal injury. "Initially, I didn't realize what could happen," said Hubbard. Also, a driver would have to put device on over his head, necessitating a large hole. That made it so wide a driver could hit his arm while steering. The juncture of the collar where it met the yoke became a problem, too. It was not sufficiently strong for the device to work under the anticipated demands of a significant crash and impact. "It would not withstand more than 100 pounds of load," said Hubbard.

From the outset, Hubbard considered military applications of the device. A project for the U.S. Army, where sometimes parachutists suffered basal skull fractures from the shock of a parachute opening, helped him jettison the "breastplate" approach in favor of two "legs" on the yoke. Using the original hard mold at Demmer, Hubbard and assistants at Demmer made a device for Joe Haley, head of the Army Air Medical Reserve in Ft. Rucker, Alabama. Although the Army decided against using it, the paratrooper version was the inspiration for having legs in the yoke portion of the HANS device.

Haley wanted jumpers to be able to remove the device within three seconds once on the ground. Also, it needed to be narrow enough to allow a parachutist to hold his arms over his head while manipulating suspension lines during descent to alter direction. Although the device was not taken up by the Army, these two criteria were the origin of using legs on the base of the HANS, a name that gradually presented itself as the project unfolded.

The Army project marked the first use of friction

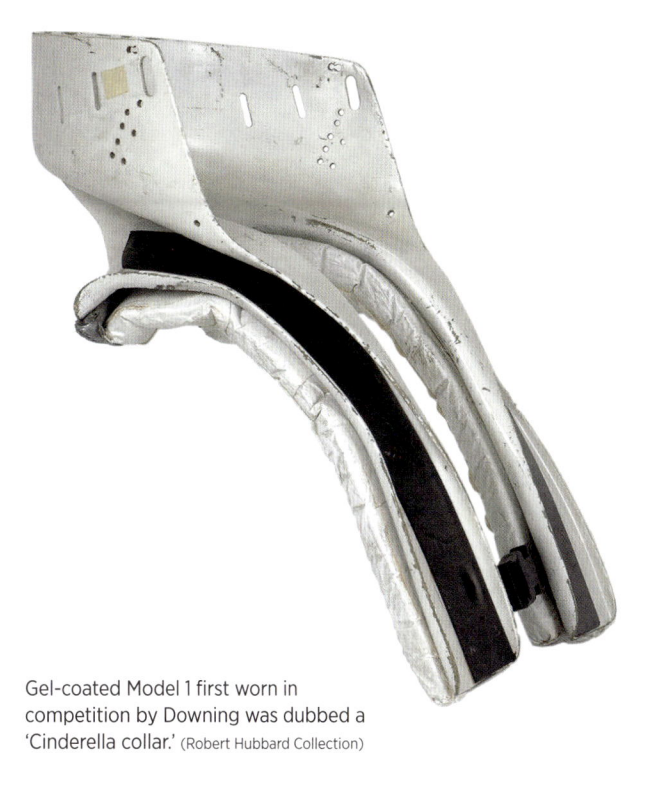

Gel-coated Model 1 first worn in competition by Downing was dubbed a 'Cinderella collar.' (Robert Hubbard Collection)

rubber, a thin strip of lightly sectioned rubber that ran the length of the legs and back over the shoulders of the yoke. In a car crash, as the driver's body exerted pressure on the harness belts, the device would initially slip toward the rear under them—until the friction created between the sectioned rubber and the belts held the device in place. The former Ph.D. advisor and a racing safety enthusiast who would be an important ally in the development of the HANS, Melvin suggested the sectioned rubber to create friction.

Once Hubbard had the requisite shape, he needed to create a more robust device so that Downing could actually begin wearing it in competition. Like the first two devices, epoxy resins and fiberglass were used to make the original Model I, which was finished with white gelcoat. The general shape, the friction rubber on the legs and horizontal slots for the tether attachments had been established. The "third-generation" device

Building the HANS

had another significant improvement. It was far more robust, thanks to a more complex curve between the collar and yoke.

Having clinched the Camel Light championship for 1986, Downing decided to test the device in the final round of the IMSA season at a race where not nearly as many people would be present as at the season-opening Daytona 24-hour event. Downing did not make a big show of using the HANS, but it certainly caught the attention of competitors any time he emerged from his Mazda-powered Argo with the white "monstrosity," as Crew Chief Steve Conover called it, on his shoulders. "That's how Jim would do things," recalled Conover. "He was very low key and didn't try to draw attention to himself."

Although Downing and his co-driver John Maffucci didn't win the race, there were two important results. Downing raced comfortably with the HANS on and got out of the car to quickly to transfer it to his co-driver on the pit road while wearing the rather large device. Thereafter, a low-key sales campaign for the HANS was engaged in by the driver nicknamed "Senator Jim" for his quiet ability to persuade fellow drivers and IMSA officials about such things as rules governing performance of the various cars.

By wearing the HANS, it inevitably spawned conversations with fellow drivers, giving Downing an opportunity to promote the new safety device, conversations that usually led to no result in either perception or the desire to buy and wear a device. At least the IMSA sanctioning body had been drawn into the discussion and allowed Downing to wear the HANS in official practice and competition.

During this period when the first HANS devices were created, Hubbard pursued his patent. This came after consulting a Michigan State administrator, who determined the HANS was not part of Hubbard's professorial research duties, i.e., an independent project.

Throughout the development of the HANS, Hubbard, who had two children headed for college, had to find a way to fund this part of the project. To

Curved transition between collar and yoke gave the Model I needed strengthening. (Robert Hubbard Collection)

pay the patent expenses, he did some legal consulting, mostly human injury cases from vehicle crashes. The key element of the patent: the mounting point of the tethers. Applied for in 1985, the patent was granted in 1987, followed by continued scientific verification of the HANS Device through sled testing.

Hubbard launched Biomechanical Design Inc. (BDI) in 1988 so he could apply for a State of Michigan small business start-up grant for funds to build HANS prototypes that could be sled tested. The funds would also help pay for the sled testing. "In starting BDI, I was encouraged and advised by Mike Martin, who was at Michigan State working to help develop tech transfer," said Hubbard. "With money from the state, I contracted a local mold maker who was unemployed to make the mold and prototypes for crash testing."

Hubbard had several of these HANS devices made for use in the inaugural sled tests. In addition to fiberglass and epoxy resins, HANS used in the initial sled test had a carbon fiber layer to add strength. "I didn't want the efficacy of the HANS to be compromised by the strength of the device itself," he said.

"They were similar to the carbon fiber black 'Darth Vader' collar that Jim first used and that we started selling in 1990. We did not know how strong to make these prototypes since nobody had measured the severity of racing crashes up to that point." Hubbard reasoned that the HANS prototype should carry a total load of at least 1,000 pounds through the tethers to the helmet, a load that would correspond to more than 60 Gs, at the time believed to be the threshold for fatal chest acceleration.

"At this early stage, we really did not know the upper limits of human impact tolerance and had to rely on the criteria used by the auto industry," said Hubbard. Subsequent testing by Melvin would discover the limit for chest acceleration was much higher. By the mid-1990s, after progress using data recorders to document crashes, it was recognized that race drivers emerged uninjured in crashes that were much more severe than the passenger car injury tolerance criteria, particularly for chest deflection.

But in the late 1980s, such data on race car crashes did not exist. The only way to get it would be the same method that had been done for highway crashes, but instead simulate racing crashes with sled tests. The site for HANS testing would be Wayne State University, where Hubbard worked with Begeman, an expert on spinal injuries.

The tolerance limit for neck shear (pulling the head straight forward) was 3,100 Newtons (700 pounds), while the limit for loading in the direction of the long axis of the neck was 3,300 Newtons (740 pounds) in tension. "These shear and axial loads, or stretch loads, are really component parts of the same load," said Hubbard. "Although the auto industry tolerance limits treated these as separate criteria, in reality the tension and shear are parts of a single load that tends to pull the head and neck from the torso."

For their subsequent scientific paper, Hubbard and Begeman suggested an important change in criteria. They believed the two forces of neck shear and neck stretch should be regarded as one single criteria. The combined single criteria for total neck load should not exceed 3,100 Newtons for a safe outcome.

But how would they measure the success of the device in keeping the forces below 3,100 Newtons? The answer: run sled tests

"The available dummies and injury assessment methods were not ideal for evaluating HANS, but they were close enough," said Hubbard. "The Hybrid III dummy was then the state of the art. This is the dummy that I helped design and develop while at GM in the 1970s."

Begeman and Hubbard ran a series of tests at Wayne State in 1989 involving frontal (0 degrees), right frontal (45 degrees) and right lateral (90 degrees) impacts. The data they later presented included measurements of forces from the computer model built by Begeman as well as the data collected in the actual tests. Neck forces and torques were recorded for x, y, and z axis. The comparisons of "with" the HANS and "without" confirmed the device fulfilled its mission, a source of great satisfaction to Hubbard and Begeman.

The following year, the two presented a paper to the Society of Automotive Engineers for peer review titled, "Biomechanical Performance of a New Head and Neck Support." The paper underscored the breakthrough of an inaugural scientific study of the forces at work on the neck in a crash—as well as an evaluation of a device to hold those forces below the injury threshold.

The speeds at which the sled hit the barriers were relatively low compared with racing crashes. Although these Barrier Equivalent Velocities (BEV) were just 30 mph and 35 mph, they created potentially fatal circumstances. The acceleration profiles had a duration of 140 milliseconds, peak values of 22 G and 25 G, respectively, and total velocity changes of 34.4 mph and 40.3 mph.

Building the HANS

(When Dale Earnhardt was killed at Daytona, the car's velocity changed 42 to 44 mph.)

Interestingly, the computer model had underestimated some of the forces at work on a driver wearing a helmet but no HANS Device. In the actual sled test impacts, despite the relatively low acceleration the injury threshold was approached or exceeded in tests with the helmeted dummies without the HANS. In the frontal (0 degree) impacts and using Hubbard's suggested measuring method of consolidating the stretch (z axis) with the shear (x axis), the neck forces far exceeded the threshold of 3,100 Newtons for either one when the dummy was fitted only with a helmet and no head restraint.

Without any device, the combined stretch (x) and shear (z) sums were 4,084 for 30 mph and 4,360 at 35 mph, well exceeding the 3,100 Newton injury threshold. There were similar results for the right front and right lateral impacts.

It represented a remarkable presentation of new data and new analysis of that data about the potential for head injury in motor racing impacts—in addition to some of the first extensive computer modeling of racing crashes. Most significantly, the tests included a solution to the problem described by the injury thresholds already recognized and understood by the automotive industry.

In the frontal sled test at 30 mph, the dummy with a HANS Device registered 467 Newtons of combined neck stretch and shear—a significant reduction from the 4,084 Newtons in the same test without the HANS. Similarly, at 35 mph the dummy with a HANS Device registered 569 Newtons of combined neck stretch and shear compared to 4,360 Newtons on the dummy without the HANS. As photographs and videos taken during later tests would show, the HANS also significantly reduced head excursion.

"The results," stated the paper's conclusion, "from the model and dummy tests show marked reductions in neck loading and head motions with the HANS in these crash environments. The reduced neck loading corresponds to a reduced likelihood of neck injury. The reduced head excursions correspond to a reduced likelihood of head injury by impact with surrounding structures."

The scientific paper began the process of persuading those interested in motor racing safety that the HANS Device presented a bona fide response to head injuries. The paper armed Hubbard with verification that would eventually persuade enough knowledgeable people in motor racing that the HANS, or at least the concept of a head and neck restraint with tethers and a tall collar, could make a significant contribution if fatalities were to be reduced and possibly eliminated.

In the same year that he presented the paper, Hubbard and Downing formed their own company to sell the HANS Device. Conversations with existing motor racing safety equipment companies had made no progress. Armed with the knowledge they could save lives, Hubbard/Downing Inc. was launched, doing business as HANS Performance Products from Downing's new location for his racing operations on Peachtree Rd. in Chamblee, Georgia.

6

Fame, Wealth, Tragedy

ONCE HANS PERFORMANCE PRODUCTS had been established, Hubbard, Downing and their new company were up against not only skepticism about racing's first head and neck restraint and resistance to it from drivers because of the considerable bulk of the wrap-around collar. There was also ongoing resistance to driver safety in motor racing.

Two years after the company began doing business, underground artist and hot rod aficionado Robert Williams released a large-scale illustration in Los Angeles, a drawing that perfectly captured the often-splintered attitude by fans and participants toward auto racing and safety.

Titled "Death on the Boards," Williams' giant poster depicts a crash in 1920 at the Beverly Hills board track that killed one of America's earliest motor racing stars, Gaston Chevrolet, in front of a large crowd and a bevy of Hollywood newsreel cameras. Williams' love of speed, hot rods and racing resulted in perfectly accurate details on each of the cars. But his poster is provocation as much as artwork. Its explosive colors evoke the curious sensations of excitement, admiration, and horror.

The race took place on Thanksgiving Day at what is now the corner of Santa Monica and Wilshire Boulevards. This new board track featured a covered grandstand and a 1.25-mile track in full view to spectators. Driving a Frontenac made by the car company he and older brothers Louis and Arthur had founded, Gaston Chevrolet had become a star by winning the Indy 500 earlier that year and clinching the American Automobile Association's National Championship.

A gaudy and grim rendition of the crash that killed driver Eddie O'Donnell and his riding mechanic Lyall Jolls in addition to Chevrolet, "Death on the Boards" captures the high-banked speed and momentum of the track's smooth arc. It portrays the Frontenac of Chevrolet and the Duesenberg of O'Donnell flying through the air above the railing in Turn 1 along with the hapless Jolls, who would be crushed as his driver's car rolled down the track.

Much like comic book panels, the poster features different insets, including a goofy, scary and depraved gorilla-like monster whose head is composed of flames and an ace of spades playing card. The gorilla, using hands and feet, twists the cars numbered 6 and 9 like pretzels. In another inset, an imposing yet composed, even heroic-looking driver stands in victory lane. With a leather racing helmet atop his head, he looks eminently human except for a green satyr-like body with furred legs and a pointed tale curled at his feet. With an air of confident authority, the green devil himself accepts the trophy with his arm around a stunning, naked female beauty.

The Grim Reaper, portrayed as a flag man wearing knickers and a straw boater, has a chess board at his feet. With the checkered flag, he flicks off a king, a knight and a pawn. In the bottom corner, one of Williams' cartoon characters lies crushed in an overturned green car numbered 13. Such was the stunning impact and renown of this crash, for much of the 20th Century the fact Chevrolet died in a green car led American racers to religiously avoid that car color as if it were a bad omen, or worse.

Crash! How the HANS Helped Save Racing

Fame, Wealth, Tragedy

The crash that claimed Indy winner Chevrolet became the subject of 'Death on the Boards.' (IMS Photo Archives)

In addition to drawing attention to a famed intersection in the Los Angeles area, Williams' drawing stands at the intersection of the sacred and profane in motor racing. Many fans and participants drawn to the sport held sacred the willingness of individual drivers to cheat death in the name of victory. Even for the most conservative and safety-conscious drivers, the sport was no doubt dangerous. When drivers failed in this endeavor, the price could be human life. Throughout the 20th Century, this continued to be held to be the right formula. Without the physical risk, could there be any racing?

Williams' drawing begged this question about a sport that from its very beginning lost participants to fatal accidents captured in motion pictures and in front of packed grandstands. In a bitter and telling irony, his drawing appeared two years before the death of F1 champion Ayrton Senna in a crash televised worldwide from Italy to an audience of as many as 50 million.

A short 16 years before the high speed, dangerous American board track phenomenon first emerged at

Playa Del Rey in California, public roads in Europe and America gave birth to motor racing. These earliest formal races were sedate and relatively slow due to the rudimentary cars involved and prevailing attitudes about the changes in mobility occasioned by the invention of the automobile.

Held in 1894, the race between French cities Paris and Rouen is credited as the first formal automotive competition, followed in 1895 by a race in Illinois from Chicago to Evanston sponsored by the *Chicago Times-Herald*. These inaugural major events held on public roads had a keen focus on safety, because they were designed to foster greater acceptance of what was regarded as unwelcome new machinery in the eyes of some entrenched politicians, newspaper editors and other social commentators.

This prevailing negative attitude towards cars moved organizers of the Paris to Rouen event for "horseless carriages" to invoke a very conservative format, lest their efforts to promote automobiles draw ire from the establishment.

Judged on safety, economy and ease of handling, the French race required competitors to complete the journey in less than eight and a half hours. More than 100 applicants were winnowed down to less than one third of the original entrants to insure only reliable cars made the trek, lest the effort to showcase the machinery be sundered in front of those who saw cars as suspect.

A little less than a decade later, the attitude toward racing had changed radically within the ranks of those who pursued it. Gone were the almost pious city-to-city tests of reliability. In their place came something entirely different as the size, power and speed of cars increased. The more enticing prospect of men racing one another and the hands of time had taken over like an elixir among the racers and the general populace, which previously had to make do with bicycle racing. The majestic allure of men onboard thunderous automobiles traveling at rates of speed more like locomotives evoked old-fashioned bravery and romance coupled with an irresistible new circus-like excitement. Safety and reliability were relegated to secondary consideration. Manufacturers and event organizers began to bank on this excitement to sell their wares.

In 1903, the disastrous Paris-Madrid race, organized by the Automobile Club de France, drew as many as 175 entries, each with a driver and riding mechanic. Scheduled to cover 750 miles, the winners would be the car, driver and riding mechanic who covered the distance in the least time after being released individually, with elapsed times compared to determine the winner. But it was clear to each driver that if he passed slower cars up ahead, his superior speed would be hastened and confirmed.

Tens of thousands of spectators, more than a few expecting to see a car for the first time, were said to be lining the route. There were entries built by Panhard, Mercedes, De Dietrich and Mors that accounted for almost one-third of the field, confirming the link between selling cars and racing them. Most of the cars were powered by gasoline engines, an accessible means to acceleration and power, in place of steam, electric or kerosene power, all of which had been represented among entrants in that first race from Paris to Rouen nine years earlier.

The participants in this tragic race never reached Spain. Forced to start in darkness due to the high number of entries, the frenzied participants aboard rudimentary cars with relatively powerful engines chased glory at a reckless pace previously unimaginable. It would be the first time, and unfortunately not the last occasion, when technology outstripped the ability of organizers to keep car racing safe. Between Le Mans and Bordeaux several accidents claimed the lives of two drivers, two mechanics, at least two spectators and two policemen in charge of trying to sustain crowd control. The race was halted at Bordeaux due to the carnage in the worst sense of a double meaning.

In more conservative quarters, where racing was perceived as a pursuit of suspect men and their noisy, fearful machines and a source of unwanted change, an enormous backlash in public opinion erupted. Europe's

Fame, Wealth, Tragedy

great city-to-city races thus came to an end almost as soon as they had begun.

One of the drivers killed was Marcel Renault, who along with his brother Louis, had established the eponymous French car company. The brothers saw the event as an opportunity to make a name for their cars. Louis, who had made it as far as Bordeaux in his Renault, eventually succeeded in manufacturing. Marcel had crashed when he sped into another driver's accident amidst dust and difficult visibility. For the remainder of his life, Louis would be haunted by the loss of his brother on the road behind him and the disdainful rebukes over the racing accident that had claimed Marcel—as if the Renault company had been built with the blood of those who died in the mayhem of multiple crashes on the road to Bordeaux.

For the first time, the debacle of the Paris-Madrid race forced those in Europe interested in motor racing—promoters such as newspaper publisher John Gordon Bennett, car clubs, car builders and participants—to alter their course in the name of safety. The city-to-city races where crowd control became so problematic gave way to the loop circuits near cities, led by a series of races established by *New York Herald* publisher Bennett and sanctioned by the Automobile Club de France. Participants would run a number of laps on cordoned off public roads, ostensibly where control of spectators could be more effective and entries more limited. This fascination with racing the ongoing stream of new cars, each with distinct designs, engines and philosophies, helped create the permanent circuit at Brooklands. The banked, concrete track opened in 1907 in England, where racing on public roads had been made virtually illegal due to a national speed limit of 20 mph.

The combination of loop circuits and the excitement generated by Brooklands eventually led to the circuits of Autodrome de Linas-Montlhéry in France, the Nürburgring in Germany and Autodromo Nationale Monza in Italy after World War I. These four tracks were the high-speed, demanding primogenitors of modern circuit racing in Europe, where ticket sales, spectators and the racing could be handled more effectively.

In America at the turn of the 20th Century, the Vanderbilt Cup introduced by W.K. "Willie" Vanderbilt as well as the short-lived American Grand Prix were conducted on what were effectively loop circuits on public roads, eventually including a turnpike funded by Vanderbilt on Long Island. There were other races on the East Coast as well, designed to attract the leading manufacturers from France, England, Germany and Italy to compete against American-built cars.

Crowd control and safety in the American events proved problematic. The winner of the 1906 Vanderbilt Cup race, Louis Wagner, suggested it was a miracle that more spectators were not killed after one suffered a fatal injury when hit during the race.

According to W. David Lewis's biography of World War I flying ace Eddie Rickenbacker, whose lust for dangerous action began in racing cars, the initial Vanderbilt Cup events were unruly affairs. Drawing on a variety of articles by writers such as Beverly Rae Kimes of *Automobile Quarterly,* Lewis cites one eccentric spectator dressed in a Civil War uniform, "who stepped onto the road after each car had passed and shook his fist, challenging the next to hurry up. He had enough sense to stay out of the way of oncoming vehicles, but other people did not and paid the price for recklessness. A man who walked in front of an oncoming Hotchkiss was struck, flew through the air, and landed dead at the feet of some terrified women."

In addition to one spectator, three riding mechanics were reported killed in the races run between 1904 and 1909 on Long Island. In 1910, four spectators were killed during the race, possibly more as a result of injuries that later proved fatal. The Vanderbilt Cup received heated rebuke from the American publishing world as newspapers denounced the event's focus on wealthy sportsmen and lack of consideration for the public, a campaign that eventually scuttled the event. The Vanderbilt Cup would be revived briefly in the 1930s at Roosevelt Field, but by then the major focus

Fame, Wealth, Tragedy

An ingenious driver as well as a brilliant self-taught engineer, Lockhart died on Daytona's sands. (IMS Photo Archives)

of American racing had moved on.

The Indianapolis Motor Speedway, also said to have been inspired by Brooklands, proved over the long haul that a closed course offered the best method of pitting American cars and drivers against the Europeans in a manner that generated excitement and, as importantly, large crowds of ticket buyers. Once the 2.5-mile dirt oval was paved with bricks for the first Indianapolis 500 in 2011, the number of entries and fans filling grandstands grew steadily. Until World War I curtailed racing in 1917 and 1918, Indy racing enthusiasts watched powerful cars from companies such as Fiat, Sunbeam, Stutz, Duesenberg, Buick, Peugeot, Mercedes and Frontenac that were driven by greats like Ralph DePalma, Jules Goux, Dario Resta and Louis Chevrolet. After the war, stars such as Gaston Chevrolet, Tommy Milton and Jimmy Murphy emerged.

Future flying ace Rickenbacker drove in the first Indy 500. He started the race as a riding mechanic before replacing the original driver, Lee Frayer, in the early going. Rickenbacker, who began racing five years

Fame, Wealth, Tragedy

earlier as a riding mechanic, would drive in five of the six pre-war Indy races with middling results.

"Nothing could have pleased Eddie more than to be engaged in the most dangerous sport on earth, one even more likely than bullfighting to result in death or serious injury," wrote Lewis. "Safety devices later used to protect drivers did not exist. Drivers wore 'simple cloth helmets' and protected their faces 'from flying gravel and dirt by googles and cloth masks.' Seats were purposefully made tight to keep occupants from falling out. Riding mechanics, who sat beside the driver, had the most hazardous job of all. Unlike drivers, they could not brace themselves with the steering wheel if a car went out of control. Indeed, in some race cars a riding mechanic could not sit at all but merely clung to a strap behind the driver's seat, on the right-hand side of the vehicle, and braced his left foot on a projecting piece of metal."

At Indy, many of the journalists carrying typewriters and film cameras came from Europe to cover the exploits of their native drivers and manufacturers. In 1921, Chicago's far-reaching WGN radio station began broadcasting each Indy 500 race in shows featuring advertisers of automotive products. The manufacturer of the winning cars, meanwhile, basked in publicity that reached around the world due to Indy's reputation for speed, mechanical innovation and heroics.

In an age when cars were considered technical marvels by enthusiasts, fans of racing offered unalloyed admiration to the drivers who thrilled at the prospects of putting themselves at risk. They were special men, and occasionally women, a breed apart whose love of the chase evoked the human spirit in a manner unlike any other. Some like Rickenbacker lived and others, such as "Wild Bob" Burman, died.

Burman was an early star of the National Championship, created in 1909 and sanctioned by the Contest Board of the American Automobile Association (AAA). He became one of the first major stars in racing to die behind the wheel, a pattern that would be repeated every decade throughout the 20th Century.

In the first year of the National Championship, Burman won the inaugural race at the gargantuan new Indianapolis track, a 250-mile event contested on dirt. Then Burman set a speed record of 141.7 mph behind the power of the Blitzen Benz's 21.5-liter engine on the sand at Daytona Beach in the spring shortly before the first 500 took off at Indy in 1911. Burman drove in the first four 500s (onboard a Burman chassis in 1914) and eventually earned victories in six of the AAA's National Championship races for the Indy-type cars. When a tire blew, he was killed during a California road race shortly before the Contest Board launched its 1916 season.

"The death of Bob Burman from multiple injuries in a California road race that had no bearing on the national rankings," read one obituary, "cast a pall over the upcoming season before it even began."

Following the success of the inaugural Indy 500, ovals soon replaced public road courses as the favored type of race track in America, initially in the form of board tracks. Modeled after cycling velodromes where speeds in tight packs reached a mere 35 mph, the motor racing tracks were built on a far grander scale. These ultra-fast tracks where speeds exceeded 100 mph could be built quickly by a horde of carpenters from tons of wooden 2 x 4s and thousands of pounds of nails. As a result of the board tracks' speed, glamor and locations near major population centers such as Sheepshead Bay on Long Island and Beverley Hills, race car drivers became popular heroes by the end of the Golden Era of American sports in the 1920s. An Indy winner and speed record holder like Frank Lockhart, also a master of the board tracks, rivaled boxer Jack Dempsey and baseball's Babe Ruth in terms of fame.

As profiled by writer Burgess Meredith, Lockhart grew up poor and almost illiterate despite a towering intellect. He stood a mere five feet, three inches tall. Fascinated by the Model T as a boy and efforts around Los Angeles to race these Fords, Lockhart schooled himself about cars, anything he could learn in books, and mechanical drafting. In school, he ignored everything except his penchant for drawing cars. Cal Tech discovered his mathematical genius by testing him, but Lockhart's single-parent mother, who supported her family by sewing, couldn't afford college.

Exploiting his extraordinary gift for engineering, Lockhart leveraged himself from racing Model Ts to an opportunity at Indianapolis in 1926, where he used dirt track-style slides through the corners in his Miller chassis to improve his times. When rain fell midway during his inaugural appearance at the Brickyard, washing the track clean, Lockhart's broad-sliding technique on the slick bricks annihilated the field and he won the 500 as a rookie, then won four more National Championship races on board tracks later that season and finished second in the points.

The vulnerability to disrepair, fire and rising real estate values would eventually scupper the board tracks on the schedule in favor of dirt ovals on the National Championship trail and the Brickyard in Indianapolis. The stock market crash, which meant the end of ready money needed by men such as Harry Miller and the Duesenberg brothers to build race cars and find buyers, became the final blow to the board tracks. By then the brilliant Lockhart, a recognized mechanical genius, had died on the sands of Daytona Beach while attempting to establish a new land speed record in a Stutz Black Hawk, a car much of his own devising, that touched 225 mph before crashing.

The racing on the board tracks, at Indy and on the permanent European circuits was not much safer than risking all in land speed record attempts. The permanent circuits afforded better opportunities for promotion, ticket sales and crowd control—but did little to improve the safety of the participants. Led by the Fédération Internationale de l'Automobile (FIA), which began organizing racing in Europe in 1922, and the American Automobile Association Contest Board in the U.S., sanctioning bodies, promoters and car manufacturers continued to count on a formula of drivers willing to risk their lives in the name of glory and fans willing to purchase tickets to witness its pursuit amid that curious combo of fascination mixed with the potential for horror so well identified by the poster art of Robert Williams.

The packed grandstands at permanent circuits stood testimony to the exhibition of raw courage unfolding on the track, the kind of attention which no doubt helped spur drivers toward the risk. For the independently wealthy, racing became a path to prove one's self beyond mere financial capacity. The crowds generated a relatively large sum of money, a great incentive for some drivers seeking their fortune such as Lockhart and Rickenbacker, who would later start a car company and buy the Indianapolis Motor Speedway as a member of an investment group in 1927.

Beyond personal satisfaction, a driver who won regularly could earn far more than in almost any other available line of work. Lockhart's mother could not afford college, so he went racing. Orphaned and forced to quit school after his father was killed in a fight, Rickenbacker found racing to be his best shot at a lucrative path forward. He would eventually win seven AAA National Championship races before World War I intervened. Flying fighter planes brought more fame for his concentration, determination and daring before he returned to his interests in engineering, cars and racing.

Ten years after Lockhart's demise in 1928, the equally famed and popular young German hero Bernd Rosemeyer died in a crash while traveling at over 260 mph aboard an Auto Union streamliner on a closed portion of the Autobahn in Germany. He hoped to set a land speed record that would produce a bonus for Audi from the fascist government of the Nazis. Rosemeyer, whose death followed a record-setting drive by Rudolf Caracciola on behalf of Mercedes-Benz earlier that same day, had been a multiple winner at the Nürburgring and had won one of the Vanderbilt Cup events during the race's revival in the 1930s. But as a result of Rosemeyer's spectacular demise, the allure of land speed record runs began to lose their luster. As an avenue to fame and fortune, the pursuit of such records fell by the wayside for car manufacturers and race car drivers, except for the pursuit by a select few specialists after World War II.

Fame, Wealth, Tragedy

The 17th Marquis de Portago pursued the noble cause of becoming a world driving champion. (The Klemantaski Collection)

One of those fascinated by the serious demands of motor racing in post–World War II America, which sometimes meant drivers losing their lives, was future race announcer Ken Squier. A native of Vermont, where his father helped promote harness racing by working as a track announcer at county fairs, Squier thought the pursuit of horse-drawn sulkies far less exciting compared with the AAA's National Championship races that occasionally used the same dirt tracks on county fair weekends. His favorite driver, Ted Horn, won the National Championship in 1946 and 1947 before being crowned posthumously in 1948 after a fatal crash on the challenging and fast clay mile of the Du Quoin State Fairgrounds in Illinois. Horn, who cut his racing teeth among the rough-and-tumble at Legion Ascot Speedway in Los Angeles, won an impressive 24 National Championship races during his career.

With an immediately recognizable voice that seemed to carry both the timber of the Vermont woods and the brimstone of New England religion, Squier went on to become one of motor racing's most riveting storytellers behind the microphones of radio and then TV. On the night of his induction into the National Motorsports Press Association's Hall of Fame in 2013, he summed up the fascination with the risks of racing, as if in a pulpit, starting with his own attraction to the sport.

"From the time I was a young boy I got to see the original Joie Chitwood drive on a half-mile track in sprint cars. I also got to see the others like Wild Bill Holland and Johnny Parsons. My hero, my hero when I was just a little kid, was Ted Horn from California.

"I think it was 1948 when he was killed at Du Quoin. That was not only a tragic day. But it was a day that it really brought home to me, because this was my hero. I had seen him in 1945 in Vermont on the Essex Junction Fairgrounds, the first National Championship race after the World War II. And Ted Horn from California beat Lee Wallard by about six feet.

"For a kid, I felt about that victory like some people feel about the World Series. This was it. Then in '48, he was gone. But it brought up the whole business about what this business was. This was no joke. This was the real game. This was not a sport that was a children's game played by adults. This was a game played by adults with all the risks that there is in the activities of our lives. If sports are a metaphor on life, the one that I began to believe as I grew older came closest to it was this motorsports business.

"Here were men who believed so wholly in what they did and were so committed to what they did that they were willing to take the risks. They weren't silly, they weren't foolish. They were people who were committed and trying to do something better than others could. If one fell, the greatest tribute one could pay was be there the next week and race in their honor of those people."

During the 1950s, another driver considered noble in more ways than one joined the list of racing greats who lost their lives in the course of events.

It's not as if Don Alfonso Cabeza de Vaca y Leighton, the 17th Marquis de Portago, needed another title. But the idea of pursuing a title that even a member of the nobility must earn—that of a world champion driver—drew him to racing. Celebrated for accomplishments in airplanes, on polo ponies, in bobsleds and swimming, the Spanish nobleman, who drove in his first race before knowing how to shift gears, became one of the world's best sports car drivers not long after buying his own entry, a 3.0-liter Ferrari. Typical of such an accomplished man's attitude, a world championship became the next goal.

In the late winter of 1957, many of the world's best drivers gathered amidst the fragrant orange groves of central Florida for the annual 12-hour race over the concrete runways of the former Army Air Force training base near the town of Sebring. An event on the calendar for those aspiring to win the world championship of sports cars, the entry list included de Portago, a driver who would later be described as "The Man Who Could Do Everything" in a magazine story by Ken W. Purdy.

The dean of American automotive and race writing at the time, Purdy regularly wrote fiction stories published in magazines in addition to his reporting. He met with "Fon" at the Kenilworth Lodge at the edge of Lake Jackson in Sebring. Over the course of a wide-ranging interview recorded on tape, they discussed the Spaniard's surprising lack of interest in cars, his love of racing and what it meant to compete at high speed with fate perennially perched on one's shoulder.

After more than an hour of exchanges, Purdy offered a question that cut to the quick of what it meant to be a world class race car driver. "I have a quotation in a story," said Purdy, "a piece of fiction, something that, I thought at the time, you might have said: Of all sports, only bullfighting and mountain climbing and motor racing really tried a man, that all the rest were mere recreations. Would you have said that?"

"I couldn't agree with you more," replied the handsome and lithe Spaniard, who at 28 years old had a mane of curly black hair that covered his ears and a propensity for smoking but not inhaling. "You're quite right," he said. "I've thought of bullfighting, of course, but the trouble is that you must start when you're a child, otherwise you'll never really know the bulls. And the only trouble with mountain climbing for me is the lack of an audience! Like most drivers, I'm something of an exhibitionist."

Few exchanges in motor racing history better summed up the motivation of race car drivers. They sought the adulation of fans after beating an entire field of similarly disposed drivers and enjoyed the self-confidence that came from defeating the fear of one's own annihilation.

That helps explain why the phrase of Purdy's

Fame, Wealth, Tragedy

fictional character, inspired by de Portago, entered the popular lexicon among racers. But people regularly attributed the phrase to Ernest Hemmingway, the more renowned macho fiction writer who wrote eloquently about bullfighting and could easily be considered one of those who admired motor racing. Certainly Hemmingway-like, the bromide was modified as it became lore and altered to end with "…all the rest are just games." The saying that showed up on T-shirts sometimes dropped mountain climbing in favor of boxing, another of Hemmingway's passions.

"Bullfighting, boxing and racing are the only real sports. All the rest are just games." So went the legend. It underscored the emphasis on risk in racing versus safety, which for an entire century was considered the right formula. If not dangerous, with the laurels going most often to the drivers whose skill brought him closer to the edge, then it wasn't really racing.

Standing in sharp contrast and an exception who proved the rule was American Phil Hill, who also began competing in the 1950s and eventually became the first American to win a Formula 1 World Championship. An avowed contrarian who could be quite cantankerous in later life, Hill did not warm to the limelight, did not enjoy beating others particularly and refused to be egged on by the adulation of fans or his own ego when it came to self-glorification during his days as a competitor in F1.

"I would so love to get out of this unbent," Hill told author Robert Daley for his seminal racing book *The Cruel Sport*. "I have a horror of cripples," continued Hill. "I guess I've always worried about ending up that way myself. I want to get out of this in one piece."

What motivated Hill to race? "Because I do it well," he said. Daley expounded on the intelligent, shy world champion's brief summation with his own observations. "How can a man not do something which he knows how to do brilliantly?" wrote Daley. The satisfaction of succeeding at the sharp end of racing, he observed, was leveraged by the physical and mental challenges presented by a world class event,

The demands of Formula 1 racing are evident on the face of Hill after finishing second at Monaco in 1962. (The Klemantaski Collection)

during which the body takes a pounding, the brain gets inundated by the demands of driving at speed and the risk of crashing, possibly causing serious injury or worse, has to be ignored.

It was not ironic that Hill won his world championship in the final race of the 1961 season versus Ferrari factory teammate Wolfgang von Trips, a German nobleman, known as one of those more reckless, glory-bound drivers who often chose risk to gain an edge and by the nickname "Count von Crash." The fatal incident of von Trips at Monza, where debris from his car sailed into the fans pressed against the fences, took the lives of as many as 15 of the Italian *tifosi* at the Autodromo Nazionale Monza and also took the lion's share of media coverage on the day that Hill finally won his championship.

Although granted his wish to be left out of the glare of the limelight, Hill was nevertheless miffed that his accomplishment did not bring more recognition after the bulk of attention was spent on the death of von Trips and the fans. Hill would soon begin concentrating on sports cars before retiring from racing to focus on restoring old cars and writing about cars and racing.

As for de Portago, he died several months after his 1957 meeting with Purdy, behind the wheel of a factory Ferrari in the Mille Miglia and scant miles short of Brescia and victory. In his mind's eye, he could see yet another stupendous accomplishment based on endurance, reflexes, balance and nearly 1,000 miles of determined risk-taking. He gambled that a front tire being rubbed as a result of a suspension that had been bent on a curb would last until the finish despite a mechanic's suggestion to replace it at the final checkpoint. When the tire blew at 150 miles per hour at Guidizzolo, the horrendous flailing of the Ferrari killed nine Italian fans gathered alongside the road, including two children, plus de Portago and his navigator Edmund Nelson. Before the Ferrari came to a rest in a ditch, the displaced hood had sliced through the Spanish nobleman like a buccaneer's sword, cutting him in half.

Daley, who covered sports in Europe for *The New York Times*, where his father Arthur Daley was a sports columnist, had also befriended de Portago. As eloquently as Daley had written about the demands of danger, the way it could destroy a driver's ego and human spirit, he considered the driver's willingness to accept risk part of the sport. "There are those who wrote afterwards that de Portago was in love with death but they do not know him and this statement is absurd," wrote Daley in his first racing book, *Cars at Speed*. "Alfonso de Portago was in love with life."

A form of competition he loved and considered art on wheels, Daley saw the cruel sport as a noble, romantic choice, all of which was embodied by de Portago, who "seemed to me the most alive man I had ever known," he wrote. "He was sensitive, restless, curiously gentle, and it is impossible to describe the impression of straining vitality which he communicated, nor to do justice to the overwhelming disbelief his friends felt when news of his death arrived."

Purdy voiced a more dyspeptic final observation of de Portago, one he attributed to the British attitude toward racing, which he quoted. "There are two kinds of drivers: those who get killed before they get good, and those who get killed afterwards."

Although the Targo Florio would continue in Sicily until 1977, the de Portago crash brought the end to racing on public roads in Italy. After half a century and following Pierre Levegh's crash in France at Le Mans that had killed or injured as many as 100 spectators in 1955, the era of major events being run on the public roads comprised of loop circuits in Europe would soon disappear in the name of safety as had already happened in America. But that safety at permanent circuits focused on spectators, not the drivers, who would continue to accept the risk of death as their stock in trade.

By the end of motor racing's first century, five of the world's fastest and oldest major circuits—Le Mans (a combination of public roads and private track), Monza, the Nürburgring, Indy and the Daytona International Speedway would account for nearly 200 driver fatalities.

After professional motor racing had been established in 1909 by the AAA, racing crashes claimed the lives of at least one driving star in every decade of the 20th Century. Greats like Bob Burman, Gaston Chevrolet, Jimmy Murphy and Frank Lockhart all died before 1930. When Formula 1 World Champion Ayrton Senna and CART star Greg Moore were killed in the final decade of the century, followed by NASCAR champion Dale Earnhardt's death in the first decade of the 21st Century, it continued a long-standing pattern.

7

The Fire Next Time

DEATH WAS A CONSTANT COMPANION TO drivers in auto racing throughout the 20th Century, but no decade suffered more fatalities than the 1960s, which hastened a sharper focus on safety. As a result, harnesses, improved helmets, fuel cells, fire suits, and stronger cars stemmed the horrid tide by the early 1970s. These changes, adapted from the aircraft industry, maintained racing as an accepted professional sport and defused criticism from sportswriters like Jim Murray of the *L.A. Times*, who famously dropped this line on the Indy 500: "Gentlemen, start your coffins."

While the safety innovations may have helped keep technical innovations and greater speed from overwhelming the sport and broader society's sensibilities, physical risk remained a beckoning lure for drivers and fans alike. Speeds continue to increase as racing hurtled into the future and risk continued to be measured in occasional deaths.

Emblematic of racing's most disastrous and fiery decade, the 1964 Indy 500 led to two deaths before drivers had completed two laps. When rookie Johnny Rutherford lined up on the outside of the fifth row to start that race, he had no idea that he would soon be driving through one of the most infamous wrecks in racing history. Another rookie, Dave MacDonald, was starting inside of Rutherford's Watson roadster in a low-slung, skate-type chassis built by Mickey Thompson. Poor MacDonald, a young up-and-coming driver, had committed to doing what his ilk had always done. He accepted an offer to drive a car he knew could be dangerous to further his career, not unlike Jim Downing agreeing to drive a Mazda with no ventilation at the harrowing Mosport Park circuit 16 years later.

Thompson's Indy car handled poorly enough that Graham Hill, the accomplished F1 ace, had declined to drive it and instead chose to sit out the race even though fellow Grand Prix drivers Dan Gurney and Jimmy Clark would garner worldwide attention for participating in the Lotus chassis built in England. After crashing during practice in the Thompson chassis, whose front end had a tendency to lift off, F1 regular Masten Gregory quit the team.

At a time when all teams were paying keen attention to the amount of fuel carried and pit stop strategy, MacDonald's Sears All State Special carried a 45-gallon hard rubber tank of gasoline on the left side, a choice that figured prominently in the ensuing disaster. Directly behind MacDonald, starting in the middle of the fifth row onboard a Shrike, sat Eddie Sachs, the popular and unofficial "clown prince" of the Brickyard. Another relatively small rear-engine car, the Shrike packed gasoline into several different tanks, including an external metal tank on the left side.

In his authoritative book *Black Noon*, Art Garner provides a detailed, blow-by-blow account of MacDonald's second ill-fated lap. When he lost control of the front end of the car, which lifted off the ground as he maneuvered in traffic, the right side of the Thompson chassis hit the inside wall at the exit of Turn 4 with enough force to break off the gas tank's filler cap on the opposite side, starting the conflagration. The burning car threw up a wall of flame as it slid back across the track

The Fire Next Time

The huge gasoline-fueled fire that killed MacDonald and Sachs at Indy led to rubber fuel bladders and methanol. (IMS Photo Archives)

and into the path of the oncoming Shrike of Sachs. With few options, Sachs collided into the left side of MacDonald's car and the already broken gas tank. The Shrike had a small auxiliary gas tank in the front and the resulting fireball produced a towering black cloud as one flaming wheel and tire assembly bounded over the fence and landed in front of the grandstand. Sachs died immediately and MacDonald succumbed to burns a short while later.

Rutherford, following Sachs, miraculously cleared MacDonald's car, rammed his right-side wheels up against the outside wall and continued before the Novi of Bobby Unser hit him. As he motored around the track under red flag conditions, Rutherford, a future three-time Indy 500 winner, noticed track workers positioned on the inside of the oval waving at him. He came to a stop along with rest of the drivers in a grassy area inside the track. "When I got out and walked around the car," said Rutherford, "I saw gasoline leaking at the back." Considering his roadster's large tail-mounted tank had been cracked by his impact with

Crash! How the HANS Helped Save Racing

The Fire Next Time

the wall followed by the collision with Unser, he had been very lucky to go over MacDonald's car, escape the gigantic fireball, and avoid his own car catching fire.

Unser, another future three-time Indy winner, had decided that standing on the accelerator was his only option and drove his Novi through the fire without braking, although hitting the cars of both Rutherford and Ronnie Duman.

Once again, the pursuit of speed and technology had overwhelmed the sport. The rule makers at the United States Auto Club (USAC) had little choice to make changes to protect fans, drivers and their event, stopped by a red flag for the first time since the inaugural race in 1911. With some prominent exceptions such as the crashes of Salt Walther and Swede Savage, the threat of fire was soon diminished by rule changes. Minimum car weights and fuel tank maximums were introduced and gasoline or more exotic racing fuel mixes were replaced by the less volatile methanol. Most important were the military-style, rubber-lined fuel cells, the type long in use in military aircraft, which helped prevent fuel spilling during crashes.

The week before the MacDonald-Sachs crash, Fireball Roberts received severe burns at the 600-mile NASCAR race at the Charlotte Motor Speedway. Nicknamed for the speed of his fastball as a baseball pitcher, Roberts became NASCAR's first hero of the ultra-fast, high-banked tracks that emerged in the 1960s following the opening of the Daytona International Speedway in 1959. In Charlotte, Roberts was engulfed in flames when fellow driver and friend Ned Jarrett, caught in the same crash, arrived at the car. "Help me Ned," shouted Roberts. "I'm on fire." Jarrett bravely helped pull him out, but Roberts died later in the hospital. NASCAR soon mandated the use of fuel cells and the readily available technology from aviation.

Just two years after these horrendous incidents, future three-time Formula 1 world champion Jackie Stewart luckily escaped fiery doom after a multi-car crash during a sudden rainstorm at the circuit located in Spa, Belgium, in 1966. In an account by Charles Fox in *The Great Racing Cars & Drivers*, Stewart became trapped in a ditch with his legs pinned under the steering wheel and woozy from a concussion. He could hear the fuel pump and motor in his BRM continuing to run, soaking him with gasoline. Graham Hill and American Bob Bondurant, who had been involved in the same incident, tried to shut off the engine and to remove the steering wheel—initially to no avail because the control panel built into the cockpit's bulkhead had been crushed.

By the time Hill and Bondurant succeeded in removing the steering wheel after finding a wrench nearby, Stewart had been soaking in gasoline for nearly half an hour. He suffered chemical burns to his skin in addition to broken bones and a concussion.

Brian Redman, in his memoir *Daring Drivers, Deadly Tracks*, summed up the similar dangerous circumstances in sports car racing's world championship for prototypes, where one in three drivers died in the years 1965-75. "It was as if an unseen sniper haunted the tracks and picked off random victims without warning, unsparing of veterans and even legends."

Stewart's accident led to one immediate safety improvement in F1. Drivers and teams began taping a wrench to the side of their cars, in case one was needed, a smack in the face to the Fédération Internationale de l'Automobile, the organizer of F1. Stewart decided to take the protest a step further. He continued to race, but his hospitalization had turned him into a radical on the subject of safety. He began an effort by the Grand Prix Drivers Association (GPDA) to force the FIA to introduce better safety on all fronts.

"We began to ask every track owner to have potentially life-saving barriers installed around their circuits," said Stewart in a retrospective article in Britain's *The Telegraph*. "We also started to demand that every F1 driver be compelled to wear flameproof overalls, thermal underwear, officially certified helmets, six-point safety belts or harnesses, and high-quality thermal socks and gloves to protect against burns. Through 1968 and into 1969, we raised the issue of safety at every opportunity, alternating dire warnings with new demands."

F1 drivers had long refused to wear seat belts. Stewart was among the first when he began using them in 1964. American Masten Gregory, a winner in sports cars who competed in 38 F1 races through 1965, became famous for leaping from his cars during crashes. The great British F1 ace Stirling Moss won 16 poles and 16 races in F1, but never once wore seat belts in 66 starts. Considered a driver who helped define F1 as a racing pinnacle and regarded as one of the sport's all-time greats, Moss relished the danger. "In my era," he said, "if it was too hot in the kitchen, fine, don't come in the kitchen. What I'm saying is that if you make racing safe, you obviously lessen the challenge." A crash in 1962 in an F1 Lotus-Climax put Moss in a coma for 30 days, injured his back and forced his retirement, but did little to change his admiration for the marriage of risk and racing.

Americans had long worn seat belts. Early stock car drivers used ropes as well as aviation-type harnesses to better hold themselves in the stock bench seats while driving, which led NASCAR to require belts. Open-wheel racers in America competed on ovals and often enough suffered flips and rollovers, where getting thrown out was not considered the best option. A safety harness helped when upside down.

In Europe, the significant change of attitude toward seat belts in F1 began with Dr. Michael Henderson's 1968 book, *Motor Racing In Safety,* which persuasively documented that remaining secure in the seat during a crash produced a better outcome. The best way to remain secure, observed Henderson, was a six-point harness in place of the more common shoulder harness and belt, because what he termed a "crutch belt" held the pelvis tightly.

Along with four other engineers, Henderson also helped design the Sigma Grand Prix in conjunction with Ferrari and the Italian design firm Peninfarina. A concept car dedicated to F1 safety introduced in 1969, in addition to six-point belts, the Sigma featured a driver safety compartment and a fuel cell. It arrived two years after Ferrari driver Lorenzo Bandini suffered death by an inferno at Monaco as a result of crashing into hay bales—not long after Stewart escaped fire at Spa. In a particularly gruesome scenario, safety crews dragged Bandini, then dropped him while getting him out of the flames—all caught by TV cameras. Like stock car driver Roberts, and MacDonald at Indy, Bandini survived long enough to expire in the hospital from extensive burns.

As at Indy prior to 1964, the European teams in F1 and sports cars considered building a fast car first and built the fueling system accordingly and without much regard to driver safety. Although World War II aircraft built in Europe usually did not have fuel cells, the technology was readily available and from the mid-1960s had been adapted to racing in the U.S. Once the chances of fire were greatly diminished by the use of fuel cells and Nomex fire suits, European drivers were persuaded that the strength of the cars could keep them safe relative to being thrown out during a crash. Henderson suggested that avoiding injury and being able to climb out after releasing one's seat belt comprised a better scenario for a driver in a burning car.

The final argument in favor of six-point belts, believed Henderson, resulted from the fatal crash of Jochen Rindt, the posthumously crowned champion of the 1970 F1 season. Rindt had declined Henderson's suggestion to wear a six-point harness in favor of using only a shoulder harness and lap belt. Henderson later reported that the buckle from the lap belt had hit Rindt underneath his jaw in the head-on crash into a barrier at Monza, contributing to a fatal outcome. A six-point harness, in addition to securing the pelvis and preventing a driver from submarining beneath the steering wheel, also helped keep the lap belt in place.

There had been resistance to safety harnesses in America as well. Two-time NASCAR Grand National champion Joe Weatherly thought it better to "flop around" in a crash and wore his shoulder belts loosely even though they were required by the sanctioning body. He died in a high-speed crash at the Riverside,

California, track in 1964 while defending his second title. Soon, five-point harnesses were required by NASCAR with a single center-mounted crotch belt that connected to the central buckle and helped keep the lap and shoulder belts in place. But it would be three decades before NASCAR acknowledged that six-point belts improved performance by keeping a driver's pelvis more firmly in place during a crash.

Helmets likewise brought scorn from some drivers. Dick Rathmann wore a cork-lined Cromwell leather helmet designed for polo players in the same Indy 500 that claimed MacDonald and Sachs when all around him were wearing fiberglass helmets modeled after those used by jet pilots and designed for racing, first introduced in the 1950s. Certification of helmets for racing by the Snell Foundation began in 1957.

Improved safety could not arrive soon enough in the 1960s, a time when individual choice reigned supreme and the mindset of World War II and the fatalistic attitudes towards death were just beginning to wane. In 1964 alone, seven drivers were killed in USAC and NASCAR. In addition to Sachs and MacDonald, USAC driver Bobby Marshman died from burns sustained in a testing crash onboard a Lotus-Ford. NASCAR drivers Billy Wade and Jimmy Pardue were killed in separate tire tests following the deaths of Weatherly and Roberts.

Eight of the 16 drivers who started the Monaco Grand Prix in 1968 would eventually be killed in racing accidents. That list did not include legendary Scotsman Jim Clark, whose fatal accident had occurred a little over a month earlier onboard a Formula 2 machine at the Hockenheim circuit in Germany, a track with no barriers between the track and the surrounding trees.

The arrival of new safety elements like five-point and six-point harnesses, improved helmets, fuel cells and fire suits all originated in the aircraft industry, much like performance enhancements in race cars such as aerodynamics and fuel-injected engines. The U.S. space program contributed DuPont-manufactured Nomex, which led to lightweight fireproof clothing for drivers championed by safety pioneer Bill Simpson, who regularly set himself alight to demonstrate his wares. Drivers had been wearing asbestos suits in U.S. drag racing, but the material proved too cumbersome in other forms of racing.

Sanctioning bodies in general continued to allow drivers to choose the risk or decline to race for increasingly better pay—particularly at Indy—as well as the ongoing prestige and glory from winning. Sanctioning groups expected safety improvements to be generated by outside influences and adopted by participants on their own. The aircraft industry, the space program, and vendors who convinced the racers to use products like Nomex fire suits and certified helmets helped drive the process far more than sanctioning bodies.

Sanctioning groups, which were sued regularly by angry family members of injured or killed drivers, preferred the legal position of having the drivers accept liability. But racing organizers often faced opposition to change in the name of safety from the drivers themselves, too. As epitomized by Rindt, Weatherly and Rathmann, drivers often declined new advancements in safety until they had been proven over time. Eventually, rulebooks would usually reflect a change once accepted by the majority of drivers.

Cooperation by drivers as a group in the name of safety rarely occurred, as might be expected from such a group of iconoclastic, free-spirited, strong-minded individuals who thrilled to the risk of racing. Cooperation among drivers was a contradiction for individuals who always seemed ready for a fight with City Hall, i.e., the sanctioning body, as well as their fellow competitors. Fans, too, endorsed the risk element and Jackie Stewart's protest in the name of safety sometimes drew derisive comments.

In the same era as Stewart's campaign with the GPDA, one rare event took place in NASCAR in Talladega, Alabama. In 1969, the NASCAR drivers went on strike prior to the first race at the track known as Alabama International Motor Speedway due to concerns over tires exploding on the new track's 33-degree banking. That short-lived movement

Stewart began a safety crusade in F1 after his BRM crashed at Spa and the cockpit became a bathtub of gas. (The Klemantaski Collection)

included Lee Roy Yarbrough punching NASCAR founder "Big Bill" France and the drivers walking out before the first race at the Alabama track. But the strike organized by a group called the Professional Drivers Association, according to the group's executive director Leonard Laye, resulted from disgruntlement with purse structures as much as safety. In general, drivers favored bravado and the admiration of peers and fans versus looking sheepish in the face of their sport's danger. It was the same tough-minded psychological outlook they used in races to dare one another to go faster at the risk of crashing—or give up a position.

Nothing seemed to persuade race organizers to make the protection of drivers a bona fide priority. GM, Ford and Chrysler all withdrew from NASCAR during the 1970 and 1971 seasons due to some deadly accidents, particularly at the Daytona International Speedway, and pressure in the U.S. Congress resulting from Ralph Nader's crusade built around his exposé of highway cars in his book titled *Unsafe at Any Speed*.

The sport of stock car racing went into a major economic depression in the absence of factories occasioned by the safety concerns in Congress. But few significant safety changes occurred in NASCAR cockpits during the 1970s—as if the issue of safety would just blow over. If there was a change in NASCAR, it was the sanctioning body regularly touting the safety of its cars in the 1970s by pointing to fuel cells, produced by tire manufacturers, and tube frames, both having arrived in the 1960s.

Introduced by Ralph Moody of Ford's Holman-Moody factory team, the tube frames greatly enhanced driver safety, no doubt, by making cars stronger. But the new cars were also typical of safety improvements suggested by competitors. They provided a more stable platform for the suspension, hence allowed cars to go faster in the corners. In 1967, Mario Andretti drove one of the new tube-framed cars to his first major victory in the Daytona 500. "I would go into the turns in the bottom lane and by time I got out, I was up by the wall," recalled Andretti, who used his experience from the Indy 500 to take advantage of the tube-framed car's better, albeit hair-raising, speed in the corners.

The tube frames were also relatively cheap to build. Ultimately, the influence of the aircraft industry was again at work as it had been in other racing series. The tube frames and riveted bodywork were just like an aircraft's space frame and fuselage.

The economic depression in NASCAR during the 1970s that followed the factory withdrawals also slowed the pace of speed increases, which was an indirect benefit to safety. That did not prevent the death of Daytona 500 winner and fan favorite DeWayne "Tiny" Lund, killed in a crash in 1975 at Talladega, one track in NASCAR where speeds continued to climb. It was one of four fatal accidents in NASCAR's premier series during that decade and the second at Talladega after the death of Larry Smith.

At Indy, a radical story emerged when it came to speed. USAC and the owners of the Speedway recognized the correlation between increased speeds at the Brickyard from rear wings and the resulting fan excitement. In 1971, the McLaren team, in a move copied by team owner/driver A.J. Foyt overnight, was the first to outfox the rulebook, which had outlawed rear wings. McLaren's interpretation that a rear wing attached to

Jim Clark's luck would not last. But he and Colin Chapman of Lotus, pictured here in 1966, enjoyed success at Indy.
(The Klemantaski Collection)

the main body of the car could be considered bodywork instead of a wing quickly evolved into all cars sprouting rear wings. Predictably, the speeds escalated dramatically. Following the excitement of 1971, rear wings of limited height were endorsed for the next year by rule maker USAC. From 1971 to 1972 alone, the pole speed at Indy jumped 17 miles per hour. The magic mark of average lap speeds of 200 mph soon became the standard. And the driver fatalities continued—Jim Malloy, Art Pollard and Swede Savage died in crashes before the decade was out.

Ironically, a rear bodywork problem led to driver/team owner Bruce McLaren's death while testing one of his Can-Am cars in the summer of 1970. Not long after leaving that year's Indy 500, the New Zealander first broached the idea to his team of how to add a rear wing to McLaren's Indy car in anticipation of the 1971 race.

In F1—where skyscraper-tall rear wings were outlawed—speeds continued to climb and circuits continued to leave competitors vulnerable in crashes. Despite changes wrought by Stewart's campaign, the equation of the drivers deciding how to gauge their own risk remained in place. In *Chasing the Title,* longtime F1 writer Nigel Roebuck underscored the occasionally slack attitudes toward safety by the sanctioning FIA. "Different regimes at the FIA took different attitudes toward safety," he wrote, "some paying lip service, others treating it with outright contempt, others again taking it seriously."

Whether it was at Talladega or at Barcelona in Spain, where drivers disputed guard rail conditions prior to the Grand Prix of Spain in 1975, promoters and sanctioning bodies in major series always had pressure on them to proceed with races even if conditions were dangerous for drivers. Once NASCAR introduced restrictor plates at Daytona and Talladega to keep cars from flying into the grandstands, the resulting large drafts of cars made racing more dangerous for the drivers. But ticket sales continued.

In a situation made famous by the movie "Rush," midway in the 1976 season the F1 competitors were allowed to vote on whether to race in heavy rain on the always dangerous Nürburgring. Some, thinking they could find advantage, voted to continue in the absence of any authority stepping up in the name of safety. Allowing the drivers to vote exemplified a case of lip service by the FIA to the cause of safety.

Niki Lauda, who had voiced his opposition to racing that day, famously crashed. When hit by the car of American Brett Lunger, the Ferrari of Lauda caught fire and the driver was severely burned. (Lunger immediately jumped out of his damaged car and ran to the burning Ferrari, helping Arturo Merzario pull Lauda out, saving his life.) As the movie portrays, Lauda gallantly fought lung damage suffered in the fire to compete against James Hunt for the world championship after losing a sizeable points advantage while in the hospital. But in the season finale on the Mt. Fuji circuit in Japan, Lauda withdrew from the race due to what he considered unsafe conditions of heavy rain and foggy conditions, losing the title to Hunt by one point. He would follow on the heels of Stewart by pushing for safety improvements—and like Stewart go on to win three world championships.

Despite the high-profile crash of Lauda, which was covered by the wire services and numerous racing trade publications, the effort to change the odds in favor of safety always ran up against the acceptance and admiration by the racing culture, which held that racing at high speeds necessarily carried inherent risk. Instead, the focus was on giving medals to the two drivers who helped save Lauda, Lauda's gutsy comeback after only six weeks, and Hunt's incredible comeback to win the title.

When the much loved, free-spirited and effervescent Canadian Gilles Villeneuve died at the Zolder circuit in Belgium in 1982 when he guessed wrong on which way a slower car would move to allow him through during a banzai qualifying lap that turned into a literal flyer, it shocked and saddened the racing world, but did not take it by surprise. Similarly, when Villeneuve's brilliant young counterpart in rally driving, Henri Toivonen, fatally crashed in Corsica four years later, shock mixed with grief, but the fatal crash was not totally unexpected.

The FIA summarily banned the Group B cars used in rallying at the time of Toivonen's death—the so-called Killer Bs. Otherwise, not much political fallout occurred. But eight years after Toivonen's death, when three-time F1 World Champion Senna died at the Imola circuit in Italy, it became an entirely different matter. The entire world responded with shock and surprise, which in turn shocked the FIA and participants in F1, beginning a new era of racing safety.

Max Mosley, the FIA president at the time of Senna's death, had competed in the Formula 2 event in which celebrated champion Jim Clark was killed. In fact, it was his first race. Mosley, a man who believed strongly in individual choice, continued his driving efforts and later became a part-owner of the March Engineering team in F1. As the FIA's leader, he found himself stunned by the backlash from the media and the public in the aftermath of Senna's fatal crash. In response, within weeks of Senna's death Mosley made a major decision on safety.

Nearly a half century after the shift began to permanent circuits to protect fans, the FIA was forced to radically change course to protect the sport. This time, the focus was on making the safety of drivers an unquestioned priority.

8
Death of Senna

THE GRANDSTANDS AND HIGH BANKS OF the Talladega Superspeedway rise up from the flat soil where the foothills of the Appalachians spill like an estuary into the plains of Alabama. On May 1, 1994, the morning of the Winston Cup season's ninth race, a pall had been cast over the massive racing facility's garage. In an age when every major international race appeared on satellite or cable TV, it was learned that Ayrton Senna, the great Brazilian, had been in a serious, possibly fatal, crash in Italy during the San Marino Grand Prix.

Those drivers and mechanics who watched the early morning telecasts of F1 races in team haulers and journalists who also followed international events were all trying to process the unthinkable. There had to be news eventually that Senna would make it—anybody but Senna. As the morning wore on in the vast garage, emptied of cars already pushed to the starting grid, the people familiar with this emerging tragedy occasionally stopped one another to ask about any news on Senna?

Roger Penske, whose driver Mark Donohue had suffered a fatal head injury in one of his F1 cars in 1975, was there. When I saw "The Captain" for the first time that day walking across the garage, I shook his hand in greeting and we talked briefly about Senna. He had an unusually stoic look in his eye and moved on.

Once the race started, it was learned the Brazilian driver had died in hospital. Dale Earnhardt, who often primed himself for his own races by watching F1 events via satellite in his motor coach in the early morning, won the 500-mile event and immediately afterward asked his team by radio about the fate of Senna. Once he climbed from his car in Victory Lane, among Earnhardt's first words were condolences.

"I want to send our thoughts and prayers to the Senna family and his fans," said the seven-time NASCAR champion during the TV interview. "He was a great racer and it's a shame to see him go the way he did. You know, it's tough."

In route to three Formula 1 World Championships, Senna became a mercurial hero, tenaciously fighting for position on the track with brilliant car control and unique lines while taking the risks necessary to win. Yet, outside the car, the Brazilian was deeply spiritual, committed to his religion and to the well-being of others, occasionally moved to tears in moments of others' distress. His athleticism, determination to win and brilliance behind the wheel were coupled with a rarely seen charisma, even in the world championship.

Senna's arrival in 1984 had coincided with the development of F1 into a media powerhouse under the guidance of Formula One Management boss Bernie Ecclestone. From his earliest days driving for Toleman, then Team Lotus, McLaren, and finally Williams, Senna's exploits were shared throughout the world by TV, radio, newspapers and magazines.

In the broadest sense, Senna was The Man in international motor racing. But in Brazil, he became more of a demigod due to the mixture of unmistakable confidence, religious conviction and a genuine concern about his countrymen backed by low-key charity projects. But above all, he gave Brazilians a sense of national pride. With his yellow helmet, he carried an extraor-

Death of Senna

Benetton's use of traction control proved problematic for Senna, here with Williams team manager Head. (LAT Images)

dinary stature as a three-time F1 champion and had managed to leapfrog four-time champion Alain Prost of France and Britain's own heroic everyman champion Nigel Mansell in popularity.

Despite his religious humility, Senna clearly grasped his own significance. "Senna had a vital arrogance, a sense of his own worth—an artistic awareness of his own value—that no one came close to," wrote Keith Botsford not long after Senna's Williams-Renault ran into a wall at the Imola circuit. "He was the spirit of the times, and he could see no end to faster and faster."

Longtime writer Roebuck, one of the deans of F1 reporting, rated Senna at the top. "Any racing journalist of my generation has written more words by far about Ayrton Senna da Silva than any other driver," he wrote in his book *Chasing the Title*. "Like (Michael) Schumacher, he was a genius; unlike Schumacher, he also had charisma to throw away. Ayrton was a presence, a special force, in a car and out. As with Gilles Villeneuve, you would go out on the circuit to watch him qualifying, choose a particular corner, and wait."

As is typical in sporting circles, some in the paddock had a less enthusiastic view of Senna than others. They saw him as an emotional product of his South American environment. The critics focused on his tenacious refusal to give ground on the track, or to give in to circumstances that might slow him down or preclude victory. People judged him to be primitive—not unlike some views of Earnhardt—creating an undercurrent of debate that only added to the mystique.

Senna believed the track belonged to him unless someone else proved otherwise. This was especially true at the street course in Monaco, F1's most cherished arena and the same place where others believed to be singularly great—Tazio Nuvolari, Juan Manuel Fangio and Graham Hill—had left their mark. Senna won at Monaco six times. He might have won seven straight, but he crashed in 1988 while leading Prost by more than 50 seconds, hammering home the point that the track was his without regard to humiliating the Frenchman, his McLaren teammate, in the process.

Roebuck's book also quotes Senna's chief rival on the less admirable aspect of the Brazilian. "He would talk about his religion," said Prost, "his upbringing, and so on, and I used to wonder how, then, he could do some of the things he did on the track. Now, looking back, I believe he really didn't know he was sometimes in the wrong. He played by his rules, and he wasn't interested in anything else."

This was after Senna infamously took Prost off the track in the first turn in Suzuka, Japan, in 1990, a high-speed and dangerous coming together that Senna later acknowledged had to do with him being denied the world championship by the FIA the previous year in Japan on a minor technical ruling in favor of Prost. Many acknowledged the technical ruling to be a bit of a joke on behalf of one Frenchman, Prost, by another—FIA President Jean-Marie Balestre. But most also thought Senna crashing Prost the following year to be equally dishonorable and horrifically unsafe.

Those in racing who were closer to Senna tended to present him in a more nuanced light. One of those was Dr. Sidney Watkins, the head of neurosurgery at the London Hospital. The medical officer of F1 and a

Death of Senna

former professor of neurosurgery at the State University of New York at Syracuse, he was known as Professor Watkins or "Prof" Watkins. He became a friend and confidant of the Brazilian driver, who arrived not long after Watkins first took responsibility to ensure a prompt medical response to drivers involved in crashes. (This was at the behest of F1's hard-driving business boss Bernie Ecclestone, who perhaps foresaw the need for greater safety and the politically risky prospect of drivers getting killed during live TV coverage he had been so instrumental in organizing.)

Watkins, in his book *Life at the Limit, Triumph and Tragedy in Formula One,* recalls the time when Senna made a visit to the Loretto School, Scotland's oldest boarding school located near Edinburgh. Watkins' stepson Matthew Amato was enrolled at Loretto and had requested a visit from Senna in a letter hand-delivered by Watkins. He further encouraged Senna to come to Loretto and then enjoy some fishing with him in the River Tweed.

The Loretto school and its students have more than a casual interest in F1. The two-time World Champion Jim Clark had attended the school and the Clark family's farm was located in the rolling hills of the nearby Borders district. Senna's visit came prior to the start of the 1991 season and shortly after he had won his second world championship—the one he had clinched by intentionally taking Prost off the track in Japan. After walking through the memorial to Clark in the chapel, Senna addressed the high school enrollment during the mandatory bi-weekly Saturday evening lecture, which usually featured speakers from industry or medicine.

"We thought Ayrton would be a good one to have," recalled Amato in an interview 20 years later. Age 15 at the time, Amato found it easy to recall the visit he had requested through his step-father. "He gave a really good talk about what it takes to be a F1 driver and about Jim Clark. He said he liked the fact that Jim Clark always had a smile."

The bulk of the lecture was a question and answer session. The first question came from a future barrister about rival Prost and what he thought of him? "Wow, first question!" said Senna, who went on to praise his rival in some detail.

"It was the etiquette that we had to address the lecturer as 'Sir' before we asked a question," said Amato. "About three or four questions in, he said, 'You don't have to call me sir.' The next question he got, the guy called him 'Ayrton,' and he said, 'Yes, like that.' By the end, everyone was calling him Ayrton. He answered a lot of good questions about the pressures of the job and even about sponsorship by tobacco. At the end, he said he was impressed by the caliber of the questions that were asked. It went on for a couple of hours."

"He talked about how he had to come over and how he had to work hard," continued Amato. "He gave advice with an ear to a young audience about how important it was to work hard to achieve a goal. He talked about sacrifice and being away from his estate in Brazil and his boats and water skiing. He gave very good, thoughtful answers to the questions, which I think is not a given for many sports people. He was very comfortable talking about his faith in God. It was more from the perspective of answering questions about the danger of his job and was he scared of losing his life? He said he had faith and that helped."

The Bishop of Truro, at the school to conduct the Sunday service the following day, attended the gathering and later in the day had a heart-to-heart conversation with Senna before the driver returned to Portugal for testing. "On Sunday, the Bishop of Truro began his sermon," wrote Watkins, "with the confession that he had been spiritually and verbally outclassed as a preacher by Ayrton Senna."

Unbeknownst at the time, the setting at the Loretto School would eventually be ironic. If there was a comparable driver to Senna, it would have been Clark—the only other F1 driver considered truly great who died in his race car.

Mesmeric behind the wheel, Clark won everything worth winning, including the Indy 500 and two world championships. His fame invariably preceded him, but Clark, who became the youngest F1 champion when he won the 1963 title, sustained a down-to-earth outlook more fitting of the mechanics who worked on his cars, an attitude one might expect from the son of a Scottish farmer.

On the track, Clark's hallmarks were all-round skills and success in a variety of cars, head-and-shoulder dominance of F1 and an ungodly ability to coax speed from even the most ill-handling or demanding machines.

He had an easy manner and smile, but Clark detested the hoopla surrounding such events as the Indy 500. "I started (racing) as a hobby with no idea and no intention of being world champion," he said in some rare video footage. "I wanted to see what it was like to race on the track."

Clark's dominance of F1 can best be summed up by 25 victories and his eight Grand Slams in 72 race starts. A Grand Slam meant he started on the pole, led every lap, set the fastest lap and won the race.

Apparently, Clark was happiest behind the wheel plying his other-worldly skills. He raced practically non-stop, spending his winters Down Under driving in the Tasman Series for F1 cars, winning the championship in a Lotus 49T in 1968 and presaging what many expected would be a third world title. He drove anything, including a Lotus Cortina taken to the championship in the British Touring Car Series and even a Ford Galaxie at the North Carolina Motor Speedway in a NASCAR Grand National event. He was onboard a Lotus Formula 2 car at the Hockenheim circuit in Germany when a suspected rear tire failure sent him off the track, into the trees and to his death from a broken neck and skull on April 7, 1968.

In an eerily similar response to Senna's death 26 years later, fans and participants in the sport found it hard to believe Clark had died. During a sports car race, an announcement about his crash at the Brands Hatch circuit in England, where Clark had scored the 1964 British Grand Prix victory, silenced the crowd. "The place was stumped," said future racing executive Ian Phillips, a teenager at the time. "People were just staring blankly at one another, standing about in complete and utter silence. The whole place went numb, really."

One of the drivers who had looked up to Clark, future three-time champion Jackie Stewart, also found himself astounded. "It was the most confusing day of my life," said Stewart in a TV interview, "because Jim Clark was not going to die in a racing car. Maybe other people might, but not Jim Clark."

The day Clark died, he drove a Lotus chassis in the gold, red and white livery of Gold Leaf Tobacco Company, not the traditional green colors representing Britain that had been used by Lotus and team owner Colin Chapman previously. It marked the beginning of the commercialization of F1, the initial step away from being considered a sport by participants. Instead, it would soon be looked upon as a sport that needed to run itself as a business.

After Clark's death, concern arose that the sport would be outlawed due to the obvious lack of safety represented by the fatal crash of its greatest driver. But the absence of scale when it came to motor racing's popularity and the lack of broad commercial involvement precluded any great backlash. The tragedy was significant enough to warrant a same-day announcement in America on the Wide World of Sports by host Jim McKay, who was the broadcaster for the Indy 500 during Clark's assaults on the Speedway. But regular live TV coverage of F1 remained years away. That, too, helped keep in check the tide of public criticism about the dangers of motor racing.

The death of Senna, whose estate was valued by some as high as $400 million, occurred on the opposite end of the spectrum when commercialization had fully bloomed. His crash in a car powered by Renault and sponsored by the Rothmans International tobacco company was beamed into homes, bars, motor homes and public houses globally, the same medium that had made the Brazilian driver a leading light in the daily march of sports heroes across TV screens everywhere.

9
Safety Gone Awry

ONLY THE SECOND TIME TWO DRIVERS HAD been killed at the same Formula 1 race meeting, the 1994 race at Imola was the darkest day in F1 history. When coupled with three other serious accidents, two involving fans and crew members who were injured, the weekend at Imola felt like the wheels had come off in a series regarded as the ultimate expression of motorsports by participants, journalists and fans around the world.

In what would become a haunting foreshadowing, the problems began in the first practice on the high-speed track of bending straights linked by corners. A crash by up-and-coming Brazilian star Rubens Barrichello knocked him unconscious and sent him to the hospital with a concussion after a frightening crash at Variante Bassa. His Jordan-Hart flew into the catch fence and stood upright on its side afterward. Barrichello had overcooked the corner, carrying considerably more speed than his previous lap.

During qualifying Saturday, well-regarded journeyman driver Roland Ratzenberger was trying desperately to get onto the grid with a qualifying time but instead ran off the track, damaging the front wing on his Simtek-Ford. Ratzenberger, not realizing the damage, continued. When the wing broke on his approach to Tosa on the next lap, the driver lost control and clouted the wall nearly head-on. He suffered a basal skull fracture and was dead by time safety crews reached him.

A somber race day arrived on Sunday, the sort most of the participating drivers had never experienced—getting into their cars in full knowledge about a fatal crash on the same course just 24 hours earlier. Then Ayrton Senna's Williams-Renault shot off the track at the high-speed Tamburello bend into a concrete barrier. He left the track at more than 190 mph, but he managed enough braking and pedaling of the throttle to reduce the speed to 135 mph at impact, which sent the car back across the 35 meters of concrete runoff and grass to the track's edge.

"Prof" Watkins quickly arrived in the medical car. Once Senna was removed from his Williams and laid down next to it on the track, the neurosurgeon checked for vital signs and knew immediately that the Brazilian had suffered a fatal head injury. The right front wheel had caromed off the wall and a piece of the suspension had pierced Senna's visor and then his skull.

Senna still had a pulse. The safety crew quickly carried him to a nearby helicopter, then transported him to the Maggiore hospital, where he would die of cardiac arrest absent any vital signs later that evening, his strong heart finally giving up.

Incredibly, another major race day incident had already taken place. Prior to Senna's crash on lap 7, a frightening start line incident where J.J. Lehto's stalled Benetton-Ford had been run over by the Lotus-Honda of Pedro Lamy resulted in a wheel bounding over the fence into the crowd, where several spectators and a policeman were injured. Then, in the closing laps, a wheel on Michele Alboreto's Minardi-Ford flew off while he was leaving the pit lane, hitting three mechanics and seriously injuring one. That was the final incident in a day of disaster marked by Senna's blood at the side of the track.

Safety Gone Awry

What had gone wrong?

From a driver safety standpoint, the writing had already been on the wall. During pre-season testing Lehto had suffered a broken neck when his Benetton B194 spun and backed into a wall at 140 mph at the Silverstone circuit. After the season's first race, Jean Alesi spun and backed into a wall at 150 mph at the Mugello circuit while testing a Ferrari 412 T1. Where Letho had broken his fourth and fifth cervical vertebra, Alesi broke the fifth, sixth and seventh. In each case, the impact broke the driver's seat.

The clear message: cars were hitting the wall with enough force to exceed the existing safety standards of the cockpits.

At Imola, the season's third race, three drivers had major frontal impacts and two of them died while a third, Barrichello, went to the hospital with a severe concussion. Then in the season's fourth round at Monaco, Karl Wendlinger hit the barrier at the Chicane in his Sauber C13 and suffered a concussion so serious "Prof" Watkins put him into an induced coma to allow his brain to heal.

In retrospect, veteran and less experienced drivers alike were having serious spins and high-speed crashes in their 1994 cars. And those cars were not equipped to provide the needed safety for drivers in such high-speed incidents. The situation comprised the age-old tragic tandem of speed outstripping the safety of cars, and speed exceeding the abilities of the last vestige of safety—the drivers.

The high-speed crashes could be traced to a radical rule change announced at the end of the 1993. Active suspensions and driver aids of any sort, including traction control, were banned for the 1994 season. But the flat bottom cars, first introduced in 1982, would remain. The flat bottoms helped sustain high speed. Some discussion took place among teams of introducing a "stepped" undertray to re-direct air under the chassis in way that would slow them down and help keep speeds in check. But the discussion never reached the stage of a formal presentation by teams to the governing FIA.

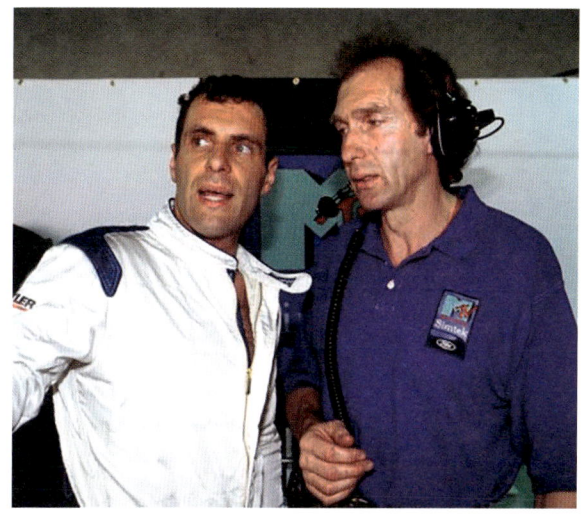

Ratzenberger with his engineer Humphrey Corbett. 'They were a small team. Everybody liked Roland.' (LAT Images)

The flat bottom chassis had first been introduced to do away with the "ground effects," or negative lift, that sucked cars to the ground by underbody tunnels and side skirts. A decade later during the 1992 and 1993 seasons, active suspensions that controlled ride heights with hydraulics became overwhelmingly successful for the Williams team. The front-running teams of Ferrari, McLaren and Benetton were all experimenting with active suspension in order to beat Williams. But the FIA abruptly introduced a ban on such driver aids prior to the 1994 season. The ban arrived in the form of an edict by the FIA that outlawed the hydraulic suspensions and traction control.

Putting the genie back into the bottle proved impossible.

After more than a decade's experience, the teams at the forefront of the active suspension era had enough data to replicate the cornering ability with the flat bottom cars absent the driver aids. When the teams finished qualifying at Imola in 1994, Senna's pole speed was half a second faster in the Williams FW16 than the previous year's pole winner. That had been Prost, who won the 1993 pole onboard a FW15C equipped

Crash! How the HANS Helped Save Racing

Safety Gone Awry

with active suspension and traction control. Given the absence of driver aids, Senna's performance amazed everyone in the paddock as well as fans.

Michael Schumacher earned second on the grid during what became the blackest of weekends in a Benetton B194, which was also faster than Prost's pole speed from the previous year. Although not quicker than Prost, Gerhard Berger picked up nearly two seconds in the Ferrari 412 T1 compared with his qualifying time from the year before.

How difficult was it to perform better in the 1994 cars than the previous year? Apparently, the challenge proved extremely difficult, despite the fact brilliant qualifier Senna, who had switched to Williams during the offseason from McLaren, won the first two poles in the team's FW16 chassis.

Having dominated the world championship for two straight seasons with its active suspension, the Williams team saw itself as marked for careful inspection by the FIA and other teams when it came to the new rules and committed to the new era of flat bottom chassis with no driver aids. Under pressure after replacing Prost, who had retired following his fourth world championship in the active suspension FW15C, Senna committed to trying to match his old rival.

But after starting on pole in his first race for Williams on the Interlagos circuit in Brazil in front of his adoring fans, Senna spun and stalled his Renault engine. Afterward, he confessed to driver error by going over the knife edge of control while trying to keep up with the Benetton of eventual winner Schumacher.

In the second race at Japan's Aida circuit, Senna spun his wheels at the start, then got hit at the first corner and knocked out of the race. Schumacher cruised to the victory.

But in Japan, it began to come to light that Ferrari and Benetton were using an indirect method of traction control by electronically manipulating the engine's output. (This was in place of the banned traction control that electronically signaled the individual wheels.) Ferrari and Benetton were altering the engine RPM

The Williams chassis of Senna and its steering became the subject of much debate over why he crashed. (LAT Images)

via the Electronic Control Unit (ECU) to provide maximum grip while avoiding slippage. The situation confirmed what some team principals had worried about when the FIA first announced the rule change banning traction control. They worried that computer systems in the ECUs were so sophisticated that the FIA would not be able to decipher or detect the presence of traction control.

After his crash in Japan, Senna stood trackside to listen to Schumacher's Benetton in the corners and came away convinced he had traction control, supposedly outlawed by the FIA's edict. He made that determination by listening to the rise and fall of the engine revs. It further fanned flames when Nicola Larini, the replacement driver for the injured Jean Alesi, said to the media during the Japan race weekend that the Ferrari team had asked him to "turn off the traction control" during one of the pre-race sessions.

Ron Dennis, team principal at McLaren, led the call for allowing traction control, since he was skeptical it could be policed. "You can call it variable engine output or torque control. And it is undetectable," he said. "It could take years to crack the software in the management system and so you are putting too much responsibility on teams not to run it."

In the third race of the season at Imola, following two of his own offs and two straight victories by rival Schumacher, Senna felt himself to be under tremendous pressure to measure up to expectations at Williams and to rebound from a 20-point deficit in the championship. Able to call upon his skill and commitment—as he had done in Brazil and in Japan—Senna took a third straight pole at Imola with Schumacher in second.

Senna's plight at the front of the field also put a lot of pressure on the back of the field and the smaller, lesser-funded teams. Although the smaller teams had never used active suspensions, they, too, had to maintain the incremental leaps in speed without traction control. Because of the rule that disqualified any driver whose time fell more than 107 percent above the pole starter, the ill-fated Ratzenberger and his Simtek car were not yet qualified after the first day at Imola and he was trying to find his way into the field on Saturday. Unsuccessful with a lap time of 1:27.584 on Friday (compared with Senna's 1:21.548), Ratzenberger continued. Approaching Tosa, the front wing damaged in an off-course excursion on the previous lap caught him out.

Senna, like all but two drivers on the grid at Imola, had never been present when a Grand Prix driver had been killed. There had been tears in Senna's eyes on Friday when he visited the hospital to see his fellow Brazilian Barrichello after his concussion. On Saturday, he went to the Tosa corner to learn more about Ratzenberger's crash.

Once Ratzenberger's body had been brought into the medical center by the track ambulance, Senna sought to gain access to see his friend Watkins, getting past the security fencing in the back. Watkins had the sad duty of telling both Charles Moody, the team manager at Simtek, and Senna that Ratzenberger was "beyond medical help." Senna broke down and cried on Watkins' shoulder.

Watkins recounts the incident in his book. "I felt I had to tell him what I thought," wrote Watkins. "'Ayrton, why don't you withdraw from racing tomorrow? I don't think you should do it. In fact, why don't you give it up altogether? What else do you need to do? You have been World Champion three times. You are obviously the quickest driver. Give it up and let's go fishing.'"

Senna calmly told his friend, "'I cannot quit. I have to go on.'"

That evening, Senna celebrated the birthday of his physiotherapist Josef Leberer along with some other friends in a dinner at the Williams compound, where the group marveled at the Italian fans known as *tifosi* who had gathered at the paddock's fences to watch crew members work on the preparation of the Williams chassis.

Despite the occasion, the mood remained somber. "We had the big accident in the first session and Rubens walks away after getting battered about," said the Williams team's press officer, Ann Bradshaw. "Obviously, the Ratzenberger crash hit everybody. When it's one of the extended family that happens to, you can't help but be affected. They were a small team and struggling. They were nice guys, everybody liked Roland."

Race day arrived without any foreboding. "I've seen so many comments from people who weren't there, saying, 'Ayrton didn't want to race,'" said Bradshaw. "Prof Watkins did suggest to Ayrton not to race. But it's your job. You get in. Ayrton was a great race driver. He was a professional. He didn't make a big show of the warm-up session. He got on with what he was there to do, which is what he loved doing."

With Schumacher in close pursuit, on the seventh lap Senna's Williams bottomed out at the bumpy new pavement at Tamburello, shooting sparks from the titanium undertray as in previous laps. But at the corner exit, the car shot to the right and into a fateful collision with a wall situated close to the track and necessitated by the river just on the other side of it.

Following behind him for the sixth and seventh lap at full speed after a safety car period to clean the

Safety Gone Awry

track from the debris of the starting line crash of Lehto and Lamy, Schumacher said Senna's car "seemed very nervous" at Tamburello and was "bottoming quite a lot." Then the rear titanium skid plate touched and the Williams was "a bit sideways and he just lost it."

By 1996, legal charges were brought against team principal Frank Williams, technical director Patrick Head and car designer Adrian Newey. For years, an Italian prosecutor tried without success to prove that the broken steering column found at the crash caused Senna's death. Prosecutor Maurizio Passarini charged that a supposedly faulty weld used to adjust the steering to Senna's liking after the race in Japan was at fault.

The accused members of the Williams team, charged with "culpable homicide" by Passarini, all argued that the column had been snapped as a result of the crash.

An entire book written by an engineer tried to support the idea of a partially collapsed steering column. This author's rather dubious methodology was based on the tiniest of mathematical calculations made from a pastiche of video and data. Technical director Head declared the data could not have been recovered from the car unless the steering column had been intact at the time the car left the track.

Newey admitted the steering column's installation and design were not ideal, but he denied it had broken before the car met the wall. He said he believed a deflating rear tire was the cause. Goodyear engineers, with deep experience in post-crash analysis, heavily discounted the idea of a slow puncture, possibly resulting from the crash debris run through during the safety car period. The Goodyear engineers said no evidence could be found of a problem in the tires examined after the crash. Another theory was that the new safety car procedure had allowed Senna's tires to cool down and lose just enough pressure to change the handling of his car.

Driver error was Head's assessment immediately after the race, expressed to journalist Joe Saward. In the end, Senna went off trying to stay ahead of a car that in all likelihood had illegal traction control. The Brazilian had been making his usual superhuman effort to win a championship with the cards dealt him.

The accident certainly left a big question mark hanging about the Benetton of Schumacher. In his autobiography *Formula One and Beyond*, FIA President Max Mosley acknowledged that officials had collected the ECU in Schumacher's Benetton after his victory at Imola to try to ascertain if the team was using traction control. But the tragic events forced the sanctioning body to focus elsewhere and returned the ECU to the team.

Later in the year, FIA officials discovered the Benetton team's computer program in the ECU had "launch control" that enabled Schumacher to get better starts. The team and driver were penalized. If the team had been willing to hide this particular menu in its ECU software, it seemed fairly certain it had used traction control early in the season as described by McLaren's Dennis.

Six years after the crash at Imola, a peculiar thing happened shortly after Schumacher tied Senna's career record of 41 victories while driving for Ferrari. In the formal but also familiar post-race press conference with the other two podium finishers conducted on TV, the announcer reminded race winner Schumacher that he had equaled Senna's victory total. The normally unflappable German started crying. Not just tears but heaving sobs. The two other drivers, Mika Hakkinen and Schumacher's younger brother Ralf, attempted to console Schumacher, who never raised his head in one of the most unusual post-race interviews ever televised.

Crocodile tears or not, the scene appeared to confirm that Schumacher knew how his traction control had helped him keep so much pressure on Senna at Imola—without taking nearly as much risk.

10
The Black Sport

IN THE DAYS IMMEDIATELY AFTER THE Imola race, the officials at the FIA headquarters in Paris did not have to cast their net very far to judge public reaction to the black weekend in Italy.

Le Monde, the largest circulation evening paper in Paris, dedicated two pages to the death of Senna in the May 3 edition. Stories included a minute-by-minute rundown of the accident, Senna's journey to the hospital, plus the time and cause of death. The coverage included the effect of Senna's accident on the image of Renault. How much insurance he carried ($11 million) in the case of death behind the wheel generated another story.

Le Figaro, France's other newspaper of record, was the more conservative of the two. Its headline blared, "Le Sport Noir", or "The Black Sport." Meanwhile, in the left-leaning *Le Monde*, a professor wrote an article in which he described F1 as a vehicle for advertising and not really a sport. He declared Senna not worthy of being regarded as a hero.

This comprised just a microcosm of stories elsewhere in the Fleet Street tabloids in Britain and in the newspapers in Italy, where prosecutor Passarini would eventually bring his charges. The sheer volume of the examination of F1 from every conceivable angle, especially whether it was too dangerous, prompted an emergency meeting in Paris led by Mosley. Convinced he needed to act, Mosley wanted to avoid the death of another F1 competitor followed by more unwinding by the media and possibly action by legislative bodies in the various countries where the World Championship had races scheduled.

It wasn't just a matter of hand-wringing. Switzerland had famously banned motor racing after the crash at Le Mans in 1955, a law that still stands. Not long afterward, Italy banned racing on public roads after the tragic crash of Alphonse de Portago in the Mille Miglia in 1957.

Editorials in the Vatican newspaper, *L'Osservatore Romano*, had been instrumental in the banning of the Mille Miglia. After the weekend at Imola that claimed the lives of Senna and Ratzenberger, *L'Osservatore Romano* again excoriated motor racing as an affront. "The roar of the motors and the spark of the sponsors prevailed over death, silencing man," said the editorial, which further accused F1 of being driven by money and condemned the role and influence of commercial sponsors.

Even those who supported Senna and motor racing weighed in. The FIA was criticized by Brazilian publications for the ban on active suspensions, saying the radical change was at the bottom of the Senna crash. There was a school of thought in many quarters of motor racing that faster—in addition to being the essence of the sport—was safer than abrupt rule changes.

In the midst of this firestorm, the FIA officials, who all had various levels of friendship with Senna, had to cope with their grief and the ongoing politics within F1 as well as the world at large. One of the sanctioning body's critics was Alan Jenkins, the designer of the Arrows chassis. He chastised the FIA for its lack of safety research and wondered aloud how it was qualified to

The Black Sport

By time Mosley and Ecclestone returned to Imola in 2003, F1 safety had undergone a complete makeover. (LAT Images)

direct a new safety push. "If you run into somebody at the traffic lights," he said, "there's probably more analysis of what happened there than there is after an F1 accident." Jenkins also faulted the secretiveness of the teams as a contributing factor for the dearth of safety information.

In the wake of Senna's state funeral in Brazil, where President Itamar Franco had declared three days of national mourning, the next race fell a fortnight after Imola in Monaco, where Senna had established his greatest legend. Out of respect for him, Williams withdrew from the season's fourth round.

After announcing a few relatively minor rule changes, Mosley mounted a public, moral defense of F1 prior to a race held on the streets of Europe's gambling capitol, a location that seemed oddly appropriate, given the question about risks in racing that were hanging in the Mediterranean city's fresh sea air. "There is a fundamental point of personal liberty," he said. "If people want to participate in a dangerous sport, they should be free to do so." Mosley cited his own experience as a race car driver. When he moved from the lower ranks into Formula 2, he entered his first race Hockenheim in April of 1968, the day Jim Clark's Lotus launched into the trees.

"I knew what the fatality rate was, but I wanted to do it," he said. "And I did it for no money—I paid to do it. If you start prohibiting dangerous sports, you have to prohibit everything—rugby, hang-gliding, mountaineering, never mind the really dangerous things like climbing K2, where you've got a 50 percent death rate at the moment."

Then Karl Wendlinger crashed at the Chicane on Thursday and suffered a severe concussion requiring expert on-the-scene care from Watkins to prevent another tragedy. In four consecutive days of F1 practice, qualifying or racing, F1 had witnessed four head injuries.

This was too much for Mosley. On the next day, he convened an extraordinary meeting at Monaco to announce sweeping technical changes designed to slow the F1 cars and make them safer. The Concorde Agreement, by which the FIA and the participating teams governed the sport, called for unanimous approval of all teams before any rule changes could be implemented. But Mosley, an accomplished lawyer, invoked the Force Majeure clause that gave the FIA legal latitude in the case of an unexpected emergency and made clear his resolve.

The rule changes Mosley announced were more

than stunning to the teams. They were mind-bending.

In Phase One, front wings and rear diffusers had to be reduced prior to next race meeting at Barcelona later in May. In Phase Two, teams had to strengthen the lower front wishbones to reduce the possibility of an incident similar to the one that had killed Senna. The cockpits needed to have increased lateral protection for the driver's head and more padding. The minimum weight of the cars increased by 25 kilograms, the engine air box had to be removed and teams could use only pump fuel. These latter three items specifically addressed reducing speeds and had to be made before the Canadian Grand Prix, which was four weeks away.

Phase Three called for the change in flat bottoms that had been under discussion prior to the second round in Japan. A center section on the underbodies would remain unchanged, but the cars' flat bottoms on either side had to be increased by 50 millimeters, which would force air through the middle of the floor and reduce speed. This was prescribed for the end of July at the German Grand Prix. The FIA also mandated a reduction in rear wing height and raised the location of the rear diffuser at the back of the chassis by 50 millimeters.

Phase Four focused on 1995. It called for a reduction in aerodynamic downforce and, after some discussion, a reduction in engine power by reducing displacement from 3.5 liters to 3.0 liters in the current generation of V-8s.

Predictably, the teams howled in protest. After the initial meetings in Paris, Mosley had only announced rule changes affecting the pit road, saying the sanctioning body needed to avoid a reaction that might introduce unintended new problems and consequences. For this, the French and Italian racing media roundly criticized the FIA president for not slowing the cars. In an about-face after the Wendlinger crash, Mosley decided the risk of unintended new problems meant the FIA had to slow the cars.

Once Mosley acted in Monaco, the teams roundly criticized him for not following his own previous

Clark was as much admired by racing fans as Senna, but the general public's response to their fatal crashes proved dramatically different. (The Klemantaski Collection)

cautious approach. "We're being presented with a *fait accompli*," Ferrari designer John Barnard told *Autosport* magazine reporter Andrew Benson. "I doubt the measures would have been announced now were it not for Wendlinger's accident. It's only a week or so since Max Mosley emphasized the importance of avoiding a knee-jerk reaction to events at Imola. This has undermined that statement.

"As much as anything, the FIA wants to be seen as doing something," continued Barnard, sharpening his knife. "It remains to be seen if the measures will have the desired effect. My fear, like a lot of other technical people in the pitlane, is that we've seen these sorts of proposals introduced overnight before, and they've backfired."

Mosley never broke stride. He immediately organized the Expert Advisory Group to be chaired by Professor Watkins. Charlie Whiting, the F1 technical delegate, driver Gerhard Berger and Roland Brunyseraede, the FIA safety delegate, were appointed to join Watkins along with car designer Harvey Postelwaithe. Other outside experts were to be nominated by the committee. Mosley promised all the necessary funds to undertake the research needed.

The brief handed to the Expert Advisory Group included investigating cockpit and overall car design, the integrity of crash barriers, circuit configurations and the protection of people working the pit lanes and those in public areas at the tracks.

When drivers revived the Grand Prix Drivers Association (GPDA) at Monaco over the issues of safety, Mosley quickly endorsed the idea. "The drivers can make a lot of contributions and anything they have to say will be listened to with the greatest attention."

But as if on cue after criticism from the teams about too many changes too soon, Pedro Lamy suffered a horrendous shunt at the Silverstone circuit during a private test of the new rear diffuser on the Lotus 107C. The change in the diffuser size meant a different mounting for the rear wing, which disengaged at speed. The tub of the broken Lotus vaulted over a spectator fence, went down an embankment and came to rest at the opening of a pedestrian tunnel. Lamy broke both legs, fractured his knees, dislocating one of them, and broke his wrist. Fortunately, no spectators were at the track and this time there were no head or neck injuries.

Following a fourth straight Schumacher victory at Monaco and a relatively safe race, if not practice, two weeks later the contentious introduction of new rules continued at the Spanish Grand Prix in Barcelona, albeit with some give-and-take compromise from Mosley. With the ongoing support of Mosley's longtime compatriot and F1 commercial director Ecclestone, Mosley made the sanctioning body's position clear. "The FIA owns and runs the F1 World Championship," he said. "Teams will participate on this basis or not at all."

Officials placed a temporary chicane on the Barcelona track's back straight to help reduce speeds. But that didn't prevent a huge shunt at the entrance to the long front straight by Andrea Montermini, ironically the replacement driver at the Simtek team for Ratzenberger. After getting the left side wheels on the grass, the Simtek snapped to the left and hit the wall at 140 mph, which destroyed the front end. The crash left the hapless Italian stunned while sitting in a car with "for Roland" written across the peak of the air box, his feet sticking out of the ravaged front end of the chassis. He suffered a broken heel and concussion, leaving F1 with head injuries in each of the three race meetings in May.

In the midst of the chaos highlighted by the backbiting and political fighting between teams and the FIA, often played out in the media, not much attention was paid to a new development at Mercedes-Benz, whose engines were powering the midfield entries of Swiss team owner Peter Sauber. The company wanted to get more engaged in F1 and offered to help on the issue of driver restraints.

The Mercedes-Benz C-class cars were competing in the German Touring Car Championship using airbags, which prompted a decision to look into upgrading the technology for the higher speeds of F1. "We are trying to put something together," said Norbert Haug, the company's motorsports boss, in the week after Imola, "but our technicians are still in the early stages of development."

During this research, the HANS Device would be recognized as a restraint with far more attractive qualities than airbags activated according to electronic algorithms.

11

Hubert and HANS

THE TESTING OF COCKPIT SAFETY IN F1 launched by the Expert Advisory Group after the Imola weekend soon crossed paths with another significant initiative—the GM Motorsports Safety Technology Research Program.

The GM safety program had been conceived and launched after two horrendous crashes in the U.S. in 1992. The first of these crashes occurred at the Speedway in Indianapolis, where three-time World Champion Nelson Piquet suffered crippling injuries to his lower extremities after hitting the wall in a frontal impact aboard a CART Indy car. Later that summer, a second accident involved heralded young star Tommy Kendall at Watkins Glen, where the American also suffered similarly grievous injuries to his ankles, feet and knees while competing behind the wheel of an Intrepid-Chevy in the GTP category.

A GM factory driver, Kendall's fateful crash greatly affected Gary Dickinson, the GM Vice President of Technical Staffs. He and his wife had become personal friends with Kendall. Just the summer before, Kendall had led the NASCAR Winston Cup race at the Sears Point Raceway for 12 laps in the late going aboard the Chevy entry of Felix Sabates. He was on the verge of becoming a winner in the GTP series when the accident occurred at Watkins Glen. By then he'd already been an IMSA GTU and SCCA Trans-Am champion. His plight of being suddenly shunted aside from a star-bound trajectory at age 24 was a major factor in Dickinson's decision to combine the resources of GM Motorsports and the GM Research Laboratories to create the first full-scale, scientifically driven investigation into motor racing safety.

Two years later, the deaths of Ratzenberger and Senna at Imola led to the launch of the Expert Advisory Group under the direction of Prof. Watkins. But it wasn't until the crash of Mika Hakkinen at the Australian Grand Prix 1995—18 months after the Senna crash—that the search for a solution to head injuries in F1 really accelerated.

In much the same manner that a personal connection to an injured driver helped motivate GM's safety program, so the crash of Hakkinen motivated Mercedes-Benz and the FIA. Hakkinen, a well-regarded future star, suffered a basal skull fracture but survived after some internal bleeding—a near miss of another fatality, which confirmed that cockpits remained unsafe for F1 drivers.

It was revolutionary for a sanctioning body like the FIA to start its own research and development, but otherwise the safety projects on both sides of the Atlantic were remarkably similar. Both the FIA and GM were relying on anthropomorphic test dummies. Each was taking a scientific approach using sled testing and high-speed cameras to determine what happened to the Hybrid III dummies in cockpits during racing crashes and to test what might reduce the threat of injury. Each followed a path initially started by the automotive industry. A key difference was the far greater interest in the HANS Device by John Melvin, the manager of GM's safety project and longtime advisor to colleague Bob Hubbard from the conception of the HANS.

For his part, Watkins would eventually become a

staunch supporter of the HANS and one of the main reasons why the FIA eventually adopted it. But at the outset of the Expert Advisory Group, the professor of neurosurgery and president of the F1 Medical Commission had a more classic view of what were the biggest threats to brain injuries in general and in motor racing in particular.

In his book outlining the safety push over the years in F1, completed shortly before Hakkinen's accident, Watkins' primary focus on head injuries concerned the skull getting struck by direct contact, or the brain suffering action and reaction injury stresses at the sudden arrest of the skull. Neck injury only entered his consideration when it came to side impacts and lateral bending. In angled impacts, he wrote, "the trajectory of the head becomes compound as lateral and anteroposterior forces, depending on the angle of impact, produce a vector." By this he meant "front and back forces" combining with a movement to the side simultaneously. It would be just this kind of a vector of combined forces that caused Hakkinen's near miss, casting new light on the HANS Device for Watkins.

F1 participants knew about the HANS Device. After the death of Senna, within a matter of weeks two helmets arrived from Ferrari at the HANS Performance Products headquarters in Chamblee, Georgia. The helmets belonged to Gerhard Berger and the Ferrari team wanted them fit with HANS Devices. Ferrari, at least, examined every possible angle and the helmets were duly shipped back to Italy after being fitted with Model I devices. What then became of Ferrari's interest remained unknown to Downing and HPP.

In general, suspicion continued about a device that had been designed specifically for motor racing cockpit safety. Where seatbelts had been greeted by some drivers with dismay and refusal, at least these harnesses and belts had proven their effectiveness in aircraft. Fire suits made with flame-retardant Nomex had been endorsed by NASA and were eventually adopted by drivers and sanctioning bodies due to their relative ease of use. But to many, this bulky device made specifically for motor racing looked more likely to cause problems in the cockpit instead of resolving them.

Math whiz Gramling switched from air bags to the HANS after finding one in a 'dust bin.' (Photo by William Thom)

"There was some restriction of motion in the cockpit with the HANS under any circumstance," said Hubbard. "We could never be sure that drivers would actually use it. But we felt it was important to take that chance."

Former F1 driver Jonathan Palmer, who had a medical degree, was quoted in *Autosport* shortly after the Imola tragedies about why tethering the head would be detrimental without mentioning the HANS Device specifically. He rejected the notion of finding a way to strap a driver's head to the torso, saying it would be counterproductive.

"You can't hold the head rigidly, or the brain will rattle around the skull and you'll get killed from that," said Palmer, who like many others believed Ratzenberger had been killed by his head hitting the wall rather than by head whip. "If a head is restrained in a strap," he continued, "I think it would become distracting and uncomfortable for driving. It could well cause more accidents than it helped."

Downing and Hubbard had heard this familiar litany before. The over-all attitude meant the HANS Device received little attention as a possible solution for F1 or seemingly any other major sanctioning body. Downing, in fact, became discouraged enough by the time and money spent with few sales and little interest from sanctioning bodies that he was ready to give up on the possibility of mandates and concentrate on his own racing. After all, he could use a HANS Model I and continue to build them as demand dictated for individual competitors.

The overall suspicion of the HANS eventually found its way into the testing process launched under the aegis of the Expert Advisory Group. Watkins and his group had commissioned a program of high-energy testing with a team of engineers and biophysicists at the Motor Industry Research Association (MIRA) in Britain. Sled tests at a variety of impact angles were conducted to gain information from test dummies about the forces acting on the human body in a crash. They wanted to find out how to employ standard racing restraints such as the harness and to supplement them with air bags.

During the course of these tests, a HANS Device underwent experimentation at MIRA, located in Nuneaton. But it generated little interest and was discarded. Perhaps the focus was on keeping heads from hitting something in the cockpit and the HANS actually introduced a foreign object to the cockpit. Or perhaps the bulkiness of the device confirmed the initial thought that air bags, which had been successful in highway cars, would work best for motor racing. Hubbard concluded that many still did not have an understanding that tension in the spine and neck created the most critical problem, not necessarily contact of the helmet and head with something in the cockpit—or the arresting of the head by a device.

There was a slightly irrational element to the rejection of the HANS. If the goal was to prevent the helmet from making contact with anything inside the cockpit or outside the car, by keeping the head restrained and aligned with the torso, the HANS accomplished precisely this goal. Once again, it seemed, the HANS got caught out in a sport where hidebound thinking by racers often followed a singular rule: "If it looks right, it must be right." The ungainly bulk of the Model I helped obfuscate its effectiveness. Once again, problems were encountered getting it to work for a driver in a reclining position. In a standard F1 cockpit, the HANS collar tipped back, contacting the head rest, and interference occurred between the full-face helmet under the driver's chin and the yoke. So, the FIA soldiered on with its air bag concept.

Preventing the head from making contact became a consistent theme in the response by the FIA. In its Phase II rules announcement at Monaco, better lateral, or side protection was called for by raising the cockpit sides and increasing the padding. To better prevent helmeted heads from hitting the steering wheel, longer cockpit openings were mandated for the race in Canada, four weeks after the Monaco announcement in 1994.

Imagine the surprise of Whiting, the technical delegate, when he learned over the course of his research and through phone calls at the end of 1994 that Indy car drivers were likely being saved from severe head injuries *because* their helmeted heads were hitting the steering wheels. "When I called to find out why more Indy car drivers weren't being killed by head injuries on high speed ovals, I was told it was because their heads were hitting the steering wheel," said Whiting. Instead of critical or fatal results, the contact with steering wheels left drivers with what was believed at the time to be a temporary problem—concussions. This explained why Indy car drivers hit the wall on ovals regularly at high speeds without constantly getting killed.

The FIA found itself under pressure to find a solution. The Expert Advisory Group had done yeoman's work in a short period of time to address the issues of safety when it came to circuit layouts and certain corners. The number of high-risk corners had been reduced from 27 to eight in a project directed by Harvey Postlethwaite. Crash barriers had been reviewed and improved. Protection of participants and spectators had also received a thorough review with recommendations for better debris fencing.

What forces the human body underwent during a crash and the human body's tolerances for those forces remained the greatest challenge. Short term, after Whiting attended a conference on motor racing safety hosted by the Society of Automotive Engineers in Dearborn, Michigan, at the end of 1994, he became fully persuaded that a driver's head hitting the steering wheel might not be such a bad thing due to discussions with Melvin, well into his tenure as the manager at the GM Motorsports Safety Technology Research Program. Others such as Drs. Terry Trammell and Steve Olvey were also persuasive. They were assisting in the GM safety program by gathering data about crashes in CART races and the Indy 500 in their capacities as medical officers and corroborated what happened to drivers' heads in Indy car crashes.

When the cockpit dimension rules emerged for F1 in 1995, the series adopted the high sides of the Indy cars for better lateral protection of drivers' heads and the steering wheel location had been re-designed to bump-stop drivers' heads in a fashion similar to Indy cars.

A nearly fatal accident quickly changed the thinking within the FIA and accelerated the search for a solution beyond catching drivers' heads with a padded steering wheel. At the end of the 1995 season, Hakkinen actually stopped breathing after his crash on the Adelaide street circuit in Australia while onboard a Mercedes-powered McLaren. A basal skull fracture occurred and internal bleeding, but not enough to be fatal. Still, a close call.

A cut tire had sent Hakkinen's car backwards over the curb at Brewery Bend, a 125 mph, right-hand corner. The car literally tripped over the curb, lifted off, spun 180 degrees from its backward course and slammed nearly sideways into a concrete wall covered by one row of tire barrier. An in-car camera shows the left front corner hit first, just before the left rear. As a result of this staggered forward and back side impact, Hakkinen's head shot violently to the side, just the sort of impact and vector of energy that Watkins had written about.

"I remember sitting in the car and trying to move my hands, but I couldn't," Hakkinen would recall later. "I tried again and again and so I knew that what had happened was bad."

The corner was near the station of medical specialists from the Royal Adelaide Hospital working as part of the safety crew established for the race by Watkins. Quick, expert work by this crew, which included the proper care in removing a driver with a potentially severe head injury, saved the Finn's life.

Initially, Hakkinen received a cricothyroidotomy from Jerome Cockings, which could be administered quickly and despite concerns about a head injury while the driver was still in the car. An incision was made just below the "Adam's apple", or thyroid cartilage, then a second incision in the cricothyroid membrane underneath followed by a tube insertion, which allowed air to get into Hakkinen's lungs.

After arriving at the scene within seconds of the Royal Adelaide team, Watkins waited until the driver was properly extricated and performed a tracheotomy, a more permanent solution to the driver's breathing difficulties and the standard follow-up to a cricothyroidotomy. The ambulance took the driver to the nearby Royal Adelaide Hospital and soon Hakkinen began a rapid recovery from what could have been the last crash for the future two-time world champion.

Not long afterward, the Mercedes division of Daimler-Benz became actively involved in the idea of developing air bags for F1, which up until that point had been a project mostly in the hands of the FIA with communication back and forth to Mercedes.

"The whole (Mercedes) project started because of Mika Hakkinen's accident in Adelaide," said Peter Wright, the longtime engineer at the Lotus F1 team who had been appointed the Technical Advisor to the FIA at the outset of the 1995 season. "The initial solution was thought to be an air bag. The FIA started working with MIRA, but little progress was being made. I went to a German Touring Car Championship test in Hockenheim, and spoke to Gerhard Lepler of Mercedes, and asked him whether they would get involved, as the car company knowing the most about air bags. The answer came back in the affirmative."

Hubert Gramling, an engineer and mathematical whiz, was the man Mercedes put in charge of its air bag project for F1 under the direction of Lepler, who had risen through the ranks of the company's motorsports program as an engineer. His resume included directing work on the redoubtable C-Class Mercedes in Germany's famed Touring Car series, the first racing vehicles to carry air bags in the early 1990s.

Gramling's biggest challenge concerned the fundamental problem presented by activating air bags using algorithms. The math would have to be applied to a very complex circumstance. How much impact would be enough to fire the explosive devices that activated the air bags? How quickly could they be deployed? In testing, the bags were fitted inside a slot above the steering wheel, then deployed over it, preventing the head from hitting it, or undergoing violent head whip in a vector-type crash.

The FIA provided Gramling with all the information that had been gathered, including data from the FIA's own testing of the HANS Model I by MIRA. With an eye toward neck tension and shear forces being a problem, when Gramling reviewed the MIRA test of the HANS Device, he saw that the neck tension figures looked good and were comparable with the goals for air bags to prevent the kind of injury that had killed

Heinz Knoll, Hubbard and Gramling at the Mercedes-Benz 'crash hall' in Stuttgart. (Photo by Theo Seidens)

Ratzenberger and had nearly killed Hakkinen.

"There was already communication between Mercedes and the FIA after the drivers were killed at Imola," recalled Gramling, an articulate, talkative and high-minded engineer fluent in English who became a key figure in the development of the HANS. "Mercedes was already developing an air bag parallel to the Senna accident. The FIA was already having communication with Mercedes on the subject of air bags.

"The accident of Mika Hakkinen in Adelaide when he was nearly killed made Mercedes extremely nervous. (The FIA) approached Mercedes and asked if it would help with the development.

"This would have been a very unique air bag, because of the sensor and triggering with algorithms. They asked me if I would help with the development. I said, 'Yes.' I reviewed what had been done at MIRA and found that the HANS had been tested. You could see in the tables of results that this looked good."

Gramling asked Whiting for more information on the HANS. "I thought the HANS would be a quick solution—maybe 90 percent—while I developed the air bag," said Gramling. "The values were the same with

Hubert and HANS

The Model 1's success in protecting boat racer Anderson from fatal injury during his 1991 flip at Bay City, Michigan, would help persuade FIA officials to look more closely at the HANS.
(Photo courtesy of Andy Anderson)

what we achieved. This was a surprise for the Americans, who didn't believe the air bag would do the job. It was a surprise for the Europeans that the HANS would do the job."

There were snags in the air bag plan. The triggering mechanism is extremely complex at high speeds and the resulting violent chassis accelerations. Air bags require careful selection of parameters such as volume, inflator capacity, and vent size to control the forces on the head and upper body. Once arriving at the speed needed for deployment by gas generation, a problem presented itself. The impact from the rapid deployment of the air bag might not be much different than the driver's helmeted head hitting the steering wheel. The force of the air bag might cause even more injury, possibly death.

Since the air bag had to be deployed from a slot above the steering wheel, it meant that coordination between the restraint system and the driver's position could not always be guaranteed. Given the air bag had to come over the top of the steering wheel, a hazard could be presented for a driver's hands on the wheel. Unintentional deployment and multiple impacts also presented issues.

By comparison, the HANS Device presented a static option, always available for use. But the Model I did not fit properly into a F1 cockpit. If that problem could be remedied and unintended safety problems could be avoided, the HANS looked like the best piece to fill the gap in the puzzle, thought Gramling. He wanted to know more.

At the end of 1996, just before Hubbard and his family were leaving their home to celebrate the Thanksgiving holiday as dinner guests at another family's house, he heard the phone ring. It was Whiting, calling from England. The dinner plans were slightly delayed as an inwardly excited Hubbard readily answered Whiting's questions.

"He asked about HANS performance in sled testing and the injury experience in racing," said Hubbard. "At that point, we had sold at least 100 Model I devices since 1991 with no cases of head or neck injuries in some apparently severe frontal crashes." He also told Whiting that Melvin had conducted his own sled tests with the HANS Device as part of the GM safety project and those tests had confirmed the findings from the 1989 test by him and Paul Begeman at Wayne State.

The conversation led to a meeting in Michigan in early 1997 between Whiting, Wright, Gramling and the principals of HANS Performance Products. The trio from Europe were interested in researching the development of a smaller HANS that could fit into a F1 cockpit.

12
German Engineering

WHEN HUBERT GRAMLING FIRST CONSIDered the HANS Device for F1, he started with a relatively beat-up Model I rescued from the testing project at MIRA. It was recovered, he said metaphorically, from "the dust bin."

Following the pre-Thanksgiving call to Hubbard by Charlie Whiting, the inaugural meeting of Hubbard and Gramling was hosted by John Melvin in the offices used for the GM Motorsports Safety Technology Research Project. The FIA's Whiting and Peter Wright joined Hubbard, Downing, and GM Motorsports director Herb Fishel, an active participant in motor racing safety. It proved to be the most momentous occasion for Hubbard and Downing since the HANS Device was first used ten years earlier.

Gramling had become less enthusiastic about air bags, because of the unique challenges presented by the speed and power of a F1 car. The sensor mechanisms and triggering with algorithms would be very complex. "This would have been a fully optimized air bag with gas generation using algorithms for sensing and there would have been only one bullet," he said. "Something that is already available, extremely robust and safe was a better solution. Even if you did a little bit wrong with it, it still works."

He had spent much of 1996 working on air bag development. "It's only with extremely proper engineering that you can make the air bag a satisfactory solution," he said. "The HANS showed to be the equivalent of the air bag. I wanted to show the limits of the air bag and continue the testing to reach the limitations of the air bag. It was in this testing that we found the air bag to be the equivalent of the HANS."

The initial meeting in Detroit started a classic scientific relationship of discovery between Gramling and fellow engineer Bob Hubbard. Once Mercedes-Benz agreed to begin a testing project with the HANS, Hubbard would become a family friend after repeated trips to Stuttgart, where the American stayed at Gramling's house. Hubbard and Gramling eventually published scientific papers together not only on their HANS work, but also on the development of air bags for F1.

In the first meeting with FIA officials, Downing felt that the guests from Europe were much impressed by the fact that the HANS had been used in the field by customers for six years with some favorable outcomes in crashes and testimonials. As importantly, there had not been any adverse incidents as a result of HANS usage. "We showed them the data and the SAE papers, but I think they were even more encouraged by the fact we had people like powerboat racer Andy Anderson who had serious crashes and then walked away thanks to the HANS Device," said Downing.

Anderson, whose crash occurred in 1991, became the first racer to testify that the HANS worked. "I don't want to call it luck," recalled Anderson. "I got this device the race before and sure enough in the second race I'm using it I get into this accident."

Racing a Mod VP tunnel boat in Bay City, Michigan, Anderson's boat lifted off, corkscrewed into the air and then slammed straight into the water upside down.

Crash! How the HANS Helped Save Racing

German Engineering

The boat came equipped with a safety capsule for the driver as well as a canopy featuring a Lexan windshield. "They used Lexan about as thick as what they used for an F16 jet fighter and it completely shattered it," recalled Anderson nearly 25 years after the crash. The boat decelerated abruptly and the impact left Anderson with a collapsed lung, a broken ear drum, a shattered nose and cheekbone. His Model I HANS had a crack in it as well, but Anderson suffered no serious neck injury.

It was a common result in various forms of boat racing for drivers involved in flips where boats slammed into the water to be killed because of broken necks. That was believed to be the result in the accident of ModVP driver Christopher "Red" Hindman, a former champion who died at Lake Havasu in Arizona the year before Anderson's crash. Driver Ricky Comer, who suffered a flip on Cedar Creek Lake in Dallas in 1992, died of a broken neck.

Given these circumstances, Anderson recognized that the HANS had done its job during his accident. "There was talk about whether the HANS was worth it, was it too cumbersome?" said Anderson. "In my own opinion, I decided it was a safety issue and not a performance issue."

In addition to this testimonial, Hubbard presented to the three representatives of the FIA information from field surveys he had conducted. The surveys included other boat drivers caught in blow-over accidents who suffered no neck injuries as well as race car drivers who had serious crashes while wearing the HANS. Most of these testimonials came from weekend warriors participating in SCCA club events while driving open cockpit cars that accommodated the HANS due to upright seating, such as Formula Continental.

The comments collected by Hubbard included drivers walking away from head-on crashes in the range of 100 mph as well as weekend warriors with previous neck injuries who credited the HANS for being able to race without fear of re-injuring their necks. Whiting, Wright and Gramling, steeped in the FIA's cautious, hierarchal ways, found this type of information very persuasive. As for unforeseen side effects of the HANS, that could be fully explored by the FIA's own testing.

Mercedes-Benz and HPP reached agreement on developing a smaller HANS Device capable of fitting into a F1 cockpit. While complicated, the agreement left the production and sales of a motor racing safety device to HANS Performance Products. Mercedes would contribute a special sled test vehicle fashioned from a Lola F1 chassis, plus the technicians, led by Gramling, required to set it up at the company's facility in Stuttgart.

"After Mika's accident, Mercedes was energized," said Gramling, who regularly received emails on the subject of racing safety and air bags from Norbert Haug, director of the Mercedes racing effort. "The argument was made that 'No one puts his logo on an advertising poster covered in blood.' That's a bit crude, but it got right to the point. Mercedes as a company was committed to safety. Something had to happen. Mercedes had already spent more money on safety and research for things such as optimizing the roll cage and the fuel cell.

"You had to have a joint venture to make it work," he continued. "First, you needed an inventor. Then you needed a big car company to invest the money. And you needed a sanctioning body willing to mandate the use."

According to Watkins, the sled testing at MIRA cost about $3,750 for each run. Given that multiple runs were needed for any valid test and multiple tests would be required for peer acceptance, sled testing dictated the sort of expense that had prohibited Hubbard from additional development once the Model I had been established. The proposal from Mercedes to keep testing until all questions about development of a smaller device had been answered marked a momentous breakthrough for a workaday professor who once needed to hustle a grant from the state of Michigan for his own inaugural sled tests.

"In early June of 1997, as soon as I could be free from my academic year duties at Michigan State, I went to Mercedes-Benz with some initial HANS prototypes," said Hubbard. "Hubert met me at the Stuttgart airport.

German Engineering

The Model II started out like a hot rod—a chopped Model 1 reinforced by aluminum plating. (Photo by Hubert Gramling)

The engineers at Mercedes had free rein to 'remodel' the HANS for sled testing. (Photo by Hubert Gramling)

During my first work with Hubert, I became a little impatient since he wanted to ask questions and talk rather than work with the technicians in their crash sled as much as I had anticipated. I soon realized that Hubert was trying to learn as much as he could about crash injury biomechanics and racing safety."

"Bob was one of my main teachers," acknowledged Gramling. "I didn't have a clue about safety. We would take long walks in the woods in the evenings after spending the day testing and I learned a lot about safety."

Since Gramling spoke flawless English, he did the translations when the duo worked with the Mercedes technicians to modify the HANS devices and to prepare the sled tests. The two safety pioneers often spent time together in the evenings drinking beer and eating German delicacies like roasted pork shank, or Schweinshaxe, while discussing the day's events.

"At the end of this summer work session together," continued Hubbard, "we had made enough progress to be confident that the HANS could be adapted for use in F1 and would function well in that environment. Hubert meticulously analyzed the data and wrote his report on this initial phase of our work for Mercedes and FIA. After some discussion, we agreed that I would edit Hubert's report on our work together to make our presentation to the SAE International Motorsports Engineering Conference in 1998. Coming from an academic world, I felt that documenting our work in a peer-reviewed journal and a presentation was essential so that our work could be understood and used by others. This publication gave scientific credence to our findings."

The paper titled "Development of the HANS Head and Neck Support for Formula One" described how the engineers had modified the Model I device and then put it through sled tests aboard the Lotus F-1 monocoque, which had been cut down to the central portion housing the driver and cockpit.

A seat with lateral support was constructed for angled and lateral impacts. Visible in part through apertures cut in the monocoque, a full Hybrid III dummy

Crash! How the HANS Helped Save Racing

German Engineering

HPP's carbon version of the final Model II was soon modified by testing with CART. (Photo by Gary Milgrom)

with a standing pelvis sat in the car, because this particular pelvis allowed for angles between the torso and thighs of greater than 90 degrees. To achieve the typical F1 seating position where the legs extended up into the nose, a curved lumbar spine section belonging to a sitting pelvis model of the Hybrid III was combined with the standing pelvis.

The laborious requirements to set up tests that lasted split seconds meant no more than three could be conducted in one day. The tests were cine photographed, a process specific to capturing motion in every detail, and videotaped for visual confirmation of the dummy's responses. By the mid-1990s, computer programs produced far more information in a short time than the methods used when Hubbard first helped design the instrumented head for the Hybrid III three decades earlier.

Frontal tests were initially run without a HANS device as a baseline, using a crash pulse of 45 Gs, chosen because Melvin used a similar pulse in sled tests of Indy car crashes. The baseline test results—without a HANS Device—showed a neck tension of 3,700 Newtons, by itself well past the threshold for injury of 3,100 Newtons. The forward neck sheer of 2,200 Newtons was below the injury threshold, but the resultant, which combines the tension and shear forces, was 4,100 Newtons and greatly exceeded the injury threshold.

Quite a few prototypes were developed over the course of the summer of testing, each made by modifying an existing Model I using aluminum to reinforce the new shape. Only two of these new prototypes were reported on in the SAE paper titled "Development of the HANS Head and Neck Support for Formula One," but each effectively reduced the neck tension and shear results with a device deemed small enough to fit into a F1 cockpit.

The same 45 G frontal test was run with a standard original type Model I, dubbed 1.0, and the results predictably brought the neck tension and shear forces well below the injury threshold standard, or Head Injury Criteria, just as had been the case in the initial tests at Wayne State University a decade earlier. Next, a frontal test was conducted with a newly created HANS 2.0. It featured three tethers, but the broad, flaring collar "lapels" had been removed. The legs remained, but they were shortened considerably. The mounting for the harness belts was extended at the back of the shoulders using aluminum.

The 2.0 HANS reduced the forward neck shear to 700 Newtons, lowering it by more than 50 percent compared to the Model I, which had registered 1,700 Newtons. The neck resultant (combining stretch and sheer) dropped considerably as well, from 2,100 Newtons for the Model I to 800 Newtons for the 2.0 HANS.

The explanation? Better resistance to the forces were at work thanks to a greater area for the mounting of the shoulder belts. An extended aluminum mounting "effectively loaded the shoulder belts that restrain the HANS against the forward forces in the tethers that restrain the head relative to the torso." In other words, more energy transferred from the head and neck through the shoulders and into the torso.

The paper also covered the second new device called a HANS 2.5, which had the collar trimmed to the width of the shoulder belts and used two tethers. In place of a semi-circle of three mounting points—one at the back and one on either side of the helmet—the HANS 2.5 had two attachment points on either side at the back of the helmet. Although more toward the rear of the helmet, these attachment points were in line with the locations Hubbard had chosen for the side tethers on the original Model I with an eye on the relationship to the head's center of gravity. The 2.5 HANS also had the extended shoulder mounting area.

The test resulted in the lowest forward neck shear number (600 Newtons) of the three devices tested and the resultant came in slightly higher than the results for the HANS 2.0, because the neck compression, also used in this calculation, was greater.

The greater neck compression likely resulted from the two mounting points, but that compression also confirmed the greater resistance offered by two helmet anchors at the back and an extended area for loading the shoulder belts. The 1,400 Newton resultant figure for the smallest of the three devices was still considerably lower than the 2,100 Newtons of the Model I test—and well below the likely fatal 3,700 Newtons of the baseline frontal test with no head restraint.

Offset tests conducted at a 30-degree angle, side impacts of 90 degrees and rear impacts resulted in numbers well below the Head Injury Criteria. (The side impacts benefitted from the higher cockpit sides of the test vehicle, which acted as head surrounds.) In a rear impact, the helmet slid up the head rest by a shorter distance than the baseline test with no device.

Gramling made one of the key observations during the summer of testing: the two mounting points for tethers on the device, now located on the high collar behind the head, worked with relatively long tethers, providing freedom of head movement without sacrificing effectiveness. Tethers of slightly different lengths compared with one another worked effectively due to the attachment points on the helmet chosen relative to the center of gravity of the head.

German Engineering

A longer tether might mean slightly more head excursion, but once tightened the tether still transferred the energy effectively. Tether lengths could be longer, because the HANS slides backward initially in an impact due to the belts slipping over the device's legs and the torso moving forward. This dynamic was clear in any of the sled testing videos. The suggestion by Melvin to put rubber on top of the legs to create friction between the device and the belts remained critical, enabling the belts to catch and stop sliding due to the friction. Having moved rearward, the longer tethers are still in position to retain the head rotating around its center of gravity once the friction is generated.

Despite time away from his family, it was one of the most satisfying summers of Hubbard's life and marked a turning point for the career of Gramling, who soon went to work as a safety expert for the FIA.

Next, another ingenious racer worked some magic. To build the new devices using the model of the HANS 2.5, Hubbard turned to Jerry "Rabbit" Lambert, the fabrication and carbon fiber whiz whose usual job was helping Downing make his race cars go faster. Hubbard drew up a brief outlining the new HANS 2.5 shape and sent it to Lambert at the end of the racing season along with photos. He wanted devices to carry back to Germany in December, where they would be tested and shown to the safety personnel at FIA and to McLaren-Mercedes technicians.

A proposal for a smaller HANS did not exactly surprise Lambert. He had continued to modify the Model I to provide a better fit for drivers, but had been limited by the curvature in the transition from the collar to the yoke, i.e., the lapels, needed for strength in the bulky device. "What's crazy is that from day one, all we heard was 'It's too big,'" said Lambert. "Everybody kept telling Bob and Jim, 'They're too big, man, they're too big.' They never paid attention to that until they went overseas. Mercedes said, 'They're too big.' 'Well, OK, we'll cut 'em down.'" They needed to cut them down to start with."

Mercedes, of course, offered to fund a complete testing program along with its suggestion to downsize the Model I devices. In addition to a lack of testing budget and concerns by Hubbard about making the devices strong enough, Downing had always liked the relatively short three-tether system on the Model I, which included tethers on each side of the helmet sides that provided better neck support. Also, the side tethers could be adjusted by the driver during the course of a race. It was a very good sales tool and had worked often enough for drivers with neck fatigue problems or who had suffered a neck injury. A comfortable fit was always an issue and the larger size spread the load of the HANS across the shoulders and collarbones.

"Jim liked the pull tethers on the side," said Lambert. In fact, Downing had worn the Model I at the Le Mans 24-hour in 1996, co-driving to the LMP2 class victory in what was an arduous race decided on the last lap of the great French event. "We still tried to incorporate the pull tethers even when we started cutting the devices down," said Lambert. "They started getting too far away from the original location and it started pulling your head left and right with a smaller device." The neck support aspect that had been instrumental in the naming of the HANS and a significant benefit for Downing, actor/racer Paul Newman, and others was dropped.

Ongoing sales of the Model I used by more than 200 drivers had kept the HANS in front of potential customers. More importantly, the sales of the Model I device had kept HANS Performance Products afloat, but just barely. Once Mercedes offered its testing facility and a possible third-party recommendation to get the HANS into F1, it became an easy decision to pursue a different approach. But the idea of a relatively high mounting point on the collar for tethers, which provided the best transfer of forces from the head to the helmet and then to the torso, remained unchanged.

To build the smaller device with the newly devised additional belt-bearing surface at the rear of the shoulders, Lambert created a two-piece mold. He decided to glue the collar together at the yoke by creating a

German Engineering

The Model III evolved with a noticeably different shape from the device first developed in Germany. (Photo by David Lynn)

hollow section where the two intersected across the back, actually making the device stronger as well as lighter. As usual, Lambert kept himself up to speed on the latest types of carbon material and layup methods to achieve the strongest final piece. The two-piece gluing approach eventually led to the construction of devices that were hollow (by gluing a top and bottom piece together), which resulted in even lighter, stronger and smaller devices, important to universal use and acceptance.

By Thanksgiving of 1997, Lambert had built a "plug" used to make the molds, the molds themselves, a Model II prototype and six robust and now sleeker devices for Hubbard to carry with him to Germany for further testing. That testing went well, as did experimentation with McLaren-Mercedes drivers Mika Hakkinen and David Coulthard—although concerns about fit and comfort were again expressed.

Mercedes recommended adoption of the HANS for use in F1. After the FIA completed its typically arduous, legalistic process, the FIA announced a mandate in Formula 1 in the summer of 2000. A Test Specification was issued titled the "Formula One HANS System" in November of 2000. This specification would enable teams to build their own head and neck restraints based on the Model II, maintaining the bespoke tradition of F1 teams building everything on the car. To be certified for use in F1, a team's device had to pass the guidelines in the Test Specification, which primarily focused on the strength of the device under duress. In effect, the manufacturer, HANS Performance Products, warranted the product (in this case after extensive testing by Mercedes-Benz) and the FIA provided testing methods to be sure it didn't fail physically under the extreme demands of F1 racing.

Although FIA President Mosley announced the HANS would become mandatory for use by teams in F1 prior to the 2001 season, it would take two full seasons before F1 teams accepted the head and neck restraint.

It was Championship Auto Racing Teams that would become the first major sanctioning group to actually mandate the HANS. It took tragic accidents to get CART involved, but it also took the existence of a smaller HANS that could be used in the narrow, reclining seat of an Indy-type car, available thanks to a German engineer rescuing a beat-up Model I from the equivalent of a testing lab's "dust bin."

About the time the FIA finished specifications for head and neck restraints to be individually built by each F1 team for its drivers, two deadly crashes occurred in CART in the fall of 1999. It would be CART that moved more quickly to implement the smaller Model II HANS Device. Ultimately, what CART teams and officials learned would be crucial to the adoption of the HANS Device by both NASCAR and F1.

Crash! How the HANS Helped Save Racing

13
CART's Black Autumn

"I'M SORRY, SON. GREG IS DEAD."

These were the words George Franchitti chose when he greeted his son Dario within minutes after the final race of the 1999 PPG Indy Car World Series.

In the race on the superfast Fontana, California, track, Franchitti had lost the series championship to Juan Pablo Montoya on a tiebreaker after disastrous strategic choices by his team. Suddenly, that was nothing compared to learning his friend Greg Moore had been killed by a violent crash in the opening laps.

George Franchitti, knowing Dario had been best of friends with Moore, quickly sought out his son in the usual post-race melee to be sure he got the tragic news from someone supportive, someone who understood how much the death of Moore would hurt. It was the kindest thing a father could do under tragic circumstances.

In an eerily similar scenario to the disastrous F1 spring of 1994, the CART season of 1999 went black in the final two months. First, a young, well-liked driver who was little known outside the racing fraternity, Gonzalo Rodriguez of Uruguay, was killed by a basal skull fracture. Seven weeks later much-admired star Moore died in another violent crash.

The participants in CART had been doing what they did so well—pursuing races that wowed crowds with speed, the virtuosity of drivers and impressive technical performance. Then it suddenly went off track.

The Fontana race was supposed to be a happy occasion for Wally Dallenbach Sr., the chief steward of CART who was retiring after 20 years. Instead, he ended up giving a postmortem on the dangers of motor racing.

"The bottom line is that our cars are very safe, compared to the way they were when I started out, or even compared to a few years ago," Dallenbach Sr. told *L.A. Times* racing writer Shav Glick. "I've been in this open-wheel racing thing for 34 years, and in midgets and sprint cars before that, and it's part of the sport, sad as it is. It never disappears."

Dallenbach Sr. pointed to the accident of Richie Hearn. Like Moore, Hearn lost control at the exit of Turn 2 due to turbulence, spun to the inside and hit the same retaining wall. But Hearn walked away unscathed after his impact occurred with all four wheels on the ground. Moore's car flew into the barrier topside first, which exposed the driver to direct impact, in his case at 154 Gs. The car literally exploded into pieces.

The yawning gap of the longest off season of his life bore down on Franchitti as he hustled straight to the shelter of the team's hauler in Fontana. With a lead in points over Montoya coming into the race, it had been hoped that Franchitti, Moore and fellow drivers Max Papis and Tony Kanaan would celebrate the season by galivanting around the world in party mode like they had the year before. Driving for Team Green, Franchitti hoped to have his first major championship to celebrate and Moore was headed to CART's version of the New York Yankees, the team of Roger Penske, where the Canadian driver was destined for superstar status. He would surely win championships with "The Captain." If Penske elected to return to the Indy 500, Moore, a virtuoso on ovals, would be a contender there, too.

Franchitti had lost his championship bid under the cruelest of circumstances. "After Greg's funeral, I needed to go home to Scotland, to get away," he told writer Shaun Assael of *ESPN The Magazine* the following spring. "It was all I thought about. I wasn't in a hurry to do anything. My whole life, my thinking has been getting in the car. For the first time, I was a blank. I couldn't leave my house. My thoughts went back to Greg at the strangest times."

The off-season had been anticipated to be an encore of 1998. That year, the "Brat Pack," as the quartet of Moore, Franchitti, Papis and Kanaan came to be known, left a trail of parties from Elkhart Lake, Wisconsin, to Helsinki and Milan.

Owned and operated by multi-millionaire and billionaire team owners, CART comprised a moveable feast that raced on four continents. The teams lavished sponsors and guests with sumptuous meals in trackside hospitality tents in an atmosphere far more approachable and friendly than F1. More egalitarian competition took place amongst a host of teams and drivers, some of them refugees from F1 who managed to be quick enough on ovals and excelled on road circuits. It was a world party and the launching pad for the "Brat Pack."

The laurels of victory in 1999, including seven wins by Colombia's rookie sensation Montoya, went to a wide variety of drivers. Franchitti won three races and Mexican Adrian Fernandez won twice. Solo victories were posted by Brazilians Christian Fittipaldi, Gil de Ferran and Kanaan; Canadians Moore and Paul Tracy; and Americans Michael Andretti and Bryan Herta.

Up until the deaths of Rodriguez and Moore at the end of the season, the vaunted "Brat Pack" foursome and their five victories during 1999 helped add a cosmopolitan, youthful élan to CART versus its American rival, the Indy Racing League. The ongoing dispute between the two series, which meant CART no longer included the Indy 500 on its schedule after 1995, pitted CART's globetrotting series versus the one operated by Indianapolis Motor Speedway principal Tony George, trying to build his rival new league around the Indy 500 and American ovals.

CART's fab four had a lot in common besides being young, single, handsome athletes. They each came from upper middle-class families in which their fathers had supported their careers avidly. After success in karting, all had risen rapidly through professional racing's lower ranks in the classic way—they were quick out of the box and victorious in anything they drove. Next, they proved they had the extraordinary physical endurance needed for the longer races in major series and could handle the high horsepower.

Moore, 24 when he died, was the leader of the pack, in part because he had arrived for a full season in CART in 1996 and became CART's youngest winner at age 22 in his second season. His father Ric had raced in various series and most often in IMSA, where he competed in the GTO class for modified American muscle cars. A Chrysler dealer in Maple Ridge near Vancouver, Ric had mortgaged much of the family's property to help keep Greg moving through the racing ranks. Like his son, Ric enjoyed himself socially but took racing very seriously. They started in karts, first in the Chrysler dealership's parking lot, and then at the Westwood Motorsports Park in the hills above Vancouver. A reasonably challenging road course with one bad hump, trees instead of any runoff and frequent rain, the track helped Moore develop his phenomenal car control and confidence.

Before arriving in CART, Moore proved himself in the Indy Lights series, winning 10 of 12 races in 1995. Approachable and friendly once he made it to CART's big show, Moore remained highly focused on his racing. But he also pulled pranks such as stealing keys to a fellow driver's scooter on the far reaches of a circuit, forcing the hapless victim to push the scooter back to his team's hauler. Moore, who could be enthusiastic to the point of ebullience, insisted on wearing red driving gloves to highlight his Canadian origins. He soon became fast friends with Franchitti, who migrated to

CART's Black Autumn

CART in 1997 from the German Touring Car Championship under the umbrella of Mercedes.

Moore continued to live at home, in part to keep his feet on familiar, more settled ground, such as nearby trout streams, in between pursuing fame and fortune at a banzai pace. Also, he needed a place to stay. Moore had been signed by team owner Gerry Forsythe to a modest contract while the driver was on his way up in the Indy Lights Series. The CART team owner obtained a long-term contract and paddock rumors had it that Moore initially signed for a mere $150,000 per year, a relatively paltry amount. When the four years of the contract with Forsythe drew to a close in 1999, a bidding war ensued for a well-recognized driver who could win and keep sponsors happy. Penske won the bidding with an offer believed to have been $3 million per year, setting up Moore as a major star in all respects of the racing game.

Franchitti's father George was an ice cream distributor who helped keep his talented son moving through the racing ranks. The Scotsman would eventually become the most decorated of the fab four, winning the Indy 500 three times and four Indy Racing League championships. His marriage to actress Ashley Judd added jet setter status to the man who flew his own helicopter. Franchitti had met Judd through actor Jason Priestly, a Vancouver native and one of the wide-ranging group of friends that Moore seemed to create in the draft of his outsized personality.

An ex-F1 driver from Como, Italy, Papis earned the nickname "Mad Max" from TV commentator Bob Varsha in IMSA sports cars aboard Ferrari 333 prototypes before his passionate personality and skills carried him into CART. At age 30, Papis had more experience and, in addition, held seniority due to his friendship with Ayrton Senna. As an entry-level karting aspirant, Papis, whose father designed neckties sold through the Milan fashion markets, had the same coach as an early teen who coached the older Ayrton Senna in the 16-to-19 age group. The young Italian became friends with the future three-time world

The 'Brat Pack' of Papis, Moore, Franchitti and Kanaan partied around the world. (Photo by Mike Levitt)

champion, who occasionally stayed with the Papis family in Como.

Kanaan lost his father to cancer at the age of 13, but not before promising to continue his racing career the two had sought so passionately in karting. After a family squabble over the ownership of a factory formerly operated by his father in Santiago, the young Brazilian of Lebanese ancestry had to make it on his own. He upheld a promise to his father to keep racing. But he had to work his way up the racing ladder by

Crash! How the HANS Helped Save Racing

apprenticing himself to teams in Brazil and then Italy. He also came to CART's premier series through the Indy Lights. Like many Brazilians of that era, Kanaan, aged 24 during the 1999 season, enjoyed the status as a driver likely to bring in sponsorship from his race-mad country, where all the CART events were televised live and which hosted an event in Rio de Janeiro.

If their racing was fierce, spirited and professional, the quartet's partying qualified as world class. The night after Franchitti's first CART win at Road America in 1998, Moore and Franchitti drank most of the night at Siebkens, the slightly rustic resort on the shores of Elkhart Lake, whose crowded bar with swinging screen doors and outdoor beer garden traditionally hosted raucous all comer parties after races. The Scotsman missed an 8 a.m. flight back to Scotland after he and Moore reportedly first took comfort from the Siebkens lawn while sleeping off the celebration. Papis said that he woke up in his bed at the resort—fully clothed.

More than just image and partying, they were a band of brothers who traveled together in Moore's motor home to U.S. races as well as hosting each other during the off season in their respective countries. Where the F1 circus of the 1960s had been an atmosphere of live and let live, full of hijinks to defuse the overhanging threat of fatalities from fires or crashes, the CART era of the 1990s skipped the fatalism due to the relative safety of cars, driver safety equipment and circuits. As with all major pro series, the sun rose and set only on the CART paddock. If a similar series such as F1 had gone through a spell of safety problems and fatalities, the CART drivers could afford the usual viewpoint held by racers living so close to danger. It will happen somewhere else, to someone else, not here. Everybody was ten tenths, but not tense in CART.

During the carefree offseason prior to the 1999 campaign, a spooky event, in retrospect, took place when Moore and Franchitti visited the home of Papis in Como while Kanaan visited with some of his former Italian racing buddies. As a young driver, Moore had been a big Senna fan. Once he got his hands on an autographed helmet of the great Brazilian, he didn't want to let go.

"We arrived at my house, and one of the big stories that me and Greg always talked about was Ayrton, our common hero," said Papis in an interview with Andy Hallberry, a writer for MotosportRetro.com. "I was the lucky guy that actually had Ayrton as my big brother and my mentor. He helped me a lot, not only in my career, but in my life. Me and Ayrton built a special relationship.

"So, the first thing that the guys do is go into my room, and in there was Ayrton Senna's helmet, signed from him," continued Papis. "He used to come over to my house, and he brought me that helmet as a present. So obviously, I walk in the room with all the pride, and it's one of the first things I can show Greg… He picked it up, and he didn't want to let go of the helmet! He had it in his hands, and kept looking at the helmet. I told him some stories, some special things about Ayrton."

Presented a guest room with two single beds, Moore quickly commandeered the one where Senna had slept. "So, obviously, Dario had no choice," said Papis. "Greg wrapped himself into the same place that Ayrton used to sleep in and, I remember that in the morning, I had a very hard time to wake him up, and he told he wanted to spend as long as possible to 'Catch some speed' from being in the same bed that Ayrton had been!"

Before the end of the final race the next season, Papis would lose a second driver who had been like a brother to him. "He is up there in the sky, and these are the messages that God sends to us," said Papis on that horrific afternoon in Fontana, lapsing into an emotive and philosophical Italian perspective. "I am so sad. There are no words… There is nothing. Greg was a special person, in and out of the track. We are not here for this."

Seven weeks prior to the Fontana race, nobody was expecting to lose a driver to a fatal accident during a practice session at the Laguna Seca circuit. Gonzalo Rodriguez was trying to follow a familiar path—racing in CART in hopes of getting an opportunity in F1 by proving himself. He had won three races in F1's understudy series of Formula 3000 and had twice finished third. But the driver from Montevideo decided he would further prove himself in the heat of CART competition. One race for Penske Racing in the team's rotating entry for guest drivers in Detroit had resulted in a 12th place finish. The Laguna Seca race would be the amiable driver's last opportunity with the Penske team before moving on to a race with Patrick Racing.

With some sponsor and investor money behind him and a reputation for occasional impetuousness that put him in front of stewards on a few occasions in F3000, Rodriguez was essentially trying out for a full-time seat in CART. Team owners were perpetually on the lookout for talented, hungry young drivers they could sign to long-term contracts for smaller salaries as had taken place with Moore and two-time champion Alessandro Zanardi, initially signed for a relative pittance by team owner Chip Ganassi. "This is my big chance to show the world how good the Uruguayan drivers are," Gonzalez told writer Barry Goodwin. "My dream now is to stand on the podium in America and hear my national anthem."

The tryout went awry at Laguna's famed Corkscrew. Reminiscent of the accident of Roland Ratzenberger at Imola five years earlier, Rodriguez pushed to improve his pace in the Saturday morning practice after being 24th in the first qualifying session on Friday. According to an investigation of the telemetry by the National Highway Transportation Safety Administration, when Rodriguez approached the entrance to the Corkscrew high on the hill at the backside of the Laguna course, he lifted the throttle later than his previous lap and got on the brakes 100 feet later.

The report included a review of the car's telemetry and found no mechanical problems. Apparently, Rodriguez misjudged the corner or got his feet tangled in the pedals. According to eyewitness accounts, the car went straight off after not much lifting of the throttle and not much braking. The right front wheel locked up, but the rear tires of the Lola-Mercedes kept driving. Due to the terrain, the car flew from the track four feet in the air before the front nose hit at the bottom

When Rodriguez crashed at Laguna Seca, the force of impact flipped his car over the barrier at the Cork Screw.
(Photo by Dave Gallegos)

of a concrete barrier protected by a double row of tires with an enormous thud that shook the ground. The car then flipped over a 15-foot-high advertising banner and disappeared.

Dr. Terry Trammell, the well-known Indianapolis orthopedic surgeon who regularly served on the CART Safety Crew, worked at the Corkscrew that day on the outside of the track behind a concrete barrier that ran parallel to the track, open on one end for safety vehicles to exit. Sitting on the front bumper of the safety vehicle at the opening and looking at the corner when the Lola-Mercedes of Rodriguez went straight off, Trammell saw the entire incident.

"I look up and this car is smoking its right front tire like crazy," said Trammell. "I looked down to write down the car number and I looked back up and there's no car—it's gone." Before he even got to the car, which landed behind the wall and the advertising banner,

Trammell knew it was a serious situation. There was blood all over the advertising banner.

"I ran through the deepest part of the gravel. I look like I'm running in molasses," said Trammell. "All I had to do was go around it. But I took the shortest distance. I couldn't figure out how I was going to get over the fence. Somebody pulled me sideways and said, 'There's a gap.' I went to the car and the helmet visor's up. He's hemorrhaging out of his nose like a garden hose. And that's when I said, 'Oh, shit.'

Rodriguez died of a basal skull fracture, the second driver to be killed in a CART crash in the 1990s, the first being Jeff Krosnoff, whose car landed on top of a wall during the street race in Toronto in 1996. Due to the downward angle of impact, Rodriguez's helmeted head had hurtled forward as the nose of the car hit the base of the wall. Instead of hitting the steering wheel as usually happened in CART crashes, it flew up and out of the cockpit. His family would eventually bring a lawsuit against CART, but failed to prove negligence.

Uruguay's president attended the Rodriguez funeral in Montevideo. Well-respected and liked by his peers in European racing, where drivers are often far more standoffish than in American racing, Rodriguez was a virtual unknown in America. "He was one of the few guys who made friends," said fellow F3000 driver Max Wilson. "In Europe, in general, drivers are cooler towards one another than in the United States. He was one of the few guys that everybody liked."

John Bright, a principal in the Redman Bright team that ran Rodriguez in the 1997 Formula 3000 series on a very limited budget, liked the driver's promise. Rodriguez's ability and spirit helped carry the team, he said. "It's a tragedy," said Bright. "He was a great talent, a good friend of the family and put our team on the map. He fit in so well—he knew the money situation but performed miracles and made us look good."

The crash of Moore at Fontana had one unique extenuating circumstance. He had missed qualifying on Saturday with a fracture to the fourth finger of his right hand, injured when his scooter collided with a delivery truck in the paddock. Cleared to drive after an evaluation by Dr. Steve Olvey, a neurosurgeon and the man in charge of medical services in CART, the facture at the base of his finger caused only discomfort. "It was not a question of him being able to drive," said Olvey, a trusted physician and longtime participant at CART events who knew the sport and drivers well.

Driving a Reynard-Mercedes for Player's Forsythe Racing with his trademark red gloves and a special brace on his hand, Moore received 15 minutes of special practice on Saturday after qualifying and was examined again after the Sunday morning warm-up by Olvey. "He was excited about racing," said Olvey. Starting from 27th position after missing qualifying, Moore passed six cars on the first lap and had overtaken five more by the end of three laps. After a caution for Richie Hearn's spin and crash, the race restarted on lap 9. Moore lost control and spun in Turn 2 on the next lap.

According to trailing driver Helio Castroneves, who would quickly be signed to replace Moore at Penske Racing, Moore did everything right when he hit the bump at the turn's exit. "The car was almost straight," said Castroneves. "He had two cars in front of him and had no downforce on the rear wing (as a result of turbulence). The back end started to come around. He steered with the throttle on like we've all been doing. Basically, he did everything right, but the car snapped around and he went down the track."

The grass on the inside of the track meant Moore's car did not scrub off much speed and it got briefly airborne. When the left side wheels dug into the grass, it flipped the car up onto its side. Moore's car hit the infield retaining wall topside first and exploded into pieces.

After the car hit open cockpit first, Moore's injuries, said Olvey, were the type one might find after an airplane crash. They included the classic basal skull fracture due to impact on the top of the helmeted head among other gruesome displacements. Still breathing, Moore was airlifted to the Loma Linda Medical Center, where the initial task of stabilizing him failed before any surgery could be performed and he died.

14

Crucible of Opportunity

TWO WEEKS AFTER THE 1999 CART SEASON ended, an urgent planning meeting took place north of Chicago in Lincolnshire, Illinois, at the headquarters of Newman/Haas Racing. The meeting had been called by Kirk Russell. The successor to Chief Steward Wally Dallenbach Sr., Russell was working in concert with Steve Olvey, the director of Medical Affairs, and his assistant Terry Trammell. They wanted to get started on mandating the use of the HANS Device by all CART drivers, which would make CART the first major sanctioning body to require its drivers to use racing's only head and neck restraint.

Star driver Greg Moore's death had shocked the CART community. But it was the death of Gonzalo Rodriguez that pointed to the HANS Device. "Really, what got us started was the Rodriquez crash at Laguna," said Trammell. "When that happened, I think it was John Melvin who put us together with Prasad Weerappuli from Ford, who did the analysis. Weerappuli worded it very politically correctly. He said the HANS Device would have prevented the fatal neck loading, but maybe not have prevented the fatality. So, we were like, 'Oh.'"

Russell, who had added chief steward to his duties of technical director, was well aware of the new Model II HANS Device developed in Germany and Atlanta. Its availability for drivers in reclining positions in open cockpits brought theory into practice. After two deaths in the span of seven weeks, Russell believed mandating the HANS was an urgent move needed to help avoid preventable deaths in the future. But he also recognized he would need compliance from teams and drivers.

"Kirk was very upset personally and highly motivated to implement HANS in CART," said Hubbard, who was joined at the meeting by John Melvin and Hubert Gramling, the German engineer who had helped create the Model II HANS. "With emphatic assurances from John and Hubert that HANS could effectively reduce injury in frontal crashes, Kirk committed to do everything he could to mandate HANS in CART."

Beyond Russell's long tenure as a practical leader in improving safety technology in racing, this push behind testing the new HANS Model II was a nexus of prior relationships.

It was agreed the Newman/Haas Racing team and its drivers would conduct a testing program during the winter to learn how to adapt the HANS Device to the cockpits in CART. It had been just over ten years since Downing and Hubbard first established their relationship with Paul Newman, co-owner of Newman/Haas Racing along with Carl Haas. Newman had been able to race one of IMSA's extraordinary GTP cars, thanks to the HANS and its neck support. Newman's established belief in the head and neck restraint helped underwrite the project, which would certainly take budget and development time in a series where test days were limited and testing cost hundreds of dollars per lap.

Newman had already been influenced on a personal level when it came to the dangers of head injuries. In 1987, his longtime friend, driving coach and Trans-Am teammate at Newman-Sharp Racing, Jim Fitzgerald, was killed by a basal skull fracture when he hit a cement barrier at over 100 mph on a street course in St. Petersburg, Florida. Not long afterward, Newman wore a HANS Model I for neck support and protection at Watkins Glen International while behind the wheel of an IMSA prototype.

Olvey, who had also followed the development of the new HANS Model II, persuaded Newman/Haas driver Christian Fittipaldi to be one of the first drivers to help introduce the HANS. For his part, Fittipaldi had previously suffered a concussion in a testing accident at the oval in Madison, Illinois, and believed in the idea of reducing head injuries. Olvey was a longtime friend with Christian's uncle Emerson Fittipaldi, a two-time world champion and Indy 500 winner. Both Fittipaldis and Olvey socialized together in Miami.

To introduce the HANS, the politics in CART required careful navigation by Russell, motivated by a longstanding interest in safety. As a young man, Russell installed seat belts in his first sports car, an Alfa Romeo Giulietta, because he believed in the importance of safety on the highways. He was also the type who worked a 40-hour week and went racing on most weekends.

The racing stints started before Russell even left high school. He worked Formula 1 races at Watkins Glen as a teenage volunteer and later participated in the Pennsylvania Hill Climb Association, drag racing and Sports Car Club of America events, always working on the technical side. The combined sanction of the Formula 5000 series by the SCCA and the United States Auto Club brought him into USAC as a volunteer for tech director Frankie DelRoy, whose official title was chairman of the technical committee. When the tragic USAC plane crash occurred in 1978, killing DelRoy, his assistant Ross Teeguarden and six other sanctioning officials, Russell was next in line to take a full-time job as the organization's tech guru.

Russell, a 360-degree thinker, looked at things from all angles and could see through many of the typical ruses that race teams and manufacturers come up with for competitive advantage. In dealing with race teams he was generally process-oriented and respectful, in part because he admired the men behind the wheel and also because he was savvy enough to know how quickly the respect from participants could evaporate. But he was also rock solid in the face of resistance about his belief in safety.

Although USAC called him and offered a full-time job after the tragic plane crash, the pay offered failed to encourage Russell to leave his position at Bethlehem Steel, where he ran projects that enabled him to work enough hours early in the week to give him time for racing. Championship Auto Racing Teams was formed the same year following a white paper written by Dan Gurney and was destined to take over the top rung of open-wheel racing in the U.S. Organizers of the new series made phone calls to Russell, too. When big-wig team owners followed up on the phone with Russell, he accepted his dream job—racing full time as CART's technical director and director of operations.

Not long after creating his first Model I HANS, Hubbard paid Russell a visit. "The CART offices were in Troy, a few miles north of Detroit," said Hubbard. "I visited Kirk to explain HANS and its potential for improved safety. CART had been fortunate to not have any fatal crashes where HANS could have helped, which we later learned had a lot to do with drivers' heads getting stopped by the steering wheel during crashes."

Following Hubbard's visit, Russell asked to borrow a Model I. "I was very impressed," he said. "I took a HANS to Cleveland. Michael Andretti was still driving for the Kraco team. So, I go out in the pit lane after the day is over and they're a couple of things they're working on with their car. I said, 'Hey Michael. Try this on.' He said, 'What's this?' So, I explained the head restraint concept to him. He didn't object. But he couldn't get in the car. The original one was too bulky." Consideration of the HANS Model I was put on the shelf, as it turned out, for ten years.

Dr. Steve Olvey also joined CART from the outset, hired from his position as director of USAC's medical

Crucible of Opportunity

team to become the medical director. Even if he worked under contract, Olvey occupied the highest perch in the medical profession as a neurosurgeon. Politically savvy, cool but passionate about motor racing, Olvey relished the opportunity to work one-on-one with team owners and driving heroes, eventually becoming Director of Medical Affairs. In his role as a neurosurgeon, he didn't have to worry too much about maintaining team participants' respect and became a sharp operator in series politics. That ability helped his cause of improving the state of medical services in motor racing.

During the course of CART's 25-year history, it was Olvey who recruited additional medical personnel to what became the world's most sophisticated and effective racing medical team. The combination of the demands of CART racing and Olvey's pursuit of data and methodologies to improve medical services generated major steps forward for not only CART, but racing in general. Olvey worked on a par with Professor Sid Watkins, the neurosurgeon who was president of the Medical Commission in F1. But CART's medical crew operated under different circumstances. Where F1 had permanent facilities at each track—paid for by Bernie Ecclestone—and relied in part on local medical personnel, CART's team traveled to each race. At the outset, not being able to install permanent medical facilities proved challenging as did high speeds and concrete barriers found at the ovals on CART's schedule.

Olvey's most famous recruits among many talented medical professionals was Dr. Terry Trammell, an Indiana native who loved the Indy 500 as much as using his orthopedic surgical skills to get farmers in his home state back on their tractors and working in the fields, often after injuring their hands in farm equipment. While on call at the Methodist Hospital in Indianapolis in 1981, Trammell successfully applied the same surgical techniques of restoring the use of badly mangled hands to the feet of race car driver Danny Ongais, whose lower limbs had been brutally savaged in a crash at Indy.

Because of this commitment to get race car drivers back in their cars and an extraordinary ability to make it happen, Trammell became a logical recruit for Olvey. The first time Olvey called on Trammell to help out, he repaired the smashed feet—and career—of Rick Mears following a crash at the Sanair track in Canada. Olvey and Trammell soon formed a one-two punch when it came to developing new medical technology for racing injuries, better scientific data about safety and better equipment. Regarded as heroic doctors, they enjoyed status as the physicians to not only the star drivers, but the team owners as well.

Olvey pioneered proper immediate critical care responses to drivers with head injuries—usually resulting from impact with a steering wheel or the buffeting of the head in a cockpit during a crash. Olvey identified the two key elements to vastly improving an injured driver's chances of full recovery from severe head trauma: maintaining proper blood pressure and the introduction of oxygen as quickly as possible. Avoiding severe heat and possible heat stroke were also high priorities.

In his book *Rapid Response,* Olvey described the miraculous recovery of driver Chip Ganassi from what initially appeared to be a fatal head injury suffered in a crash at the Michigan International Speedway's high-banked oval in 1984. An impact to the top of the head left him with a swollen face and head.

"I thought he was dead," said Olvey, on the scene quickly in the typical response of the Safety Team. "His eyes were dilated and his pupils did not appear to react. He wasn't breathing, he wasn't moving at all. The fact was, he appeared clinically brain dead." After administering his protocols of stabilizing blood pressure and clearing the driver's airway, Ganassi began to breathe on his own prior to being transported to a nearby hospital by helicopter. Olvey told Ganassi's father it didn't look good.

Ganassi woke up 10 days later. When he later returned to the races, Olvey diagnosed Ganassi as hebephrenic, a term used to describe "a person who was abnormally jovial and inappropriately unconcerned," wrote Olvey. Those in the CART paddock who knew Ganassi thought he'd never drive again and none imag-

CART safety advocate Russell, right, talks with team owner Barry Green and driver Franchitti. (Photo by Mike Levitt)

ined that he would one day become one of the most prominent team owners in American motor racing. But that's what happened after Ganassi returned to normal over the course of the following two years—a second chance provided by the proper immediate emergency care he received from Olvey and the CART Safety Team. He briefly returned to driving, competing in IMSA sports cars prior to turning his attention to team ownership.

Olvey helped driver Roberto Guerrero return from a severe head injury suffered in a tire test at the Speedway in 1987. The decision to use a massive dose of barbiturates to reduce the metabolism of the driver's injured brain avoided the threat of death from extensive swelling. The strategy also helped Guerrero overcome a Diffuse Axonal Injury, which is the shearing of nerve fibers in the brain caused by a violent rotation of the head. Not only did Guerrero make a full recovery, he returned to competitive driving and eventually won the pole for the Indy 500 in 1992.

For Olvey and Trammell, radical procedures were undertaken to save a driver's ability to return to professional racing. The goal reflected their confidence, ability, constant research into new methods and, above all, a sense of *sympatico* with the racing heroes they were treating. Future four-time Indy 500 winner Mears broke all 27 bones in his foot in the accident in Canada; Derek Daly had his ankles shattered in a Michigan accident; Jim Crawford suffered grievous foot and ankle injuries in a meeting with the wall at Indy. These three drivers as well as others owed their ability to return to racing to the surgical skills of Trammell.

The most famous rescue came in 2001 at the Lausitzring in Germany, where the CART Safety Team led by Lon Bromley got Alex Zanardi to the hospital quickly after his car was hit at full speed by another car with enough force to tear his legs off. Getting him stabilized and to the hospital by helicopter within 20 minutes saved Zanardi's life, if not his lower limbs. That was enough, because Zanardi recovered fully, began to walk again with the aid of prosthetic devices, and then became a frequent medal winner in the Paralympics in hand cycling. Even more amazingly, he returned to his previous form as a two-time CART champion behind the wheel, driving to GT series victories in Europe as well. The ongoing success was a tribute not only to the effervescent Italian's determination and love for life, but also to the life-saving abilities of the CART Safety Team.

There was always much going on behind the scenes when it came to safety at CART. The close working relationship between CART's Safety Team and the GM Motorsports Safety Technology Research Program directed by John Melvin helped break significant new ground. They used sled testing to recreate crashes from CART incidents by employing the information from the data recorders in the cars and anecdotal reporting from Safety Team members at the scene of severe crashes. By recreating the crashes in the lab, Melvin could "develop test conditions of high crash severity with demonstrated low injury potential for the head, neck and torso."

A scientific paper written by Melvin, John Pierce, William C. Little and Edward Jedrzejczak in 1994 titled "Racing Car Restraint System Frontal Crash Performance Testing" became the first to examine, using

Crucible of Opportunity

Trammell was a member of the triumvirate that persuaded CART to introduce the first HANS mandate. (Photo by Mike Levitt)

realistic time-histories, what forces were exerted on a Hybrid III crash test dummy during an Indy car crash.

The palpable conclusion of these sled tests: a driver without a HANS and a steering wheel to hit would likely suffer fatal neck tension and shearing forces in a frontal crash at forces in the range of 37 G. (This eventually came to pass with Gonzalo Rodriguez's fatal crash at Laguna Seca when his head missed the steering wheel due to the angle of impact.) In addition to head acceleration and neck tension, the tests demonstrated the values for chest deflection and lumbar compression. The latter two were areas where a restraint could possibly introduce enough forces to cause injury. But the test confirmed chest deflection and lumbar compression were not excessive as a result of the harnesses or as a result of a HANS Device that provided dramatic reduction in neck tension.

In 1997, a significant change took place in CART cockpits that once again put any chance of using the HANS Model I back on the shelf. Full head surrounds in the cockpit came into place in CART after Emerson Fittipaldi's neck-breaking crash at Michigan in 1996—an impact that came close to paralyzing him. So, the prospects for the HANS Model I in CART were completely done. The new surrounds in CART for 1997 were computer-designed by Ford working in conjunction with on-the-scene accident research directed by Olvey and Trammell. Higher cockpit sides were introduced as well as better, form-fitting seats that kept drivers more stable in crashes.

During this same 1997 season, Gramling and Mercedes-Benz—on behalf of the FIA—began their testing of the Model I, cutting it down to find a size accessible to drivers in a reclining position in open cockpits with the HANS Model II gradually emerging by the end of 1997. Gramling's scientific paper, co-written with Peter Hodgman and Hubbard, about the effectiveness of the significantly smaller HANS was presented to the Motorsports Engineering Conference in 1998. The wrap-around used for side impact protection was missing from this new version of the HANS and soon the FIA would be referring to the HANS as a frontal impact head restraint.

Prior to the 1999 season, communication between Olvey, Trammell and the Medical Commission of F1 led to a joint meeting in London. Hubbard presented the new Model II version of the HANS and made clear on both sides of the Atlantic that the issue of too much bulk had been successfully resolved. By the end of the tragic 1999 season, Russell, Olvey and Trammell were convinced it was time to begin using the new, smaller version of HANS in CART. The next step: testing the Model II for fit and comfort during winter testing by the Newman/Haas team and drivers Christian Fittipaldi and Michael Andretti in Sebring, Florida.

"The Newman/Haas drivers, Michael Andretti and Christian Fittipaldi, agreed to work with us to get them comfortable with the HANS," said Hubbard. "Steve Olvey had urged Christian to take a leading role since he had suffered a concussion. While we eventually learned much more about detecting and treating concussions, Steve knew that repeated concussions were not good for Christian's future racing and health prospects."

This winter testing effort would be the portal needed to introduce the HANS to major league racing.

15

'Testy' Testing Brings First Mandate

DURING TESTING ON TRACK WITH Newman/Haas Racing drivers in the winter of 2000, the Model II HANS created during the sled tests in Germany by Mercedes-Benz evolved significantly. What was learned in CART soon became the basis for HANS models used for all reclining drivers, including those in F1, as well as drivers in upright seats such as stock cars.

The testing at Sebring International Raceway was relatively easier for Michael Andretti, whose beefy upper body meant the new, smaller Model II yoke did not put undue pressure on his collarbones. It was not the same for the taller, lankier Fittipaldi.

Oddly enough, this fit Olvey's strategy. He thought working with Fittipaldi the best choice, in part, because of his reputation as a prima donna. "I reasoned that if I got the pickiest driver that we had, one that can't tolerate any unnecessary discomfort in the car, or any changes and he accepted it, we could then convince the other ones," said Olvey. "I was close friends with Emerson Fittipaldi, so Emerson helped me talk his nephew into trying the HANS during the winter testing period. At first, he absolutely hated it, but agreed to continue using it."

From the outset, Fittipaldi recognized that the HANS Model II wasn't ready for the reclining seat in his Champ Car, no matter how much testing it might have undergone in sled tests. (Due to the split with the Indy Racing League, CART teams began referring to their cars as Champ Cars to distinguish them as different in specifications and manufacture, despite over-all similarities.)

"It's not easy when you go around a road course in a Champ Car," recalled Fittipaldi of the Sebring tests. "Those cars had almost 1,000 horsepower and you're flying over curbs and just running all the time on surfaces that are uneven. It's a different story than going around on an oval where you don't have the bumps like at Sebring. On an oval, you're not braking or accelerating, you're at a constant speed all the time. You're only turning one way. On a road course, you're aggressively turning right and left, sometimes when you're turning, you're flying over a curb."

Hubbard understood the problem. "Because of the complex shape and movements of shoulders, the only way to get an acceptable fit was to make HANS prototypes for the drivers, then try to find fault with it," said Hubbard. "Then, we would have to change the shape and try again. This cut-and-try shape development would be mostly the responsibility of Jim Downing and fabricator Jerry Lambert at Jim's racing composites shop in Atlanta. We also would have to search out and try several padding materials. The cooperation and patience of the Newman/Haas team was essential to arriving at shapes that the CART drivers could accept."

"Sometimes we stayed several days in Sebring and we spent a shitload of money," said Fittipaldi. "There

Crash! How the HANS Helped Save Racing

'Testy' Testing Brings First Mandate

were times that it was so bad, I couldn't drive the car on the limit. So, the laps I was doing, we had to wipe out. We were burning tires, we were burning fuel only to develop Dr. Hubbard's stuff."

The team calculated that testing at Sebring cost $1,500 per lap—including supplementary expenses like plane tickets and transporting the cars. With the testing of various HANS iterations remaining so long at the top of the clipboard list of priorities, tempers occasionally flared. "At a certain point the conversation started to heat up," said Fittipaldi. "I think Dr. Hubbard was expecting me to say something. For me, life is very black and white. So, there were times when I got out of the car and said, 'Hey dude, the thing is shit.' Even if he spent four weeks, or months or whatever, I was worried about my safety and the safety of my colleagues. I was worried for what he was trying to implement and I wanted to guide him in the right way and not be political and not tell him something wrongly."

For his part, Hubbard had a great deal of experience working with young, idealistic people. The patience developed by years as a college professor in addition to his dedication to the task at hand helped sustain Hubbard on his typically even keel. At one point, Fittipaldi looked at the HANS inventor and said, "Dr. Hubbard, you don't like me very much, do you?" Hubbard declined to answer that day at Sebring. "I thought about it and when I saw Christian the next day," recalled Hubbard, "I told him, 'Christian, I like you well enough to save your life.'"

For the HANS to be successful, drivers who found it more painful or even psychologically difficult would have to be accommodated. "Christian would call me all winter long," said Olvey. "And the calls got better. Hubbard went to the tests and made adjustments to the device. Christian at first called him Dr. Hubbard. I knew we were getting somewhere because later on he was calling him Bob. 'Bob and I worked on this, we worked on that together.' By the end of that winter, Christian could tolerate the device while driving long stretches. Then we had a driver's meeting and I presented it. Christian helped me do that. Following that meeting more drivers began to experiment with the HANS."

Although the use of padding under the yolk could relatively quickly resolve the pressure on the collarbones, getting the HANS to fit became a major project. The goal: make it comfortable to use the HANS on both high-speed ovals—where speeds were regularly exceeding 230 mph—and on street courses and permanent road circuits.

The timing was critical. The head injuries kept coming once the 2000 CART season began. The ongoing issue of cars cornering at increased speeds sustained the prospect of incidents where the existing cars, cockpits and barriers were not sufficient to prevent injury.

Dario Franchitti, for example, suffered a concussion when his car slammed into the Turn 3 wall at the Homestead-Miami Speedway during Spring Training in addition to three non-displacement fractures of the left pelvis. The accident was attributed to a broken spindle—but the driver had no recollection of the incident, indicating he was briefly knocked out.

Rookie Shinji Nakano suffered a head injury when he hit the wall at the Milwaukee Mile, driving for the team of Derrick Walker. According to Terry Horner, a consulting neurologist for CART, the accident left the Japanese driver with several small bruises on the brain. He missed two races.

After Norberto Fontana hit the wall during the race on the oval at Nazareth, Pennsylvania, he suffered a bad enough concussion that Olvey required him to begin wearing the HANS Device. It was the second concussion for the Brazilian driver within two weeks following an earlier incident at the Twin Ring Motegi circuit in Japan.

The "prescription" of a custom-fitted Model II HANS Device became one way for it to be introduced without a mandate or voluntary use by drivers such as Fittipaldi and Andretti. The day after Fontana's accident at Nazareth, Steve Knapp was required to wear a HANS Device during the Indy 500. Dr. Henry Bock, who had succeeded Olvey at the Speedway as the medical director, "prescribed" the HANS for the driver who had suffered a broken neck the previous year in an Indy Racing League accident.

Later in the summer of 2000, in qualifying for the street race at the Belle Isle circuit in Detroit, Tony Kanaan suffered a mild concussion in an accident that broke his left forearm and fractured four ribs.

Fittipaldi, too, fell victim to a head injury. He crashed at the Chicago Speedway oval, an impact recorded at 99 Gs. Because of the HANS Device, Fittipalidi likely avoided being forced out of the car for an extended spell such as when he missed five races in the 1999 season following a concussion in a testing accident at the Gateway International Raceway near St. Louis. In Chicago, Fittipaldi sat out one race under Olvey's rules about drivers losing consciousness in a crash, then passed a neurological test and returned to racing.

As would later be the case with Dale Earnhardt, Jr. in NASCAR, the HANS Device did not prevent a concussion for Fittipaldi, but it likely prevented a more serious brain bruise or contusion. Concussions occur due to abrupt rotation of the brain inside the head as well as forces from impact. The HANS Device and the cockpit-mounted head surrounds did not entirely prevent such rotation, and drivers who had already suffered a concussion such as Fittipaldi were more vulnerable.

In a conversation with reporter Robin Miller, Fittipaldi joked that the crash in Chicago might have ended his career. "It was very close to Christian turning into a gardener," joked the Brazilian after returning to competition at the Mid-Ohio Sports Car Course two weeks later and finishing third. As was frequently the case with so many drivers, the thought of a worse outcome was not verbalized by Fittipaldi.

By mid-summer, Russell formally introduced a mandate for the HANS Device on ovals, effective for the following 2001 season along with some other changes to the rulebook. They were supposed to all have HANS Devices in place for the 2000 season finale at the Fontana, California, track. The HANS mandate was a relatively low-key measure that came at a time when fierce arguments reigned, often covered by the media, between team owners and the four engine manufacturers about reducing horsepower to reduce speeds and improve safety.

"Any time you got in an Indy car or an Indy Lights car, you had to be wearing a HANS," said Russell of the mandate. "Testing, practice, anything. Well, the first thing that happened was drivers started asking questions like, 'Who gives you the authority to mandate this? I just tested at Mid-Ohio and I can't drive the car.'"

The mandate was changed at the next meeting of the CART Board to ovals only. The team owners who comprised the board were wary of the increasingly high speeds on ovals. At the same time, they discounted the fact Gonzalo Rodriquez had been killed by a basal skull fracture on the road course at Laguna Seca less than a year earlier.

While the debate among engine suppliers Honda, Toyota, Ford and Mercedes about how to reduce horsepower for the sake of safety swirled without any end in sight, the HANS was an immediate option on ovals where qualifying speeds exceeded 235 mph on the 2.0-mile tracks—Michigan and the California Speedway in Fontana. But speed was only part of the equation. The circumstances of a crash had as much to do with severe head injuries as speed. When Fittipaldi hit the wall on the Chicago Speedway oval, where pole winner Juan Pablo Montoya averaged 168 mph, the crash produced an impact recorded at 99 G.

The formal announcement of the mandate for the following 2001 season came prior to the midsummer race at the Mid-Ohio Sports Car Course. Hubbard had been present for some testing at the hill-and-dale track in the midst of Ohio farm country to help teams and drivers begin the discussion about their transition to using the HANS. One of the drivers, Max Papis, had seen Downing racing with the Model I device when he first moved to the U.S. and began driving Ferraris for team owner Gianpiero Moretti.

'Testy' Testing Brings First Mandate

"I had a sit down with Bob," said Papis. "Because of Gonzalo's accident I was thinking, 'You would have to be a stupid person not to be wearing one of those.' It would almost be like someone wanting to drive a race car without a helmet, knowing the helmet was available." Papis knew about the winter testing by Fittipaldi, a fellow Miami resident who "was almost like a second cousin," and wanted to test one as soon as the devices became available.

In the course of testing with Newman/Haas, the Model II created for Formula 1 gradually turned into the Model III, a HANS able to work for all drivers in a reclining position, including F1, thanks to the work of fabrication maestro Jerry "Rabbit" Lambert at Downing/Atlanta. But since the business practices at HANS Performance Products were still developing, the Model III HANS Devices were initially made to order for the CART drivers at a cost of $2,000. That cost included the development of a proper mold for each driver from a softer "plug" device that could be carved and re-modeled to fit each driver's physique.

"As soon as we were able to get it to fit my shoulders, I started wearing it immediately," said Papis, who had the full support of team owner Bobby Rahal. "The first one was too narrow. So, we made it wider. As soon as they made that change, I had it in the car. I was just waiting for HANS to get the proper piece."

But the changes needed to adapt to the HANS wouldn't have been approached conscientiously by all the teams without the mandate from Russell and the advice from Olvey and Trammell that the HANS could well save lives, a timely suggestion in light of the deaths of two drivers and incidents such as Fittipaldi's crash in Chicago. Coming from the men most likely to meet a driver after an accident, the message gradually sunk in.

Not all team owners were enthusiastic about making the conversion to the HANS.

"I don't remember which drivers and team owners, but they were against it for the comfort factor, and they were not open-minded to new innovations," said Papis. "I could see that someone who just wanted to put the HANS on and the seatbelts and go, it would not be the optimized thing to do."

Dario Franchitti became the last driver to be fitted with the HANS. He found that his right arm and right hand would go to sleep while using it and pushed for an exemption. "Doc Trammell and Doc Olvey were putting a lot of pressure on me to wear it," recalled Franchitti. "I told them they had two difficult options. Either I wear the HANS and don't do up my belts or I do my belts up, whichever you want."

Trammell arranged to get a "plug" device, also known as a "wax blank" for a custom fitting of Franchitti during a test in Indianapolis. "It was a gray, soft, deal that you could carve," said Trammell. "So, we took this thing and put Franchitti in the car and started grinding on this deal. It took us all day to get it to where it felt right. It looked like it was off-kilter. One side was way smaller."

When Trammell brought the odd shape to Franchitti's attention, the driver said, "You know my tailor said the same thing about making a cloak for my wedding. I broke my collar bone when I was little on a dirt bike. It healed and overlapped." As a result, he had shoulders of uneven height and numbness developed in Franchitti's hand when using a standard HANS.

Trammell shipped the "plug" to HANS Performance Products to make a mold for a custom device. "So, it comes back by FedEx and we take it out of the box and it looks nothing like what we sent," said Trammell. "Before I even showed Dario, I got on the phone with Jim Downing. I said, 'What's wrong? What is this thing that you sent?' And he said, 'We thought it got damaged in transit and it was so wrong we fixed it.'"

Trammell and Olvey each understood a single driver exemption could lead to the mandate unraveling. So, a regular HANS was cut in half and laced back together in a way that Franchitti could wear it for one race. "He never crashed and by the next race we had the one that fit," said Trammell. "When we put that first one through the sled test, it tore right in half."

If there were any doubts about the value of the HANS, they disappeared after Mauricio Gulgelmin's

'Testy' Testing Brings First Mandate

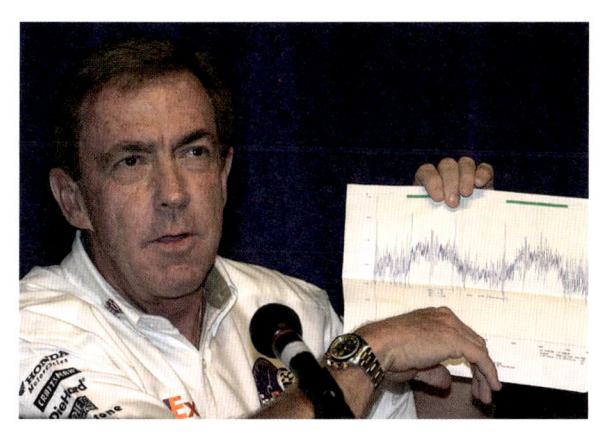

Olvey shows a chart with the lateral and vertical G-loads behind Gugelmin's horrific crash in Texas. (Photo by Mike Levitt)

harrowing experience at Texas Motor Speedway, site of the first oval race in 2001, which meant the first oval of the season where the HANS was mandated.

The Texas event turned into one of the most bizarre race weekends ever recorded once CART teams began practicing on the 1.5-mile track's 24-degree banking at speeds approaching 240 mph.

The teams and the three remaining engine manufacturers (Mercedes had elected not to continue in 2001) had finally decided that a reduction in turbo boost would be an important step in reducing speeds, particularly on ovals. Still, disaster for driver safety in Texas almost occurred in what became a political tornado for the sanctioning body, which had decided not to test before racing at a facility where the rival Indy Racing League had been making regular appearances.

If not for the quick and brilliant work by Olvey to identify the problem of cars going around the steep banking at an average speed of 232 mph, a full-blown disaster might have taken place. In *Rapid Response*, Olvey wrote about the strange loss of control by drivers Cristiano da Matta and Mauricio Gugelmin during the practice on Friday. Gugelmin's accident became particularly harrowing.

Following a normal racing line, Gugelmin suddenly veered into the Turn 2 wall in a front-end impact that registered 66 G. The impact resulted in his right foot getting caught between the brake pedal and the throttle pedal, which kept the throttle wide open. The poor driver turned into a passenger as the car accelerated down the back straight, engine screaming. After spinning 180 degrees, the car crashed into the Turn 3 wall with a massive second impact that measured 113 G. Nothing in the way of padding remained in his protective head surround, which was flattened by the two impacts. His feet were fully exposed in the absence of the nose cone once the car came to rest near Trammell at one of the CART Safety Team stations.

"When the Safety Team arrived, Gugelmin was still conscious," wrote Olvey, "and appeared to be uninjured. A double impact of this magnitude would have been fatal just a few years earlier. Thankfully, he was wearing a HANS Device. Without it he would have likely been killed." The device itself broke—which meant it had absorbed the energy that could have broken the driver's neck, resulting in a serious injury, if not fatality.

The following day, Gugelmin came to the CART medical center to see Trammell. "Why does my chest hurt?" he asked the doctor. "Because you're not dead," replied Trammell.

The Brazilian remained perplexed about why he had hit the wall. During the Saturday morning practice, Olvey worried about impending disaster as Paul Tracy posted a lap averaging 236 mph. Through comments from drivers after they were out of their cars, Olvey realized several of them were suffering from vertigo. When he checked with Tracy's team to examine the in-car data report, Olvey discovered the vertical G-load in the corners was 3.5 Gs and the lateral load 5.5 Gs. Drivers were sustaining high G-forces in the banking for an unprecedented long period of time compared with cornering on a road circuit.

Olvey concluded a connection existed between drivers' symptoms of vertigo and the G-loading. Following some very quick research, including a discussion with a former flight director for NASA, Dr. Richard Jennings, it became clear that the CART cars and driv-

'Testy' Testing Brings First Mandate

ers were carrying a combination of more vertical and lateral G-loads than human beings had been subjected to for a sustained period of time previously, even astronauts or jet fighter pilots. It explained why drivers Da Matta and Gugelmin couldn't identify why they had crashed. The loading had altered the function of their inner ear, creating temporary blindness in the left eye.

It was the ultimate example of cornering speeds exceeding previous standards with dangerous results. The Texas track had to cancel the race once it became clear that the CART cars and drivers were cornering at speeds considerably faster than what IRL teams had raced at safely. The cancellation left a lot of egg on CART's face and a debt to the Texas Motor Speedway, which successfully sued the sanctioning body. Thankfully, the HANS had been mandated for all drivers and Gugelmin walked away from his horrific crash with only a chest made sore from the loading during his two impacts, transferred to his harness and body by the HANS Device.

The debacle in Texas took place in the midst of serious business struggles for CART precipitated by its ongoing turf war starting in 1996 with the IRL for the control of open-wheel racing in America. According to TV ratings that were slipping below 1.0 in the U.S., CART was in a precarious position. At the conclusion of the 2001 season, the ESPN network was leveraged into leaving CART and committing solely to the IRL, whose centerpiece was the Indy 500, which continued to carry ratings well above 3.0 during broadcasts on ESPN's parent network ABC. After losing the $5 million rights fees from ESPN, CART had to buy TV time at a cost of $15 million per year—a negative swing annually of $20 million to its budget as TV ratings continued to fall.

PPG Industries, a longtime title sponsor of CART, departed and other sponsors in the series began questioning the cost paid to teams in light of dwindling TV numbers. Next, the Japanese officials at Honda and Toyota, who provided their teams in CART with as much as 60 percent of their budgets, decided to take

Downing/Atlanta fabricator Lambert developed a universal fit for the HANS after testing, development in CART.
(Photo by Gary Milgrom)

their engine programs to the IRL and the Indy 500 as well. Absent outlawed tobacco sponsorships that had sponsored as many as eight cars and amid complaints from promoters about high sanctioning fees, CART team owners struggled to replace the departed sources of revenue. Meanwhile, the CART teams associated with Toyota and Honda returned to competing in the Indy 500 and soon began moving to the IRL.

One of the greatest and most daring racing series motor sports had ever seen, CART filed for bankruptcy in 2003, because it couldn't overcome the appeal of the Indy 500.

16
World's Fastest Track Slow

IT WAS AN ODD TIME TO ANNOUNCE A cause of death. Bill York, the longtime manager of the Indianapolis Motor Speedway's media center, interrupted the usual hushed din of writers tapping on computer laptops while meeting deadlines to inform them that Indy 500 pole winner Scott Brayton's fatal practice crash had resulted in a basal skull fracture. Writers were working furiously to meet deadlines for stories on Carburetion Day when York made this announcement—six days after the incident.

A no-nonsense guy who also ran the press box for the Indianapolis Colts, York looked hefty enough to be a National Football League lineman. His stentorian and spare announcements were well known to reporters. A longtime official at the Speedway, York had witnessed firsthand the infamous crash of the pace car into the photographer stand in the pits at the start of the 500 in 1971.

His office had glass windows that overlooked the narrow, long and typically busy media room during the month of May at Indy, when U.S. and international journalists came to report on the world's largest single-day sporting event. This particular Carburetion Day in 1996 fell on the cutting edge of a great upheaval in Indy car racing. In three days, the first Indy 500 would be run since the Indy Racing League split from the Championship Auto Racing Teams. For its part, CART had scheduled a competing race, the U.S. 500 on the 2.0-mile, high-banked Michigan International Speedway oval on the same day.

The writers who had decided to cover Indy—or whose editors had decided for them—were busy mulling, tapping, and pounding out stories on Carburetion Day, the last time cars would appear on the track prior to the 500. The usual protocol of not interrupting one another unless it was necessary prevailed among the writers as well as the usual low-key exchanges about various points of information. While often resembling a free-flowing workplace, when deadlines prevailed, the atmosphere in the "long house" was more like a prison cafeteria shortly before a riot breaks out.

York occasionally interrupted the hallowed, daily grind with pertinent information about the day's events via an intercom-type PA system. On this day, at the peak of the deadline pressure, York intoned information about the death of pole winner Scott Brayton in a practice crash from the previous Friday, six days earlier. Brayton, he said, had died of a basal skull fracture in his meeting with the Turn 2 wall. This according to the Marion County Coroner's office.

Reporters were used to procedures at Indy that worked according to the internal logic of the track's owners, the Hulman-George family. But surely, it made little sense to make such an important announcement while writers were busy on their stories about Carburetion Day. And why had it taken six days to make this announcement?

For a column in *On Track Magazine*, I later learned the autopsy had been performed five days prior to the announcement. It was the policy of the coroner's office of Marion County, I discovered, to forward its findings in the event of a death at the Speedway to the track, which elected to announce the information in the middle of a busy deadline period after waiting five days in hopes, apparently, of writers giving it less attention. Such were the political times during the initial outbreak of open wheel racing's civil war between CART and the IRL.

Brayton's death took on all the trappings of a tragic family story. The son of former driver Lee Brayton had won the pole powered by a Buick V-6 turbo engine built by his father's engineering company. The 37-year-old Scott had had succeeded as a driver in the family business in ways his father before him had not, helping to make his achievements that much sweeter for all the Braytons, including Scott's wife Becky and a two-year-old daughter.

Lee Brayton, from Coldwater, Michigan, had run his gravel and sand company during the week before going sprint car racing on nights and weekends, taking his wife Jeanie and two young sons Scott and Todd along with him. Like so many of the weekend warriors in sprint cars who had experienced success, his ultimate goal was to race at Indy, the pinnacle of American open-wheel racing. The opportunity presented itself in the early 1970s when he was able to buy used Coyote and Eagle chassis from team owners A.J. Foyt and Dan Gurney. But in an era when speeds were jumping precipitously from year to year—hence the need to constantly build new cars and sell the old ones—Brayton did not fare well on the Champ Car trail, the year-long schedule built around the 500. From 1972 to 1975, his average start was 20th and his average finish was 15th against the formidable likes of Foyt, Gurney, Mario Andretti, Gordie Johncock, Rick Mears, Tom Sneva and other well-known speed merchants, all backed by major teams.

Lee Brayton failed to ever qualify at Indy, although his 16 Champ Car race starts included other high-speed venues such as the Ontario Motor Speedway—a knock-off of Indy—and his home-state track in Michigan. It was at Michigan in 1974 that a pit fire left him burned and put a temporary halt to his Champ Car exploits. Determined to race, he entered at Ontario on the first weekend of the 1975 season, but exited the race after 46 of 200 laps due to being too slow. He decided to leave behind the cockpits of Indy cars.

Scott's younger brother Todd was born the night after Lee won a feature at the Butler Speedway, but never had the urge to race. The determination to race was reborn in the older brother. Scott always knew that he wanted to be a professional race car driver, although his parents made him get a degree in business as a prerequisite. Diploma in hand, Brayton aced his first driving school and with the help of his father quickly moved up the racing ladder, qualifying at Indy in 1981 at the age of 22 after father and son pieced together $200,000 in loans and sponsorships and secured a chassis from team owner Roger Penske powered by a Cosworth engine.

Focusing on Indy initially with a team fielded by Lee, Brayton started second at the Speedway four years later in a March chassis powered by one of his father's Buick V-6 turbo engines. A deal soon followed to drive a March-Cosworth in CART for the team owned by Ron Hemelgarn in 1986. The younger Brayton thus embarked on a full-blown professional racing career.

The father wasn't worried about the son's safety. "Death in one of these things is a thing of the past," he had told *New York Times* writer Malcom Moran during Scott's rookie year at Indy. "Because of the safety, you can crash these babies pretty hard. When I was driving, you had 80 gallons of fuel, on both sides. Now you only carry 40 gallons. You just don't hardly ever see a fire in a race car anymore. The worst I was ever hurt was when I was burned. In the last few years you haven't had that."

The younger Brayton, enthusiastic and quick to smile, had lived and breathed American open-wheel racing from his earliest days. Indeed, he was at the track the day his father was burned in the pit fire. Among his peers, he was regarded as a racer's racer. "He was so appreciated and liked by the people in the sport and the fans of the sport," his widow Becky told reporter Bill Broderick of the *Battlecreek Enquirer* two decades after the fatal crash. "That spirit, the sportsmanship he showed, his presence around the track, that is really his legacy. That is what we all miss."

Brayton was living the dream, telling his father he couldn't believe he was getting paid for doing something he loved. The results were not dissimilar to those of his father, but the purses were far better, thanks to CART, and he no longer had the overhead of a family-operated team. Driving for the teams owned by Hemelgarn, Dick Simon and John Menard, he had led only 24 laps in his first 16 seasons, including one the year he started second at Indy. But the first year of the IRL in 1996 with its emphasis on ovals and rules allowing the stock block Buick V-6 turbo engines built by his father's company was a great opportunity, especially at Indy—where he had already qualified 14 times.

When he beat Arie Luyendyk and teammate Tony Stewart for the Indy pole in 1996 aboard a Menard-owned Lola, it was Brayton's second straight at the 2.5-mile track. The year before, Brayton had beaten his CART peers for the most coveted and fastest starting spot in circuit racing before choosing Indy and the IRL after the schism between the two series erupted. A second straight pole at Indy left him happy, voluble and anxious to engage the constant swarm of fans in Gasoline Alley and the pit area.

Brayton had fought hard for the pole, convincing team owner Menard to withdraw an already qualified chassis to take a second shot at beating Luyendyk in a back-up car. "You've got to give me a chance to drive it," he told Menard. It would be ironically tragic, because several days after winning the pole Brayton was in another back-up chassis practicing set-ups for himself and his teammates Mark Dismore and Stewart. Entering Turn 2, a left rear tire deflated due to a cut, which sent the car spinning before it caught the wall with the left rear just before the impact of the left front. That produced the same cockpit vector dynamic that had nearly killed Mika Hakkinen in Australia the year before, except Brayton hit a wall without tire barriers at a considerably higher speed.

Scott Brayton, shown here in 1994, started 14 straight Indy 500s. He won his second consecutive pole in 1996 under Buick V-6 power before his fatal practice crash. (IMS Photo Archive)

Brayton's head slammed sideways and came out over the cockpit surround, enough violent movement to generate the basal skull fracture. It was the second such fatal injury in four years at the Speedway. Jovy Marcelo had been killed after a crash into the Turn 1 wall during practice in 1992.

The cause of death for Marcelo—blunt head trauma, which generally meant a basal skull fracture—was announced the day following his crash by the Speedway. It was odd four years later that the announcement of the cause of Brayton's death would come six days after the crash. The timing certainly meant no dedicated stories to that piece of news—or how safety at the Speedway was being handled. In the midst of a CART versus IRL war, there were those who blamed IRL founder and Speedway owner George for Brayton's death—although Jimmy Vasser's pole speed at the U.S. 500 in Michigan was a comparable 232 mph and both series were using chassis built by the same manufacturers. The broader truth was the entire sport of motor racing was in an epidemic of fatal head injuries, often caused by basal skull fractures, and not much attention was being given to it by tracks, sanctioning bodies or the media.

NASCAR driver Stanley Smith had survived a basal

Crash! How the HANS Helped Save Racing

Dr. Bock holding helmet of Villeneuve. Rice's crash dispelled worries about the HANS in rear impacts. (Photo by James Penrose)

skull fracture in a 1993 Talladega crash—two years after J.D. McDuffie had been killed by one at Watkins Glen. In the midst of a battle with Dale Earnhardt for the championship, NASCAR star Ernie Irvan survived a basal skull fracture suffered at the Michigan oval in the summer of 1994. F1 driver Roland Ratzenberger had not been so lucky and was killed in the spring of that year at Imola in Italy. Including the Marcelo and Brayton incidents, that was at least six basal skull fractures in major racing series in five years.

An increase in cornering speeds and the subsequent opportunity for sudden deceleration when hitting a wall were the common theme of these accidents. At Indy, this lack of awareness, or the willingness not to worry about it, had much to do with the deaths of Marcelo and Brayton.

According to John Melvin, the Filipino driver was killed because he left the pits on a low-speed reconnaissance run without the U-shaped, padded head surround inserted into the cockpit after a driver gets in. A rookie at the Speedway following a Formula Atlantic championship the year before, Marcelo's car spun at about 180 mph, well below the usual competitive speed. But the absence of that padded surround in the cockpit enabled Marcelo's head to hit the back of the cockpit with enough force to kill him. The Brayton incident involved a much smaller, but still deadly indiscretion according to Melvin, who by this time was four years into running the GM Motorsports Safety Technology Research Program.

Brayton "jumped into a teammate's car," said Melvin. "It wasn't his seat. It wasn't his car and his head flicked over the top. He wasn't in it properly. He was just going out for a little test drive. I'm just going out to test. It's OK at 200 mph… It was pretty clear that his head was too high in the cockpit."

When the IRL introduced two all-new chassis the following year built by Dallara and G Force, potential cockpit issues were overlooked, creating a new problem. The new car specifications called for a higher front cowling to accommodate taller, and therefore larger, drivers. That changed the seating requirements for shorter drivers, pushing the seat location up higher. Unfortunately, dimensions at the rear of the cockpit remained unchanged, reducing the cockpit protection in the rear for shorter drivers in raised seats. The lack of complete containment of the cockpits was precisely the type of problem that had led to Brayton's death.

In the first race weekend for the new cars, relatively short driver Davy Jones spun and hit the wall on the oval at Disney World in Orlando. Following a heavy rear impact that broke the seat mounting, Jones' car ricocheted down the banking and made a second rear impact with the inside retaining wall. His head and neck came out of the cockpit. A veteran driver who had gained recognition driving sports prototypes for Jaguar, Jones had nearly won the Indy 500 in 1996, finishing second to Buddy Lazier, and then co-drove to the Le Mans 24-hour victory three weeks later in a Porsche prototype. The neck injury sustained in the crash in Orlando the following spring effectively ended his career at the age of 32.

"They made an error," said Melvin. "I remember seeing the new IRL car on display at Las Vegas. I remember seeing one of the features. They raised the cowl so that bigger drivers could fit in better. They didn't raise the back. I could see that drivers were going to be sitting up higher to look over the cowl and they didn't raise the structure behind them. I thought, 'Sure enough, these guys are going to be getting these head injuries.'"

Jones' injury was the first and worst. The IRL soon moved to reduce the amount of energy being transferred to the cockpit due to a heavy, bulky transmission at the back. An attenuator built by Riley Technologies located at the rear of the car helped reduce the G-forces generated by rear-first crashes into the wall. In cockpits, better padding introduced by GM's safety program helped protect drivers' heads and necks.

"Davy Jones, a whole bunch of 'em had problems," said Melvin. "We got the IRL to raise the head supports and to introduce the padding we developed at GM and of course the problem went away. They didn't realize the driver really slides up the seat quite a lot on a rear impact."

By the time the war between the IRL and CART began to wind down due to the combined sporting and commercial appeal of the Indy 500 in the early 2000s, a new generation of IRL chassis had arrived. All of the drivers migrating to the IRL from CART were used to wearing the HANS Device. Once Mauricio Gugelmin had walked away from his horrendous double impact in Texas, the CART drivers had been fully persuaded the HANS worked.

Yet, no mandate existed in the IRL to wear a head and neck restraint at Indy or any of the other tracks on the schedule in 2003, the decisive year in the demise of CART. One of those who migrated to the IRL from CART was celebrated surgeon Trammell, who once again began working with the safety crews at Indy. "They told me the HANS was not mandatory," said Trammell, who replied rhetorically, "'What do you mean it's not mandatory?'"

Instead of mandating, the IRL, which changed its brand name to IndyCar in 2003, published a white paper in January of 2003 titled "Head Restraint Device Evaluation." The paper presented by IRL technical officials Brian Barnhart, Phil Casey and Dr. Henry Bock, the medical director, essentially endorsed the use of the HANS Device as a result of private testing at the Delphi Safety Systems Test Center in Vandalia, Ohio. But that endorsement came with a disclaimer that the league could not guarantee a head restraint "will not worsen a crash condition or cause injury." The testing also included devices comprised of straps known as the Hutchens Device and D-Cell Harness, both manufactured by Safety Solutions, which had been worn by IRL competitors according to the paper. (Neither the Hutchens nor the D-Cell would pass certification by SFI that began at the end of 2003.)

Nearly ten years after extensive sled testing had been conducted independently by GM and six years since testing by Mercedes-Benz on the HANS Device, which had been covered by numerous scientific papers and video recordings, the IRL elected to conduct its own tests and came to its own conclusion, which was a cautious, legalistic recommendation. "The HANS Device controlled neck tension forces (upward pull) the best" read the report. The caveat offered by the IRL was that other sled testing had taken place at speeds below those common in IRL crashes and "at attitudes not fully representative of IRL oval track crashes."

The IRL's paper went on to remind drivers of the importance of a properly fitted seat and head surround. "It is imperative that both the seat and head surround be properly fitted…" The paper added that the "IRL cautions competitors not to modify any of the cockpit energy absorbing material in such a way as to reduce its effectiveness."

The paper made no mention of the single-most dramatic real-world crash of a HANS Device on record. Word of mouth meant most already knew about the crash of Richie Hearn in a test at the 1.5-mile Kentucky Motor Speedway oval in 2002. Wearing a HANS Device, Hearn suffered relatively minor injuries from a crash that registered an astounding 130 Gs according to a data recorder in his IRL chassis.

Dr. Bock, who had become medical director when Dr. Steve Olvey had moved to CART, believed there was still some liability with the HANS Device, particularly in rearward crashes. Drivers complained about pain in the back in the region of the thoracic vertebrae after such crashes, a development that Olvey and Trammell had noticed. Occasionally in CART, drivers suffered hairline fractures in the upper back. But the two doctors believed the benefits of the HANS far outweighed any drawbacks. A crash by 2004 Indy 500 winner Buddy Rice during practice at the Speedway in 2005 proved their point.

"Buddy had a crash here at Indy that without a doubt from the loading would have killed him," said Trammell. "I took a picture. It was the first HANS tattoo. You can see from the loading where it bruised his back. It shows the perfect loading pattern (from the device)." Instead of fatal injury, Rice, who had backed into the wall at Turn 2, was forced to miss the 500 after a neck injury and concussion, a situation that meant his Rahal Letterman Racing team would focus more attention on a promising rookie driver named Danica Patrick. Rice quickly recovered and resumed his career with the Rahal team following the 500.

Even in a rear crash, the HANS helped control potentially fatal violent head movement effectively. Although it proved to be life-saving in the case of Rice, the HANS did have a problem in high-speed, rear-end crashes, because of the interface between the device and the head surround in the cockpit. "If you went backwards, that short HANS lip would engage the head surround," said Trammell. "That's where the tall HANS came from."

The "tall HANS" was an extension attached at the top of the HANS collar which enabled it to slide over the head surround in a rear impact as the driver inevitably moves up in the cockpit. First introduced in 2007, it was invented by Jeff Horton, the chief engineer of the IRL, and essentially removed the secondary problem of back or neck injuries in a rear impact. It arrived after a similar device was worn by Michael Schumacher at Ferrari.

When Bock retired in 2006, Horton shortly thereafter mandated the HANS Device for all IRL drivers. By that time, A.J. Foyt IV was the only regular driver not using the device in practice or races.

Bock's opinion about the problems of rear-end crashes notwithstanding, the privately owned IRL had pursued the conservative course when it came to its legal liability. Fearful of lawsuits, the IRL considered it safer for the organization to wait instead of mandating equipment that might be construed as faulty in court during a wrongful death or injury case.

Under the same Hulman-George family ownership as the Speedway, the IRL pursued an age-old tactic. The sanctioning body recommended a safety device, waited for a majority of participants to voluntarily use the equipment and only then mandated it.

17
Deadly Year 2000

NASCAR'S DILEMMA ABOUT MANDATING the HANS Device began with the fatal crash of Adam Petty at the New Hampshire Motor Speedway during practice for drivers in the series known by its sponsor Busch. It was the first of three fatal crashes in each of NASCAR's three major traveling series during the 2000 season. As in other series suffering from a sudden problem with fatalities, cornering speeds for NASCAR's vehicles in the Cup Series, its understudy Busch Series, and the Truck Series were fast enough to exceed the existing safety standards.

Kyle Petty had often credited his son Adam for having more race car driving talent than he himself had. The only fourth-generation driver to ever compete in NASCAR's premier series, Adam Petty represented the future of Petty Enterprises. Then came a crash in May of 2000 in New Hampshire that ended his life at the age of 19.

The gradual increase in cornering speeds and corresponding increase in force of impact with the wall caught the younger Petty out, a problem long brewing in NASCAR. These speeds led to impacts with the wall that increased the G-loads on a driver. In the case of Petty, he did not survive because his helmeted head apparently missed the steering wheel, which often gave NASCAR drivers concussions, but saved them from more serious head or neck injuries. Instead, due to the angle and severity of the impact with the wall at Turn 3, Petty's head excursion gave him a fatal basal skull fracture.

Speed, not stiffness of the stock cars, was the key element in bad outcomes, according to Tom Gideon, who succeeded John Melvin as manager of the GM Motorsports Safety and Technology Research Program in 1997. Gideon, who later moved to NASCAR Research and Development as the director of safety initiatives, found that the increasingly well-engineered and stiff chassis were contributing to the cornering speed of stock cars. That speed, he said, was the significant factor in bad outcomes.

Many in the sport believed stiffer chassis were the problem. Gideon thought otherwise. He eventually created a mathematical model to test his theory about speed being a greater danger than stiffness in chassis. It was an important consideration. Stiffness can also be a major benefit in terms of adding strength to the cocoon a driver sits in, thus contributing to safety.

Gideon used a mathematical formula to reduce the influence of a car's structure, using existing models of crashes. Even when he reduced chassis stiffness to the minimum influence, the structure of the car could not necessarily get the energy down to a safe level—because speed was the issue. The stiffness of the chassis was a factor, but not the most significant factor in crash outcomes.

From the early 1980s, observed Gideon, the qualifying speed at Charlotte for the Cup cars increased an average of one mile per hour per year. "If you start your skid slower, you hit the wall 10 mph slower," he said. "What that means, this thing about the cars being stiffer—it's all about speed. No drivers were getting killed back in the 1980s. By time you hit the wall you

Deadly Year 2000

Heir apparent to the Petty legend, teenaged Adam Petty's fatal crash at New Hampshire's mile oval became a wake-up call for NASCAR. (Photo by F. Pierce Williams)

were going slow. That's the difference. The co-efficient of friction (for tires) doesn't change and drivers are always at the limit. That's why they do crash. This, to me, is more powerful than anything that ever happened to the car. One mile per hour per year. It doesn't mean much until you wait 20 years and then, Holy Moley! You're going a lot faster."

The problem created by stiffer chassis resulted from the better performance of suspensions in cornering, hence higher speeds. "It's all about speed," said Gideon. "All that torsional stiffness helps you go faster."

Like others researching safety, Gideon recognized that prior to the fatal accidents in NASCAR, the steering wheel was often saving drivers in crashes where the impact measured in Delta V—the change in velocity when a car comes to a sudden stop—might have been sufficient to cause a fatal head or neck injury after crashes into unprotected walls.

"Just about the time they started to pick up tension (in the neck) they'd get pushed back," said Gideon of the steering wheel impacts. "And, of course, Earnhardt missed the wheel. All the right front (impacts in 2000 and 2001) missed the wheel. And their seats had no head support. So, the driver just went out."

Adam Petty died of a basal skull fracture, according to the coroner, Dr. Thomas Andrew. His Pontiac hit the wall in Turn 3 at New Hampshire with the right front corner of the chassis before continuing down the track. Although many believed that a stuck throttle caused the crash based on what observers heard and saw, no hard evidence emerged. The other prospect was simply a loss of control. In the braking zone entered at more than 150 mph, a bump unsettled a car. If it was out of control, the car could run 75 feet before collecting the wall due to the track's wide corners. In retrospect, it was the worst-case scenario of improved car performance and speed, an aging race surface and a unique track configuration with little banking in the corners.

The young Petty's death meant a heartbreaking loss for the NASCAR community. Lee Petty, the racing family's patriarch, a three-time champion and the winner of the first Daytona 500 in 1959, had died unexpectedly at age 84 within days of Adam Petty's debut in the Cup series at the Texas Motor Speedway. At the time of that debut in April, there were a bevy of photos of "King" Richard Petty, Kyle and Adam all beaming the famed Petty smile—teeth as broad and even as white-washed fences. And then the youngest one disappeared.

The need for speed began three generations before "The King" got his nickname by Atlanta newspaper writer Bill Robinson, who dubbed him "King Richard the Hemi-Hearted" after one of his Daytona 500 victories. Lee's grandfather and Richard's great-grandfather started the family's love affair with the speed of an automobile. "He had an old T-model Ford and he took the body off and I think the only thing that was there was the running gear," said Richard Petty. "He had a long beard and he would drive down the road and his beard would blow back and stuff. And he said no matter how fast he ran, he just wanted to go faster."

Adam Petty exemplified his clan's love for speed,

pressing his father to get a go-kart in between running around the team's Level Cross compound in North Carolina as a boy. It seemed inevitable that he would become a race car driver. His mother, Patti Huffman, worked at the races in the role of Miss Winston. Before marrying Kyle Petty, her beauty and enthusiasm as an ambassador for stock car racing charmed many at the track and in Victory Lane on behalf of the Winston Cup's sponsor.

Adam was known for the same down-home humility and good humor of his father Kyle, his mother Patti and grandfather Richard, whom he called "the cat in the hat" in honor of the Charley 1-Horse cowboy hats he wore. When road racer Anthony Lazzaro switched to stock cars, Adam Petty was one of the first to seek him out.

"The only reason I met him is because he came up to me, extended his hand, introduced himself, welcomed me to the Busch Series and offered any help he could give," said Lazzaro. "I was really touched by that, and it showed what a genuinely nice person he was. The racing world lost a class individual."

It was three weeks after the New Hampshire crash before Kyle Petty, the CEO of Petty Enterprises and driver of one of the team's Pontiacs, bravely met with the media, occasionally dabbing at the corner of his eye with an extended finger while discussing his son's death. After talking about plans for the team and his ability to focus as a driver (he had skipped The Winston all-star race and the Cup race in Charlotte), Petty answered the inevitable question of any thoughts about quitting.

He sometimes had said his family farmed raced cars while the neighbors farmed tobacco and he stuck with that approach. "We look at ourselves in a lot of ways like a bunch of farmers," he said. "Just because something goes bad or something goes wrong, you don't quit and go home. You keep plugging along at it. Like I said before, and sometimes it sounds a little crazy to say or a little stupid to say, but as much as Adam loved racing he wouldn't stop, so there's no reason for us to."

Unbelievably, eight weeks after Adam Petty's death, another young star, Kenny Irwin, Jr., died at the same turn of the same New Hampshire track in the same type of accident while practicing in his Cup series car. At the age of 30, he, too, suffered a basal skull fracture "remarkably similar" to the injury of Petty, said the coroner, Dr. Andrew. In the next NASCAR race after the May incident at the New Hampshire track, NASCAR officials revealed prior to the event that they found no evidence of a stuck throttle in the Petty crash. In Irwin's case, there were long skid marks leading to the point where the right front corner of the Chevrolet entered by Team Sabco hit the Turn 3 wall. The car then continued down the track on its side and came to rest on its roof.

After following his father into racing competition, Irwin raced out of Indianapolis and had a meteoric career in open-wheel cars before switching to stock cars, where he continued to gain accolades. A rookie of the year in United States Auto Club sprint cars in 1993, he earned the same title in USAC's Silver Crown series in 1994 before taking rookie honors in NASCAR's Craftsman Truck Series and then the Winston Cup in 1998, the same year he won a 200-mile Automobile Racing Club of America (ARCA) Series race in Daytona.

Future IRL and NASCAR champion Tony Stewart competed against Irwin while coming through the USAC ranks, where Irwin won the Copper World Classic in 1994 and the National Midget title in 1996. He scored seven feature wins in the USAC National Sprint Car Series. "I have to thank Kenny for helping me get where I am," said Stewart after the tragic crash. "Racing against him made me a better driver."

A fun-loving bachelor not above drinking beer in local bars on NASCAR race weekends, Irwin had three career Cup poles and was known for his outright speed on qualifying days. But the long run aspect of 500-mile or 500-lap stock car races versus the shorter race distances in USAC challenged him. After first signing with Robert Yates Racing for two seasons, he then moved to Team Sabco.

The sudden turn of events as a result of two deaths roiled NASCAR and its participants. In a decade when the sport grew rapidly in terms of fan and media interest, there had been five previous fatal accidents in NASCAR's three major traveling series during the 1990s: J.D. McDuffie at Watkins Glen in 1991, Busch Series driver Clifford Allison at Michigan the following year, Neil Bonnett and Rodney Orr at Daytona in 1994 and Truck Series driver John Nemechek in 1997 at the Homestead, Florida, oval.

Later in the 2000 season, despite the absence of any direct evidence of sticking throttles in the two New Hampshire crashes, NASCAR introduced an engine kill switch. More significantly, the sanctioning body made clear to its drivers that it approved the use of the HANS Device. In a sad irony, Kyle Petty had been the only driver to use one previously while driving for Team Sabco. In the races at the North Carolina Motor Speedway at Rockingham in the mid-1990s, he had used the HANS Model I in hopes of relieving problems with neck fatigue. But once the new generation of cars appeared with smaller driver side windows, Petty elected to stop using the bulky device.

It wasn't until the exhaustively detailed accident report on the crash of Dale Earnhardt was released in August of 2001 that the physical circumstances of the crashes of Petty and Irwin became more accessible, albeit indirectly. The same model used to assess the Earnhardt crash could be applied to the crashes of Petty and Irwin the previous year.

There are two major forces at work when a car impacts a wall. The heading angle, i.e., the angle of the car relative to the wall when it hits, creates one major force. The other significant force, the vector angle, results from the direction of the center of gravity of the car, whose inertial forces continue to try to send it along the path of the track. In the crashes of Petty and Irwin, after impacting the wall with the right front corner, each car continued down the track toward Turn 4.

Despite being harnessed to the seat, a driver's body will follow the same direction as the first impact. It is this angle of impact that controls the load path of the initial forces. When that impact is the right front corner, the driver's restrained torso and an unrestrained head will move in the direction of the impact—possibly enough to the right for the driver's helmeted head to miss the steering wheel. In the absence of a detailed investigation, this is likely what happened to Petty and Irwin, especially given the similarities of their injuries.

In the absence of data boxes on cars midway in the 2000 season or any detailed investigation of either the heading angle of the cars into the wall and velocity vectors, which measure speed, the only thing clear about the two accidents at New Hampshire were the identical results. (The cars themselves were returned to the teams and cut up, in the case of Petty Enterprises, and buried, in the case of Team Sabco.)

Like Kyle Petty, the drivers participating in NASCAR's Busch Series and Winston Cup continued to pursue their profession despite the chilling incidents—including the Cup race two days after Irwin was killed. Most of the drivers had been involved in incidents resulting in heavy impacts without such dire results. Since corner entry speeds had been climbing at well documented incremental rates, it could be deduced a limit had been reached when it came to what a driver could physically sustain with existing safety equipment. But in the minds of drivers, no acceptable alternative to racing existed.

Prior to the second scheduled race at New Hampshire in the fall, NASCAR tested a "soft wall" at the 1.0-mile track. The sanctioning body did not comment directly about testing "soft walls," but reports emerged that NASCAR had placed what were described as Styrofoam barriers at the Turn 3 wall and sent an unmanned car into it at high speed. The resulting debris on the track proved too problematic to move farther into the uncharted waters of "soft walls."

The test likely used the Polyethylene Energy Dissipation System, which employed 16-inch diameter, high-density polyethylene tubes covered by 1-inch thick overlapping plates made of the same high-density

Winston Cup Director Nelson, left, and Bodine were key 'inside the fence' players in HANS' NASCAR saga. (Photo by Robert LeSieur)

polyethylene. The PEDS had been developed by John Pierce, a colleague of Melvin's at GM's safety research project. Testing went as far as having a PEDS barrier installed on the walls at the inside of Turn 4 at the Indianapolis Motor Speedway, a dangerous location if hit directly but also well away from the racing groove.

In the 1998 International Race of Champions (IROC) event at the Speedway, Arie Luyendyk's car hit the barrier. Not only did the driver suffer a concussion, but the impact scattered debris all the way to the track's racing groove. Because a small field of cars competed in the exhibition race, none of the trailing competitors were affected by the debris. It would not be until four years later that the SAFER barrier would emerge as a more practical way to reduce the energy of an impact into a wall during a race.

As a possible antidote to basal skull fractures, NASCAR expanded the range of safety equipment by letting drivers know it would accept the recently introduced Upright HANS following a previously scheduled open test at the Indianapolis Motor Speedway. Also known as the Model IV, the Upright had only slightly changed from the updated Model III for drivers in reclining positions. Although not requiring the use of the HANS, the sanctioning body made acceptance of it clear by inviting HANS Performance Products to a test at the Indianapolis Motor Speedway immediately after the New Hampshire race where Irwin was killed. The test had already been scheduled to precede events at the Pocono International Raceway and at Indy. Each was a 2.5-mile track and relatively flat like New Hampshire.

Jim Downing and one of his HPP field representatives, John Carver, attended the test at Indy. One driver, Brett Bodine, decided to modify his car so he could wear the Upright HANS Device at the upcoming race at Pocono. Because he believed an engineering degree would help his racing career, Bodine had earned one from the State University of New York College of Technology in Alfred before embarking on a full-time on a career in racing, following older brother Geoff, a Winston Cup competitor. Their father Eli had operated the Chemung Speedrome, a quarter-mile dirt track, on family property in Chemung, N.Y. as the three Bodine brothers were growing up, including the youngest Todd, who also became a NASCAR competitor.

"I was at an Indy test day and I don't think John Carver was getting much attention from anybody at the test," recalled Brett Bodine. "The last day of the test, I decided to change the seat in our car and try using the HANS. John Carver and I were friends. We had been talking whenever he would come to the NASCAR races. At Indy, he walked up and said, 'I can't get anybody to talk to me about this thing.' He was pretty frustrated. Part of the problem was the way the seats were set up and the way the head rests were mounted at the top of the seats.

"Since I had an engineering degree," continued Bodine, "I looked at the HANS from the perspective of an engineer. And it was being tested by engineers like John Melvin and some others at the time. So, I decided to give it a try. We had to do something to improve safety. We sawed the head rest right off the top of the seat. John fitted the tethers for me. I did a 10-lap run and said, 'That's it. I can drive with this.'"

After reworking his seat to allow for the harness to

Deadly Year 2000

fit over the legs of the HANS and moving the headrest to give the device enough room behind his helmet, the reaction Bodine got from other drivers and participants in the garage when he used the HANS at Pocono caught him by surprise.

"When I got to Pocono," said Bodine, "everybody was calling me names. Things like pansy and sissy. People asked, 'What do you want to use something like that for?'

"A few guys were truly inquisitive, like Matt Kenseth, who came over to talk to me. I also had one guy tell me that, 'You can't turn your head if we get side-by-side.' But you only need to turn your head enough to see the mirror. At Pocono, I ran all of practice with the HANS and the rest is history.

"I wasn't afraid to say we've got to fix this," said Bodine, who later became a full-time employee at NASCAR Research & Development and the driver of the pace car at Cup events. "We needed to improve safety. Regardless if people pointed and called you names, you had to step up and say this was the right thing to do. The longer I stuck it out, the more people came up to me and said, 'OK, what's the deal?'"

Attitudes continued to change when the fatal crash of Craftsman Truck Series driver Tony Roper occurred at the Texas Motor Speedway in October. The Cup drivers had their own race that weekend at the Talladega Superspeedway and as usual many of them were watching the Truck Series event, a night race, on TV after their own day at the track.

Drivers were always slightly on the edge whenever they came to Talladega due to harrowing multi-car incidents in the draft at the Alabama track and the previous fatalities there of drivers, fans, officials and crewmen. Watching the crash on TV of Roper, who died at the hospital due to a neck fracture, greatly unsettled them and other participants in a year when three drivers had been lost. "Drivers were saying to themselves, 'I could envision that same kind of accident happening to me,'" said Bodine of Roper's incident. "A couple of trucks got together and one of them went into the wall. Drivers were thinking, 'What do you mean that guy died? That doesn't make sense.'"

Roper was the 35-year-old son of Dean Roper, a three-time USAC stock car champion who had also been successful on dirt tracks in the ARCA Series. Born in Springfield, Missouri, Tony Roper struggled as a journeyman driver when it came to pursuing a career in NASCAR. In 1999, four seasons after running his first NASCAR race in the Truck Series, Roper had attempted to qualify in 20 of 32 races in the understudy Busch Series. He started in 16 races with a best finish of eighth place on the short track at South Boston, Virginia. In 2000, he entered 11 Busch races and failed to qualify nine times while driving for the start-up operation of former NFL player Joe Washington and NBA star Julius Erving.

In 2000 and with his career flagging, Roper entered four Truck races for Mike Mittler prior to the Texas event with a best finish of 21st. In the Texas race, he attempted to squeeze between two trucks approaching the dogleg shortly after the exit of Turn 4. Upon contact with the truck of Steve Grissom, Roper's truck turned right and slammed directly into the wall head-on, his truck bouncing straight back from the wall after a crash of major magnitude.

The first driver to be killed by a crash at the Texas track, Roper was unconscious and unresponsive when taken from his mangled truck and never recovered after being airlifted from the track. The physician at Parkland Hospital, Dr. John LaNoue, said the "severe neck injury caused blood flow to the brain to stop." That essentially describes a basal skull fracture. Roper's father Dean looked on when efforts to sustain his son ended by taking him off a respirator.

Like Kyle Petty, Dean Roper continued to race after the death of his son. In a poignant irony, he suffered a fatal heart attack behind the wheel during a race at the Illinois State Fairgrounds 10 months after son Dean's crash—and two days after NASCAR released its official report on the death of Dale Earnhardt in a major media presentation in Atlanta.

18
Idling at Daytona

"RED NECK HIGH HOLY DAYS" OR "THE Crown Jewel" were two traditional descriptions of the Daytona 500, which became "The Great American Race" after CBS began televising it live in 1979. By any name, the Daytona 500, the ultimate NASCAR event, generated more pre-race buzz in 2001 than any time in its history.

Dodge, one of the legendary brands during the roaring 1960s and a longtime backer of Richard Petty, returned as a manufacturer for the first time in two decades. Then in qualifying, "Awesome Bill" Elliott won the pole in a Dodge for the new team of celebrated Crew Chief Ray Evernham.

After bidding $1.5 billion to win rights to the first half of the NASCAR season, Fox Sports was gearing up to televise its first Daytona 500. Expected to be one of the most competitive races in years due to rule changes, which called for a roof blade and a 75-degree minimum spoiler angle—Dale Earnhardt's critical comments about slowing speeds notwithstanding. Both changes would help cars punch a larger aerodynamic hole in the air with the hopes of generating more overtaking.

The year marked the 25th anniversary of the celebrated last-lap scrap for victory between Petty and David Pearson. In that one, Petty clipped Pearson in the chute between Turn 4 and the finish line, which sent both cars spinning. Pearson eventually chugged under the checkered flag in his damaged Wood Brothers Ford as Petty's Dodge sat stalled in the tri-oval grass, less than 100 yards from the finish line.

But all of these landmark developments paled in comparison to the pre-race lambasting of NASCAR by the print media on the issue of safety in its premier series. Following the three deaths in 2000, the print and fledgling online media openly questioned the lack of more proactive safety efforts by NASCAR compared with other sanctioning bodies.

The *Orlando Sentinel*, already established as a thorn in the side of NASCAR, led the way. Following the deaths of Neil Bonnett and Rodney Orr in 1994 prior to that year's Daytona 500, the *Sentinel* staff undertook an extensive investigation that presented persuasive evidence the same problem—broken shock mounts in the right rear—led to the crash of each driver. Since Orr was killed several days after Bonnett's crash, it raised the question of the sanctioning body's oversight of safety issues in the garage.

The HANS Device appeared at the heart of the Orlando paper's critical coverage of the run-up to the 500 in 2001, which included an editorial on the op-ed page. A week before the race, the headline above a story by Ed Hinton practically shouted: "NASCAR Idles While Drivers Die." The lengthy story covered three broadsheets inside the sports section, including a history of the development of the HANS and diagrams of how it worked.

The *Sentinel* did not stand alone in bringing attention to the HANS. After the deaths of Petty and Irwin, the print media in cities and towns hosting NASCAR events like Atlanta, Daytona Beach and Corning, N.Y.—near Watkins Glen International—plus industry magazines such as *Racer* had started drawing attention

Idling at Daytona

to the HANS Device as a likely solution to the types of injuries suffered in New Hampshire and Texas. During Speed Weeks, the Orlando paper went a step further and took NASCAR directly to task for failing to mandate better safety practices.

Hinton's story comprised a classic case of compare and contrast, drawing the distinctions between how CART and Formula 1 approached safety versus NASCAR's approach. The comparison was unfavorable on two counts. First, CART and F1 were accurately characterized as more sophisticated technical enterprises when it came to safety; and second, the two series had begun applying their technical expertise to safety with a far greater sense of urgency about protecting participants, including the use of dedicated safety teams versus the NASCAR method of allowing tracks and local doctors to handle accidents.

Where the FIA comprised an industry organization and CART operated under its team owners, privately held NASCAR had a legal distinction. Teams and drivers were considered independent contractors, an approach that reflected unwillingness by officials to discuss any details about safety initiatives. NASCAR would soon pivot on the safety issue after the death of Earnhardt, much like F1 dramatically altered its course following the death of Senna due to public and political outcry. Eventually, NASCAR became the world leader in proactive safety pursuits by a sanctioning body.

In the short term, NASCAR saw things differently than other sanctioning groups like F1 and CART, summed up by the comment from NASCAR Chairman Bill France, Jr., who was quoted by Hinton. "They have their legal advisers and we have ours," said NASCAR's boss.

A veteran attorney familiar with motor racing summed up the dilemma faced by NASCAR at the time. "In motor racing, in particular and parallel to the NFL and the football industry with respect to head trauma, there is some feeling that these organizations have the responsibility to preserve the health and safety of the participants," said the attorney, who requested his comments remain unattributed. "That responsibility is amorphous. It's very easy to say the sentence, 'We have the responsibility for the health and safety of the participants.' The problem comes in with, 'Well, what do you do about it?' That's where the real conundrum comes in.

"If NASCAR mandates certain behaviors," he continued, "then they have a very specific responsibility, which is relatively easily attacked. If you say, 'You must wear this device' and a driver wears the device and an injury occurs, either in spite of or because of the device, a good plaintiff lawyer or someone in the public dramas industry now has a very specific target to shoot at. It's way easier to hit a target that is defined than to hit one that is amorphous. So, what did the sanctioning body do? Their responsibility for health and safety was amorphous, a kind of public relations policy, although there were some real pieces to it."

The drivers in NASCAR were generally of the same mindset as the sanctioning body when it came to the legal issues of individual responsibility and voluntary choice. They preferred making their own safety choices. In the second half of the 2000 season, only Brett Bodine and Kyle Petty used the new Upright HANS Model IV despite the three deaths. There had already been a push to try to get more drivers engaged through persuasion by officials from GM and Ford.

"In 1998 we started buying HANS Devices," said Tom Gideon of his stint at the GM Motorsports Safety Technology Research Program, "and started giving them to our drivers. We said, 'Please wear this.' We did that with NASCAR drivers, with Indy car drivers and we did that with National Hot Rod Association drag racers. You would see me at the events talking to the guys and hawking our wares, so to speak." Further drawing attention to head restraints, midway in the 2000 season, CART announced its decision to make the HANS mandatory for oval races in 2001.

NASCAR also began to change its ways when it came to the HANS. After Kenny Irwin, Jr.'s death in July of 2000, Jim Downing received an invitation from

Jarrett counseled Earnhardt about the HANS. Middle man Gordon began wearing it after the tragic Daytona 500.
(Photo by Nigel Kinrade)

the sanctioning body to the test at the Indianapolis Motor Speedway to introduce HANS Performance Products' new, smaller version of the device for drivers in upright seats. NASCAR was finally prepared to actively encourage drivers to voluntarily use the HANS. According to a story written by Rick Minter at *The Atlanta Journal-Constitution* in early August, the company had sold 35 Model IV devices for upright seating within two months and another 44 orders remained unfilled.

Winston Cup driver Kenny Wallace became one of the converts. Downing maintained that the resistance to the HANS often resulted from drivers not wanting to look like sissies compared to their peers. Wallace considered it a valid theory. "Years ago, Earnhardt started that rawhide-type image where you've got to be tough," Wallace told Minter. "Some drivers will chicken out of using a safety device because they don't want to be looked at as a wimp. You're not really being a wimp. You're being smarter."

Reporter Minter asked Gary Nelson, the Winston Cup director, if the sanctioning body would consider mandating the HANS Device. "We're not going to jump on something until we research it completely," said Nelson. "We're allowing it to be run on a voluntary basis so we can get feedback from the drivers… We're watching to see how things go."

During winter testing at Daytona, the manufacturers convened mandatory meetings to present information about the HANS Device to drivers. John Melvin, by this time working as an independent safety consultant for his own Tandelta company, explained the HANS and other points of safety to drivers in meetings sponsored by the three auto manufacturers participating in NASCAR. Drivers were mightily impressed and distressed when they saw videos of the sled testing presented by Melvin. It clarified just how much body movement occurred during a crash despite the safety harness.

"To hear a professor talk, and he's right, about critical areas on your body really brought a lot of light to me," said driver Jimmy Spencer during that year's NASCAR Media Tour hosted by the Charlotte Motor Speedway. "I always thought, 'Man, I have a big neck, 20 inches around, and I don't need to worry about it.' He said, 'Guys, you can have the strongest neck muscles in the world, and if you hit the wall right, it will break your neck.'"

Melvin also informed drivers that of the eight drivers killed in NASCAR's three major traveling series during the 1990s, at least seven likely would have been saved by the HANS Device. This led to 21 devices being sold to Winston Cup drivers during the winter by Downing and HPP, mostly through purchases underwritten by the manufacturers for a price of $1,275.

He also pointed out that a six-point harness, which had straps for each leg in place of a single strap at the crotch in the five-point version, prevented the kind of lower body movement that translated to upper body movement in a crash. Drivers were reminded that belt installation with anchors in proper position also was a critical element in reducing potentially fatal body movement.

But by time Speed Weeks and the Daytona 500 rolled around in February, only a handful of drivers planned to use a HANS Device. Drivers continued to complain about the usual issues that those in CART had harped on—discomfort and restricted movement of the head, although they weren't a bother for Petty or Bodine. The resistance to change wasn't restricted to the HANS. Driver Jeff Burton said that he could point to at least five drivers in the garage, including past champions, who had their harnesses installed improperly. As fate would have it, that included Earnhardt, whose separated belt due to improper installation and "dumping" became a point of controversy after his crash.

Beyond the HANS Device not being required by NASCAR in the same year that CART had mandated it for ovals, the article by Hinton raised questions about the lack of onboard data recorders in NASCAR, which had been in use by the GM Motorsports Safety Technology Research Program in CART entries since 1993 and later in the IRL. Also, questions were raised about the extent of post-accident investigations by the sanctioning body and the issue of so-called "soft walls."

Reporters at other prominent publications covering the sport raised the same issues. NASCAR's newly promoted president, Mike Helton, generally declined to discuss specifics about any of NASCAR's safety initiatives, even though he had already begun organizing a research and development operation to be run out of the former racing shops of driver Dale Jarrett in Conover, N.C. Veteran crew chief Joe Garone had been appointed to direct the project. He had most recently been working for the Precision Performance Inc. team, which had already started developing an improved full containment seat for stock cars made from carbon fiber.

Despite the use of restrictor plates for the first and only time at New Hampshire in the track's fall race of 2000 to slow speeds, despite the decision to slow cars at Daytona and despite the seminars by Melvin about cockpit safety during winter testing, once the 2001 season-opening race at Daytona rolled around there would be only five drivers wearing a HANS Device: Brett Bodine, Kyle Petty, Dale Jarrett, Andy Houston and Matt Kenseth.

Although Hubbard had worked directly with Bill Elliott during the days prior to the race, the driver ultimately declined to wear a HANS Device. "We couldn't get it to fit right with the way his seat was set up," said Evernham. "But I can tell you he was sure wearing a HANS at Rockingham." The Rockingham race immediately followed fateful events at Daytona, after the message being delivered by Melvin had finally sunk in with the death of Earnhardt.

When drivers returned to the Daytona track for the Cup Series' summer race in Florida, the majority of them were wearing a HANS Device.

19

Earnhardt and HANS

JUST AS DRIVERS LIKE WORLD CHAMPION Jacques Villeneuve in F1 and future three-time Indy 500 champion Dario Franchitti held out against the HANS Device, so did Dale Earnhardt, who referred to it publicly as a "noose." The similarity in responses by stars in other major racing series was direct and inescapable. Race car drivers were interested far less in what the media had to say about empirical scientific testing or in sanctioning bodies intervening. When it came to intense competition at speeds that could exceed 200 mph, they considered their own opinion far more important about what went on inside the challenging environment of their cockpits.

The NASCAR racing culture differed considerably from those of F1 and CART. All of three of these sanctioning groups approached their business with an eye on legal considerations when it came to injury or death. But NASCAR had been the most aggressive at avoiding legal liability. The NASCAR rulebook, for instance, warned that racing could be dangerous and possibly deadly, but did not specify a driver had to wear either a fire suit or a helmet while competing until the 2002 season—after the intense focus on safety resulting from four driver deaths. And not until that same year did the rulebook define how to install a safety harness.

Earnhardt had strong opinions about what worked for him when it came to his cockpit and safety equipment, starting with his open-face helmet. Unlike nearly 100 percent of the other drivers, he declined the use of a full-face helmet. Brilliant in the high-speed drafts created by stock cars, Earnhardt could "see the air" and make successful moves in traffic as a result. But drivers in the former generation like Cale Yarborough, who wore an open-faced helmet throughout his career, said it was more a matter of *feeling* the wind in the aerodynamic draft without the fully surrounding helmet. (Testing showed the HANS Device was just as effective with an open-faced helmet as with full-face models.)

Some drivers believed if the seat belts were too tight that internal organs were at risk in a crash. Until the testing done by the GM Motorsports Safety Technology Research Program, many in the automotive business and in racing also believed the chest had a limit on how much gravity forces the chest of an occupant restrained by seat belts could handle without fatal deflection that harmed internal organs. Earnhardt, who had a peculiar seatbelt installation in his race cars, evidently believed internal organs were at risk and had some reasons to back it up. Daytona 500 winner DeWayne "Tiny" Lund died in a crash at Talladega in 1975 and it was believed, accurately or not, that the 6-foot-5 driver's heart was torn from its mooring after a collision with another car.

Despite his status as "The Intimidator," Earnhardt could sometimes be easily spooked, especially when in an unfamiliar environment. Perhaps that helped make him resistant to the HANS.

Those who were aware of Earnhardt being ill at ease outside of his usual environment sometimes used this anxiety to yank his chain. H.A. "Humpy" Wheeler, the promoter at the Charlotte Motor Speedway for three decades, found out Earnhardt intended to compete as one of four co-drivers in the Daytona 24-hour race

Crash! How the HANS Helped Save Racing

Earnhardt and HANS

in 2001 aboard a Corvette and decided to wind him up (and perhaps discourage him from helping rival Daytona sell tickets to its sports car race). Wheeler told him the rules required drivers to sleep on a cot in the pits between stints for the duration of the race. "I ain't sleepin' on no cot," groused Earnhardt, completely taken in by Wheeler's fabrication.

Despite his public stances, Earnhardt sometimes went through bouts with a loss of confidence. Twice during his career, he utterly lost his swagger, not unusual for a star race car driver not getting results. The first episode came when car owner Rod Osterlund fired him less than a year after winning his first title. Earnhardt lost confidence again when a neck injury suffered at Talladega in 1996 was aggravated in the Daytona 500 the following year when his car overturned and slid down the back straight because he tried to block eventual winner Jeff Gordon.

The neck injury bothered his driving so much Earnhardt started asking his crew chief Larry McReynolds to talk him through his cornering lines at Darlington on the radio. That same year, 1997, he fell asleep behind the wheel at the start of the Southern 500, according to McReynolds, because of his regular use of pain pills for the neck problem. Earnhardt hated the thought of surgery to correct the issue, but eventually submitted to a scalpel before the 2000 season, which helped revive his career.

As the Daytona 500 approached in mid-February of 2001, Earnhardt made it clear to HANS inventor Hubbard not to bother talking to him during the time he shuttled between the cars of fellow champions Dale Jarrett and Bill Elliott in the garage to help them with the HANS. But Earnhardt, forever curious, had never been totally uninterested in safety.

Prior to the race, Earnhardt decided he would discuss the HANS issue with his friend Jarrett, who intended to wear the device. The book *Earnhardt Nation* by Jay Busbee describes the meeting between the two friends and champions in the sanctuary of the drivers' and team owners' motor home lot—a meeting that

Adamant about not wearing 'that noose,' Earnhardt liked the idea of soft walls. (Photo by Nigel Kinrade)

might have been typical except for the concerns about safety swirling through Daytona. Jarrett took the opportunity to show the seven-time champion the HANS Device he planned to use in the upcoming race.

Earnhardt posed the unthinkable question for a professional race car driver, recounts Busby's book, asking his friend, "Are you afraid of dying?"

"Dale was always inquisitive," Jarrett told Busbee, "and this incredible conversation was part of that. He was trying to get my feelings, to understand why I'd want to wear this device."

Earnhardt told his friend, "I don't think I can do it."

110   *Crash!* How the HANS Helped Save Racing

NASCAR sold tickets and TV time through the presence of star drivers. If one driver alone could have been pointed to as the reason behind an unprecedented $2.4 billion TV contract with three major networks that began with the 2001 Daytona 500, it would have been Earnhardt, the most charismatic and accomplished of NASCAR's drivers. The white working class that made up the majority of ticket buyers and TV viewers identified with his aggressive tactics and brilliant, breathtaking and brave maneuvers as well as his refusal to back down. Those who became some of his multitude of friends in the garage, including competitors, saw Earnhardt in a similar light. "He was just cool," said Steve Hmiel, a longtime crew chief on the competing Ford team owned by Jack Roush who later went to work for the Dale Earnhardt, Inc. team.

Off the track, Earnhardt, who lived on a farm in Mooresville, N.C., stayed close to his Southern roots, which his fans also appreciated. If "King" Richard Petty brought stock car racing out of the back woods with his success and personality, Earnhardt had taken it to the national stage of major league status. It could be argued that Jeff Gordon's stardom depended on being able to beat Earnhardt.

What was NASCAR to do? Earnhardt could well have refused to race if it required the HANS. Every star team owner and driver in the garage held out refusing to race as the nuclear option. It had historically been a tactic used to force favorable rule changes or prevent rule changes in the first place. From "King" Richard, who went drag racing one year for Chrysler when NASCAR outlawed the company's Hemi engine, to Junior Johnson, the last American hero, the pattern had long been established.

Early in his career, NASCAR founder "Big Bill" France tried to persuade Johnson to run all the races instead of a selected schedule, which would sell considerably more tickets to NASCAR-sanctioned events. For his part, Johnson didn't care about season-long points titles. He preferred to show up with a car prepared to lead every lap and then proceeded to try to lead them all once the race started. He believed in a classic "go or blow" approach and the idea of a points championship didn't fit into the big picture for the independent mountain man, who eventually won 50 races.

"I enjoyed racing but it weren't my whole life, and I didn't intend for it to ever be," recalled Johnson during an evening round table meeting with journalists in Daytona in 1991. "And I made that decision long, long before I ever quit."

"Big Bill" France once tried to persuade Johnson to join the championship over a now famous breakfast. "He kept telling me I was committed to racing," said Johnson. "Me and him was sitting down, eating breakfast when he said this to me. I said, 'France, you don't understand what being committed means. For instance, if you sit down to breakfast and you have bacon and eggs, that chicken was involved, but that hog was committed.'"

For years after he quit driving and became a team owner, Johnson's occasional threats to quit racing to pursue other enterprises carried a lot of weight when it came to either rules enforcement or rule changes by NASCAR, because he might decide to make good on the promise. Unlike many fellow successful team owners, Johnson indeed quit after the 1994 season.

Entering the 2001 season, Earnhardt decided to focus on winning a record-breaking eighth championship instead of changing the routine that had won him seven. And he committed himself to winning that elusive eighth title on his terms. Earnhardt thought stock car racing should be about doing what it took to win without being intimidated. When NASCAR first looked at lowering speeds prior to the Daytona 500 in 2001 by reducing the size of carburetor restrictor plates in the name of safety, Earnhardt challenged fellow drivers who supported such a change. "Tie kerosene rags around your ankles," he said in public comments, "so the ants won't crawl up and eat your candy ass."

His reputation as "The Intimidator" comprised much more than just an image or legend. Never once after his many run-ins on the track, which included putting drivers such as Darrell Waltrip or Bill Elliott into the wall deliberately, did anybody challenge Earnhardt to fight afterwards. Routinely taking the aerodynamic downforce off the rear spoiler of a car up ahead by following closely, he enjoyed destabilizing competitors. He challenged his adversaries to do the same in return.

That was the Earnhardt ethos: whatever I do to your car on the track, you're welcome to do to mine. He was forever committed to the idea his approach was fair—and accepted like kind retaliation from his opponents, which he rarely groused about. (Although he did things like flip off Jeremy Mayfield on the cool down lap after the driver knocked him askew to win at Pocono in 2000, which cost him dearly in his championship fight with eventual title winner Bobby Labonte.) Earnhardt's favorite drivers were those who fought his fire with their own such as Rusty Wallace and Gordon. His popularity became a divide-and-conquer strategy, because his approach always brought a lot of boos, in no small part because of Earnhardt's deliberate contact on occasion or over-aggressiveness.

In 1993, the year after independent driver Alan Kulwicki had scored his remarkable championship, Earnhardt deliberately banged doors with Kulwicki's Hooters-sponsored Ford—twice—at the high-speed Atlanta Motor Speedway. "Earnhardt ran into me in the middle of the back straight," said an exasperated Kulwicki, whose loss of concentration resulted in a crash shortly afterward. Turning left into Kulwicki's door on the back straight was Earnhardt's way of saying that year's championship was still up for grabs and he intended to take it back. He calculated the deliberate contact would upset the Wisconsin-born driver, who held honorable, by-the-book racing in high regard. For his part, the wily Earnhardt considered his tactics just as honorable as Kulwicki's due to an open invitation to retaliate. Kulwicki, meanwhile, lost a lot of points due to his crash.

It was the rambunctious aggression that helped Earnhardt win points championships, where every position and point mattered. He was the inventor of the now common passing maneuver known as a side draft, which he called "raking." It required delicate control of an inevitably unruly stock car and steely nerves. Earnhardt would pull up alongside the rear quarter panel of a competitor within inches at full speed. He then would suddenly break across the wake of air surging around the front end of both cars. It was a bit like catching a wave on a surfboard. If timed right, breaking across the wake of air would slow down the leading car, not unlike taking the air off the rear spoiler.

Just as CART doctors Steve Olvey and Terry Trammell knew they couldn't allow Dario Franchitti to avoid using the HANS despite his out-of-kilter shoulder, so NASCAR officials knew that any rule ignored by Earnhardt was no rule at all.

Earnhardt, who was friends and occasional fishing buddies with NASCAR owner and chairman Bill France Jr., had made it clear he was not going to race with a head and neck restraint—that "noose" he said in far more vehement terms publicly compared with when he discussed the issue with Jarrett.

Earnhardt, always astute, likely figured he had the political situation on his side. According to a personal contact high up within the hierarchy at NASCAR, Hubbard said the sanctioning body received "legal advice" against mandating the device. In other words, NASCAR had decided to stick with the age-old rule of thumb that held teams and drivers to be contractors and in charge of their own safety in the cockpit. It was the same approach that meant a written rule for helmets or fire suits, according to journalist Bob Pockrass, went missing in the rulebook for decades.

This comprised the eternal dilemma for NASCAR, always the fish in the barrel when it came to safety issues. The sanctioning body stated safety to be its first priority and had done a great deal to make its tube-frame cars safe. But NASCAR acted differently when it came to individual driver equipment out of protection against liability. The sanctioning body had a long list of lawsuits to prove that relatives, when confronted with an injured family member, were only too glad to pursue legal action. The driver who had elected to take the responsibility of injury or death was often no longer available to remind relatives that the risk had been undertaken knowing the possibility of a bad outcome. Or that they had voluntarily undertaken racing for the love of the sport as well as the income potential.

To lose one lawsuit, to be followed by others, would seriously threaten the business viability of NASCAR.

A classic example concerned driver Rick Baldwin. His helmeted head was believed to have hit the wall at the Michigan oval in June of 1986 in a practice crash, although it was more likely head whip caused his injury in a classic side-impact scenario. After 11 years in a coma, he finally succumbed. His wife sued NASCAR and attorneys zeroed in on the fact the driver's side window net—mandated by NASCAR—had not prevented Baldwin's injury. NASCAR won the case. Most persuasive, observers believed, was the testimony of star driver Darrell Waltrip, who said that all drivers know the risk and decide to pursue racing anyway. A similar outcome occurred in the lawsuit brought by the widow of longtime NASCAR independent driver J.D. McDuffie, who died from a basal skull fracture in a 1991 crash at Watkins Glen.

The long history of NASCAR only paying attention to ideas generated "inside the fence" of the NASCAR garage further complicated the issue. New developments had to be accepted, if not generated, from inside the garage. One example were roof flaps devised by engineers from manufacturers participating in NASCAR and introduced in 1994. Still in use, these flaps pop up if a car spins, dirtying the air over the front end and roof, helping to prevent the aerodynamic lift that can send a car flying, possibly into grandstands. Accepting a new idea from "outside the fence" like the HANS Device—however much it might have been proven elsewhere—was anathema to the NASCAR methodology for many participants, not just the sanctioning body.

The one group that worked inside the fence and outside it, media members who regularly covered stock car racing, applied pressure to NASCAR with stories questioning its approach to safety following the three deaths in 2000. Many of the stories in major newspapers included detailed articles about the HANS Device with graphics about how it worked.

For his part, Hubbard remained confident that his life-saving invention would eventually prevail. The sanctioning body, he decided, needed to pursue business according to its own directives. In the hierarchy of the FIA, F1 and CART, that had meant a long process by the leadership of codifying, allowing teams enough leeway to get used to the idea and then laying down the law. It was a similar circumstance for NASCAR in 2001, believed Hubbard.

"Wearing a head and neck restraint wasn't something NASCAR was going to mandate before the Daytona 500 in 2001," said Hubbard. "I never second-guessed that. They were responsible for running the racing business and it was up to us to work according to how they ran things."

20

The Fateful 500

WHEN MICHAEL WALTRIP CAME TO A MEETing in Dale Earnhardt's motorhome on the Friday night before the Daytona 500 in 2001, he expected a tongue-lashing from the team owner. Newly hired for the season to drive for Dale Earnhardt Incorporated, Waltrip had missed a shift in his preliminary Twin 125-mile qualifying race on Thursday and lost an opportunity to win it. But instead of a lecture from the seven-time champion, Waltrip got a pleasant surprise.

"We're gonna win this race Sunday," said Earnhardt enthusiastically.

Waltrip, who had not won a championship points race in 262 starts, muttered he should have won his preliminary event, but Earnhardt told him to forget about it—according to Waltrip's memoir *In the Blink of an Eye*. "Pay attention to me. I'm gonna tell you how we're gonna win this race on Sunday," said Earnhardt. "With the rules the way they are this year, it's a different animal. It's gonna be wide open out there."

The conversation was a little odd in the sense that Earnhardt drove for the Chevy team of Richard Childress while Waltrip, Dale Earnhardt Jr. and Steve Park would compete for Earnhardt's own DEI team. According to Waltrip's account, Earnhardt always used "we" when he outlined a plan whereby his Childress-owned Chevy and the DEI Chevys of Waltrip and Earnhardt Jr. would work together at the front of the field at the end of the race. "Me, you, and Dale Jr., we're gonna win the race," repeated Earnhardt, who reminded Waltrip that he had always been good enough in the draft to race at the front.

The new rules that included a short horizontal rail across the leading edge of the roof and a taller rear spoiler angle would certainly create a lot of passing in the draft due to a larger hole punched in the air by the revised aerodynamics. Earnhardt believed that by working together, he and the two DEI drivers could be the top three finishers, although the conversation fell short of designating an actual winner, just cooperation. Historically, it's not unusual for drivers with the same manufacturer to team up, although planning by two different teams two days in advance was more than a little out of the ordinary.

Earnhardt's confidence somewhat baffled Waltrip, but Earnhardt had an inside line: the Chevy engines of his DEI team were producing more horsepower than any of the other teams—an observation Earnhardt had likely confirmed by watching qualifying and one of the two preliminary Twin 125-mile events that he was not participating in. He also knew about developments in the DEI dyno room, which went unreported in the Waltrip book.

The long, high-banked and fast circuits at Daytona and Talladega were known as "restrictor plate" tracks because NASCAR required a plate with four bores underneath the four-barrel carburetors to choke the engines and keep speeds in check. Otherwise, cars tended to lift off in crashes and present the disastrous prospect of a car flying into the grandstands. Teams had tried to find ways around the plates ever since they were first introduced in 1988, the season after Bobby Allison's flying Buick nearly landed in the grandstands

Crash! How the HANS Helped Save Racing

at Talladega, where Bill Elliott had won the pole at 212.809 mph.

Once the plates were installed and average lap speeds dropped well below 200 mph, even the slightest addition of horsepower resulted in a decisive advantage. Teams tried all manner of ways to bypass the restricted opening of the plates to get more air into engines.

Media and fans, meanwhile, eternally speculated about NASCAR manipulating race outcomes by giving certain drivers and teams plates with bigger holes and more horsepower—a cottage industry rumor mill born of cynicism about the sanctioning body that never produced any proof of conspiracy. NASCAR had its hands full with teams not waiting for any handouts and piping air into engines through various clever methods, including solenoid valves connected to holes lower in the engine block used in qualifying and cylinder heads with visually undetectable leaks that produced a mysterious whistling. These cylinder heads, ingeniously produced by physicist and racer Tomoka Brady, were used by Sterling Marlin's Morgan-McClure Motorsports team in back-to-back Daytona 500 wins in 1994-1995 before NASCAR began testing more closely for outside air induction.

During the 1994 season, meanwhile, illegal inserts at the throat of the manifold were successfully used by Junior Johnson that went undetected during his team's summertime victories at Daytona and Talladega, which accounted for Jimmy Spencer's only two career victories in the Cup series. The manifolds were later confiscated after Johnson finally made good on his threats to leave the sport at the end of the season, threats which evidently had discouraged NASCAR from looking at the manifolds more carefully before the engines were sold to another team.

To prevent this problem, NASCAR introduced a round, snub-nosed block during engine inspections. Still in effect in 2001, rules also called for the manifolds sitting beneath the carburetors to have a flat floor. With the carburetor removed, inspectors inserted a snub-nosed block into the throat of the manifold. The block was long enough to reach the floor directly under the carburetor opening. NASCAR wanted to prevent any adjustments inside the manifold or at the entrance to the manifold, which sat just below the carburetor and plate.

But for several years, the team of Richard Childress had begun taking the rule literally—that the floor of the manifold had to be flat *only* where the inserted block met the bottom. While retaining enough flat floor for any visual inspection, the engine builders at Childress began carving grooves into the remaining bottom portion of the manifold to better direct the air and fuel mixture from the carburetor to each cylinder. In effect, there was a raised island in the middle of the manifold that met the rule. Otherwise, carved runners helped guide the path of the air and fuel mixture. Since combustion engines are essentially air pumps, this gained more than several horsepower—a significant edge on a restrictor plate track.

The Childress team's engine man Danny Lawrence and rival engine builder Randy Dorton of Hendrick Motorsports later confirmed this approach. Eventually, Chevy started manufacturing a standard manifold with an "island" at the bottom so all of its Chevy teams could start air flow development with the "raised" floor already in place that met NASCAR's inspection block method. Dorton pushed for this new manifold for all Chevy teams after belatedly discovering what the Childress team had been taking a creative approach to NASCAR's rule about flat floors in manifolds.

Dorton, by contrast, had mastered getting more air through the plates by developments in the carburetors above it. When Hendrick driver Jeff Gordon won the Daytona 500 in 1997, midway in the race his Chevy and Earnhardt's Childress car were visually developing the most power and speed down the back straight—a fact confirmed by their pit schedules, since more horsepower increases fuel consumption. Gordon's advantage was in carburetion and the advantage of the Childress Chevy driven by Earnhardt was in the manifold underneath the carburetor and the restrictor plate. Both drivers were taking advantage of their superior

The Fateful 500

Contact with car of Schrader meant Earnhardt's car hit the wall at an increased speed and bad angle. (AP Photo)

horsepower by getting off Turn 2, which led to the long back straight, better than their teammates driving cars with similar engines.

Earnhardt, who had suffered through years of bad luck in the 500, was hampered all day by slow pit stops in that 1997 race eventually won by Gordon. The right front tire changer for the Childress team, Gene DeHart, had missed his wake-up call that morning and new Crew Chief Larry McReynolds had fired him, necessitating a change on the pit crew and a different right front tire changer. The upshot: three successive slow pit stops and then a miscall by McReynolds to take only two tires on the final stop.

At the checkered flag, Gordon led a Hendrick Motorsports sweep of the top three positions and Earnhardt ended up on his roof after trying to block Gordon, who was on four fresh tires, in the closing laps. The following year, Earnhardt finally claimed his long-sought-after Daytona 500 victory, in no small part because of the advantage with the Childress V-8 engine in addition to his enormous skill in the draft at Daytona.

After winning the 500, Earnhardt, always loyal but never to a fault, carried the engine manifold secret from Childress to his own DEI team. In another crucial development, Earnhardt hired Richie Gilmore, the carburetor specialist at Hendrick Motorsports under Dorton, to run the engine program at DEI. As expected, Gilmore brought his carburetor expertise learned under Dorton with him.

By 2001, the combined work Gilmore did above the plate with the carburetor and the manifold development under it meant the DEI team had everybody covered when it came to horsepower on the plate tracks, an edge that would be sustained for four seasons, during which the DEI duo of Waltrip and Earnhardt Jr. won an incredible 11 of the 16 major races on those tracks.

In addition to belief in the drafting ability of Waltrip and his son, Earnhardt's confidence in 2001 resulted from this recently developed horsepower edge at DEI. His own chances, meanwhile, would rely on slightly less horsepower from the Childress engines, his own extraordinary ability in the draft and the strategy of the three de facto "teammates."

Earnhardt started Sunday's race with 34 career victories at Daytona. Three weeks earlier, he had raced a Corvette at Daytona in the Rolex 24 endurance event that opened Speed Weeks. In a 24-hour race where rain fell regularly, Earnhardt posted a remarkable sports car debut along with co-drivers Dale, Jr. plus sports car regulars Andy Pilgrim and Kelly Collins. They finished the race second in class and fourth place overall. It was Earnhardt's first racing experience in the rain. "They gave me a lap time to run," he said after climbing from his Corvette following a morning stint in the wet. "Shoot, I was two seconds below that in a couple of laps." He was as pumped as a kid who had just grabbed air on his skateboard for the first time.

That enthusiasm and confidence obviously carried over to the Daytona 500, judging by Earnhardt's conversation with Waltrip.

The new aerodynamics at Daytona were not about to slow Earnhardt down, even if the pole speed had dropped to a lowly 184 mph. Earnhardt had long since mastered hooking up with other cars in the draft to gain speed. And who wouldn't want to work with the man in the black Chevy who could "see the air" in the draft?

In the media center in the tower at the start-finish line, among the gathered reporters, including this writer, there was a lot of anticipation over the new rules and, with safety issues hanging in the air, some trepidation about NASCAR's crown jewel 500-mile race.

Once the green flag fell, the new rules and the new factory Dodges led by the silver Coors-backed Intrepid of Sterling Marlin created some furious

By 2001, newly named NASCAR President Helton was familiar with an already swirling safety controversy. (Photo by Nigel Kinrade)

maneuvering at the front of the field. In their first year back in NASCAR competition, the Dodges had a bit of an engine advantage of their own on the restrictor plate tracks. The company's new NASCAR engine was patterned on the model of "The Beast," an engine developed by Mercedes-Benz for the team of Roger Penske and the Indy 500 in 1994. This Indy V-8 took advantage of the rule book allowing pushrod, "stock block" engines. The so-called "pushrods" on "The Beast" V-8 were shortened considerably by Ilmor Engineering compared with previous standards. These highly efficient engines produced a whopping horsepower advantage due to rules allowing more turbo boost for the "stock blocks" and their "pushrods."

Seven years after "the Beast" dominated to win

The Fateful 500

at Indy, it became the model for the NASCAR V-8 introduced by DaimlerChrylser in the Dodge brand's return to NASCAR racing. The new engine for NASCAR was designed with very short pushrods located high up in the engine block like the Mercedes. On the restrictor plate tracks, the shorter pushrods meant more aggressive valve timing compared with the longer pushrods of Chevy and Ford—hence more air in the engine and power.

On lap 27, Earnhardt signaled the superiority of his Chevy versus the Dodge by taking the lead from Marlin in Turn 3. But during the first round of green flag pit stops, an unexpected braking by the Pontiac of Kenny Schrader entering the pits meant the trailing Chevy of Earnhardt banged into the rear bumper, causing some damage to the front air dam. In the ensuing laps, that would become a point of discussion on the radio with Crew Chief Kevin Hamlin about the extent of the damage. The slightest change in aerodynamics could adversely affect the handling of any car in the draft and eventually would play a role in the "three-car" strategy Earnhardt had discussed with Waltrip and Earnhardt Jr. before the race.

Undaunted, Earnhardt returned to the lead three more times. On the 183rd of 200 laps, he sliced between the Chevy of Waltrip and Marlin in the narrow Turn 3 with a breathtaking maneuver that only Earnhardt seemed capable of executing. It was a reminder that two days earlier, Earnhardt had been knocked sideways 30 yards into the grass at Turn 1 during the International Race of Champions event by Indy car driver Eddie Cheever and had responded with an incredible seat-of-the-pants maneuver to save his car. The maneuver reminded everyone why he had won seven championships. Dale Jarrett wryly commented that Earnhardt made the great save so he could get back on the track and retaliate against Cheever. After two more laps of racing, the checkers fell and Earnhardt indeed caught up to Cheever and spun him on the back straight during the cool down lap—to a mighty roar from the grandstands. Minutes before, those same fans had let out their first mighty roar after Earnhardt made his incredible save in the grass.

As the laps wound down in Sunday's 500, Earnhardt undertook his aggressive move between Waltrip and Marlin to put himself, Waltrip and Earnhardt Jr. into the top three positions and to hamper the progress of Marlin. It worked, except that the black Childress-owned Chevy's faulty air dam made it difficult for Earnhardt to hold the lead while running in clean air with no traffic in front of him. Plus, he lacked horsepower compared with his own DEI cars just behind him, which had the engines with better carburetion in addition to manifolds that directed the air/fuel mixture. Waltrip, with Earnhardt Jr. right on his rear bumper to assist him in the draft, skipped past Earnhardt's GM Goodwrench-backed car in Turn 3 two laps later, dropping the black Chevy into third.

Once in third place behind his son's red Budweiser-backed Chevy and the leading NAPA Chevy of Waltrip, Earnhardt's front air dam problem was not nearly as pronounced. The one-two-three formation in the closing laps corresponded perfectly to the pre-race meeting between Earnhardt and Waltrip—even if Earnhardt might have expected his Childress Chevy to be the one in front. NASCAR lore holds that Earnhardt next began blocking from his third position in order to insure the victory by the DEI tandem of Waltrip and Earnhardt Jr. (For his part, Earnhardt Jr. said after the race that his car worked much better in the trailing position in the draft than when in front of Waltrip's Chevy.)

The idea of Earnhardt fighting from third place to protect the DEI cars held true according to the pre-race agreement now working in favor of Waltrip. But Earnhardt had another motive. He always put an emphasis on coming out of Daytona with momentum for the year's points championship. Holding onto third versus the Dodge of two-time Daytona 500 winner Marlin and the Pontiac of Schrader, who were trailed by the Ford of Rusty Wallace, would be important to his goal of winning an eighth points title.

Waltrip and his son would not likely challenge

Earnhardt for the championship, but longtime rival Wallace, driving for the powerhouse team of Roger Penske, and Marlin, with an effective new Dodge team where successful CART entrant Chip Ganassi was now the owner, could well be in the hunt at season's end. The actual points at stake were not that great among the four positions, but the Intimidator was not about to give them up—or the psychological points at stake. His was the tenacity that had already won seven championships.

With ten laps to go, the three Chevy drivers formed a line in the bottom groove as Earnhardt began his rearguard action. On lap 196, four from the finish, he shut down Marlin's strong bid at the entrance to Turn 3 by blocking. Two laps later, Schrader failed in his move to get around by taking the high groove in Turn 1 in his yellow Pontiac. On lap 199 of 200, the leading Waltrip-Earnhardt Jr. tandem broke away as the third-placed Earnhardt blocked Schrader and Marlin again—this time at the tri-oval bend—setting up the fateful final lap.

By blocking in the tri-oval bend, Earnhardt lost the draft and the sudden yawning gap to the front-running DEI cars would be decisive for him and his car. Absent the draft by following close behind Earnhardt Jr.'s Chevy, the damaged front end of Earnhardt made his Chevy vulnerable as it traversed Turns 1 and 2, then headed down the back straight with less speed on the last lap. At the end of the back straight and entering Turn 3 for the last time, Schrader made a bid to pass the black Chevy on the high side. Marlin took the bottom groove and the Ford of Wallace pulled up close to the rear of Earnhardt's car. Still fighting the broken air damn, on worn tires now and without any drafting help, the black Chevy was surrounded by faster adversaries and turbulent air.

With his car wobbling, Earnhardt's errant left rear connected with the nose of the Dodge as Marlin bid to pass at the lower edge of the track midway between Turns 3 and 4. Perhaps caught out by the broken air dam, the new aerodynamics—or both—Earnhardt over-corrected and his Chevy's tail swerved down the track as a result and hooked its left rear tire on the apron. As both Marlin and Wallace stormed past, the black Chevy shot up the banking, caromed off Schrader's Pontiac and then cannonaded into the wall.

The resulting basal skull fracture from the impact with the wall meant Earnhardt bled to death within a matter of seconds. Andy Pilgrim, his Corvette co-driver from the 24-hour, had watched the race from the Earnhardt motor home with Earnhardt's wife Teresa. Both had the team's radio headsets, which were full of questions from Crew Chief Hamlin and Teresa without any answer.

Schrader climbed from his car and ran to the black Chevy. He frantically waved to the drivers of the rescue vehicles parked at the east end of the track to hurry up. He had seen the blood and the slumped, unresponsive driver. It was all too reminiscent of the day Jimmy Means ran to the window of J.D. McDuffie's crashed car at Watkins Glen in 1991 and saw the gushing blood of a basal skull fracture injury before he started waving frantically for the ambulance crew.

Once the ambulances arrived, Schrader rode back to the infield medical center while another ambulance carried Earnhardt's unresponsive body to the hospital. After being checked and released, Schrader then made the pilgrimage on foot from the medical center to Victory Lane, a walk of about two hundred yards. By then, the celebration was well under way for winner Waltrip.

A long-faced Schrader, partially hidden by sunglasses and a cap pulled down low, walked into Victory Lane and passed along the news to a jubilant Waltrip after first taking his friend by the arms, according to Waltrip's book.

"What's wrong?" asked Waltrip. "It's not good," replied Schrader in a shaky voice. Then he repeated the message. "It's not good. I think Dale's hurt. He's really hurt." Schrader hugged longtime friend Waltrip, telling him "I love you, bud" and then blended back into the celebratory clamor.

21
Earnhardt Was Racing

NOBODY EVER ACCUSED DALE EARNHARDT of being a fake. What you saw and heard from the seven-time champion invariably confirmed his status as "The Intimidator."

If you liked to push—or be pushed back—you were more likely to get along with Earnhardt, because that suited a driver with more restless spirit than a caged panther on a sweltering summer night. Being a bit pushy was part of the job if you were a reporter in search of a story in the NASCAR garages, but I had no expectation it would one day lead to becoming friends with "The Intimidator."

When I first interviewed Earnhardt while sitting on the back of the Osterlund Racing truck in the garage at the Darlington Raceway, he was a rookie who had just won his first race on the half-mile in Bristol, Tennessee. I had been on the Winston Cup beat for three seasons, writing for the *Durham Morning Herald*. Even then, he had a unique combination of charisma and friendliness, which could sometimes, I would learn, be overrun by a bristling moodiness.

He first got tagged with the nickname of "Ironhead," initially because he actually had a small piece of metal in his forehead from a machine shop accident and later because of his uncompromising driving style. In the late 1980s, Earnhardt and wife Teresa decided to generate the name of "The Intimidator"—the first of many successful marketing campaigns.

For years, I simultaneously admired Earnhardt's car control and disliked his driving tactics. I had little regret, for instance, while writing the lead paragraph after he suffered another miraculous loss in the Daytona 500 to Derrike Cope in 1990 due to a cut tire on the last lap while leading. "The fans with the 'Anybody But Earnhardt' t-shirts," the story began, "got their wish on the last lap of the Daytona 500 on Sunday..."

His car control and sheer bravery were extraordinary, sometimes breathtaking. Early in his career, Earnhardt alone mixed it up on the superspeedways from the drop of the green as if they were short tracks. The moral question of endangering other drivers, or using underhanded tactics, always hung in the air. Fans started booing him regularly. It wasn't until John Andretti arrived in the Winston Cup in the early 1990s that my attitude began to change after a conversation with the former Indy car and sports car driver.

During an Atlanta race, I had watched Andretti stay with Earnhardt for 15 laps on the track's daunting high banks, following him through the field to the front from their respective mid-pack starting positions. I remarked on it to Andretti after the race, asking him if Earnhardt had taken the air off his rear spoiler to get by before Andretti started following the black No. 3. "The thing about Dale is that anything he does to your car, you can do to his," replied Andretti.

I had generally accepted car racing as a test of skill and bravery among the guys on the track. The only rules that mattered were the ones decided upon by those same guys. Because of my respect for Andretti, I began to recognize that I hadn't quite seen the whole picture in place of a rather narrow, moralistic view of Earnhardt. Another influence was a story by Sandy McKee of the *Baltimore Sun* that appeared about that time on the retired David Pearson, the driver many figured had been the best in the business. In the story, the always smooth "Silver Fox" recounted how much he admired the far more rambunctious Earnhardt.

When I first began covering the Winston Cup in 1976, on superspeedways the drivers generally shepherded each other around, trying to put any competitors fast enough to block the path to Victory Lane in positions where they had to lift. Like Pearson and later Bill Elliott among Earnhardt's generation, they relied primarily on the skills of car preparation, speed and race craft.

Inevitably, there were occasions where high spirits got out of hand and drivers tried to wreck one another, but usually they were limited to late-race situations such as the infamous Daytona 500 in 1979, when Donnie Allison tried to block Cale Yarborough's winning pass on the final lap and the bantam-sized South Carolinian returned the favor. That led to one of the most famous wrecks in NASCAR history and post-race fist fight shown live on CBS Sports. When it came to entanglements on superspeedways occasioned before the checkers were anywhere near, longtime Winston Cup director Dick Beaty always advised drivers to "save your paybacks for the short tracks."

Earnhardt, a rookie the year of the infamous episode between Allison and Yarborough, soon added a new dimension to superspeedways. Where the generation of Petty, Pearson, the Allisons and Yarborough had generally saved their close quarters moves for the end of a superspeedway race or events on the slower short tracks, Earnhardt ran close quarters from start to finish on any kind of track, daring his competitors to do likewise.

"The Intimidator" represented far more than a trademarked name. His competitors knew what to expect from him, which included occasional recklessness. Once when asked what happened after a wreck in Turn 4 early in a race at Darlington, Petty wryly replied, "I forgot I was racing around Earnhardt." (In classic style, "The King" paid Earnhardt back with a body slam at Richmond's short track the following week.) Most other drivers didn't have the same resolve as Earnhardt due to less car control, less bravery, more consideration for their fellow drivers, or less desire to be the one driver everybody in the garage recognized as "The Man."

During an annual pre-season charity event in Winston-Salem, N.C., attended by most of NASCAR's biggest stars, someone once chided Jimmy Spencer that his autograph line fell far short compared to the one for Earnhardt, which snaked its way through the entire pavilion like a giant python. "Everybody," said Spencer, "wants to meet John Wayne."

As Earnhardt became the straw that stirred NASCAR's drink during the late 1980s and early 1990s, others such as Rusty Wallace, Ken Schrader, Davey Allison and Ernie Irvan began to endorse similar tactics. It became increasingly apparent that Andretti's observation about all being fair in this man's game had been taken up by some of Earnhardt's peers. The younger Allison, in particular, was inspiring as he, too, became a daredevil on superspeedways.

But after the deaths of Allison and defending champion Alan Kulwicki in aircraft accidents in 1993 and a near-fatal crash at Michigan by Irvan a year later, and before the ascent of Jeff Gordon, Earnhardt stood alone as the reigning king of stock car racing. It was my job to get the full story, not pick and choose whom I liked or didn't like. So, I began to make a concerted effort to spend more time with Earnhardt other than the usual post-race interviews or occasional exchange in the garage.

I arranged an extended interview while working on an article for the year-end special advertising sections on motor racing in *Sports Illustrated*, an annual assignment at the time, figuring it was time to fight the modern era's increasingly difficult task of getting face time with NASCAR's stars. But the real turning point came at *Autosport* magazine's year-end banquet in 1996 in London, where Earnhardt had been invited to receive an honorary award.

Earnhardt Was Racing

The funny thing about "The Intimidator" was his shyness in an unfamiliar environment. Such circumstances seemed to shove him back to his awkward, inarticulate, painful childhood and adolescence, where he struck out regularly in both school and on the baseball field. In this case, going to London for an award from *Autosport* magazine in front of the international driving stars and glitzy Formula 1 crowd, although still part of the racing scene, made him more nervous than, well, English class. Never mind that NASCAR president Bill France Jr. would also be there.

The Grosvenor Hotel ballroom, site of the *Autosport* banquet, did nothing to calm Earnhardt's nerves while sitting in the huge and impressive ballroom with its several tiers of surrounding balconies. It required binoculars to see from one side of the room to the other. Driver Dick Trickle often said running on the high banks at Bristol's short track was like racing jet fighters in a gymnasium. The Grosvenor seemed large enough to host just such an event.

Guests had to consult small books to find their name and table assignment. "What are you doing here?" said Earnhardt, already seated when I arrived at our appointed table. I replied that I covered NASCAR for *Autosport* magazine among other assignments.

"I don't hardly know what I'm doing here," he said, making it clear his awkward shyness had overwhelmed him on this occasion. Since I considered myself one of the hosts of the occasion, and with an eye on his role as a speaker later in the evening, I asked Dale if he remembered the story he had once told me of the day Humpy Wheeler, the promoter of the Charlotte Motor Speedway, had invited him to a Chamber of Commerce meeting during his rookie year.

During that Chamber meeting in Concord, Earnhardt had asked Wheeler who the speaker was going to be that day? The promoter turned to him and said, "You are." In a panic, the 28-year-old with an eighth-grade education told Wheeler he didn't know anything about business. Wheeler replied that the businessmen already knew about business and wanted to know more about racing. Earnhardt, who once was so word-struck he described short track racing as "frammin' and bammin'," quickly learned how to get over his fear of public speaking.

Not incidentally, it was the first business meeting attended by the man who took to business deals like he did to racing and would one day own a seat on the New York Stock Exchange plus a huge ocean-going yacht called "Sunday Money."

At the posh banquet in London, after reminding Earnhardt of that chamber meeting 20 years earlier, I made a grand sweep of my arm as if I owned the ballroom and said, "These people already know all about Formula 1. You're here because they want to know more about NASCAR." That seemed to calm his nervousness.

Very much unexpectedly, prior to the start of dinner and after grace, Sterling Moss, the great Formula 1 driver, was called on to deliver a eulogy in the form of a toast. Denis Jenkinson, one of the most dedicated, brave, and incorrigibly honest motor racing journalists of the 20th Century, had died the previous week. Having once worked alongside Moss as the navigator en route to their victory in Italy's Mille Miglia sports car race, "Jenks" received a heart-felt send-off from the great Formula 1 driver, standing under a spotlight at an adjoining table in the middle of the hushed hall. Unknown to many in the business, Jenkinson had actually died a pauper in a public hospital.

I was aware of Jenks' death, but this grand British gesture of a toast caught me by surprise. For reasons little known to me at the time, after Moss invited us to all raise a glass in his memory, I looked at NASCAR president Bill France Jr., seated on the other side of Earnhardt and his wife Teresa, and raised my glass saying, "And here's to Joe Whitlock." Whitlock had worked at the NASCAR News Bureau in the 1970s, then at the Charlotte track and later as Earnhardt's PR man and mentor in his first several seasons in the Winston Cup. Whitlock had committed suicide with a shotgun blast to the head for reasons unknown on the same day as a race in Talladega several years earlier, which had deeply confounded and troubled his friends, including Earnhardt.

France Jr., never a man of great empathy or compassion due to survival instincts and a lifetime at the top of the cutthroat business of racing, chortled at my impromptu toast. But Earnhardt, for whom Whitlock had been simultaneously like a father and big brother as he had learned to navigate fame, appreciated my sudden, impassioned gesture, one he knew came straight from the heart. A very talented writer, Whitlock had helped me along on more than a few occasions early in my career.

Earnhardt's loyalty after that encounter took me by surprise. He went out of his way to shake hands at the Winston Cup banquet the following week in New York City. When he won his eighth straight Twin 125-mile race the following February, I saw him in the Daytona press box afterwards. "Where've you been? I haven't seen you all week," he said with friendly concern. "I figured I'd wait until this race was over and then see you up here for the winner's interview," I replied. He looked me dead in the eye to be sure I wasn't being a wise guy and then started talking about one of his favorite subjects, the Atlanta Braves.

That year, 1997, turned out to be another disastrous Speed Weeks finale for Earnhardt, who lost his 19th straight Daytona 500, his Chevy riding in a cascade of sparks down the back straight after a late-race accident when he tried to prevent eventual winner Jeff Gordon from passing underneath at Turn 2.

The next time I saw Earnhardt, a little over a month later, a real friendship began. Drivers were required, as a result of receiving Winner's Circle bonuses, to make a select number of appearances at tracks in advance to help promote upcoming races. Earnhardt usually liked fulfilling one of these obligations in Atlanta and had signed up to help promote the spring race.

On this day, a sterile conference room located in the clubhouse of the condos at Turn 4 at the Atlanta Motor Speedway stood a long way from the Grosvenor Hotel ballroom. I arrived a little late and as a testy Earnhardt meandered through a standard answer in a monotone. I caught his eye and quickly recognized Dale's lackluster mood, in part because Earnhardt had anticipated the inevitable questions about his latest failure to win the Daytona 500. The losses didn't taunt him as much as the inevitable easy lines in what he regarded as the cheap shot media about how the greatest driver in stock car racing couldn't win its greatest race.

Still early in the media conference, I walked around to the front table and took a seat left empty where none of the gathered media had wanted to get too close to dark ol' Dale, preferring their own company. Only Tom McCollister, too close to retirement from *The Atlanta Journal-Constitution* to worry about any athlete, had taken a chair near the seven-time champion.

Confident about my relationship with Earnhardt, I waited for a question that would inevitably, on a day like this, rankle "The Intimidator." "How do you like the change in the track configuration?" someone asked. The previous fall, owner Bruton Smith had butchered the country's only high-banked, true oval, installing a dogleg along the front straight to accommodate more seats with a view of the pits and the start-finish for the rapidly growing crowds at the Winston Cup season finale hosted annually in Atlanta.

Earnhardt, who had won eight times on the true oval, loved the old configuration and dissed Smith's penchant for putting doglegs into front straights. Now that he was rolling, I interrupted and told Dale that Smith had changed the track to accommodate more room at the start-finish line for pre-race shows, hoping to wind him up a little further. Earnhardt didn't take the bait. "I kind of like some of those shows in Charlotte," Earnhardt countered quickly, easing off the throttle and referring to Smith's track in North Carolina. He recalled a five-story-high, fire-breathing robot that chewed up junked cars. "I really liked that Robo-saurus," he said.

"It figures," I casually replied in a voice that only he and T. Mac could hear, "that you would like a machine that went out and tore up a bunch of cars." It was a

Earnhardt Was Racing

none-too-subtle reference to Earnhardt's reputation for over-aggressiveness with his black Chevys.

Well, that didn't work either, Earnhardt being too sly for such tactics. But I had him rolling. Not long afterward, I started to ask him about his accident in the closing stages of the Daytona 500. But before I could finish the question, he cut in quickly with an unrelated answer. "Was I scared?" he replied testily, finally on the high lobe of an emotional cam. "No, I wadn't scared. I ain't never been scared in a race car."

The words started tumbling out involuntarily instead of his previously testy speech, which had bucked and stuttered like an old jalopy as he rebelled against questions. "I was riding on my roof, waiting for the car to stop," he said. "Then it flipped back over and slid into the grass. I got out and they was trying to make me go to the ambulance."

Sensing that he had everyone's keen attention, Earnhardt continued apace, as if among friends sitting around a camp fire telling a story. "But as they were tryin' to git me to walk to the ambulance, I looked at the wheels on one side, saw they was OK. I walked around to th' other side and the wheels were on that side. I told one of the safety workers, 'Git in and see if it'll start up.' He got in and pushed the starter button and it cranked up. I told him 'Git out! Git out!' I got back in, brought it back to the pits, they put on some new tires and I finished the race."

By time he got to the finish of describing the wreck that had ended another day of Daytona 500 futility, Earnhardt had turned the episode into a funny story ("Git out! Git out!"). Determined to avoid getting too riled up, he demonstrated that he had righted himself despite what had become one of American sports' most celebrated losing streaks.

Needling him, he recognized, had been a friendly, yet competitive gesture not unlike sharing the same boat but putting individual fishing lines into the water. With my needling him, he had something to lose and something to win as well, and equilibrium had no greater master than Earnhardt, who eventually won the day with his acid retort ("Was I scared?") and funny conclusion ("Git out! Git out!") about losing yet another Daytona 500.

And, we got our story. After completing a subsequently more relaxed sit-down meeting with the media, his first since yet another fateful loss in Daytona, the man in black quickly headed for the doors in the midst of an animated conversation with track owner Smith, who had arrived toward the end of the meeting. At the gate leading to the parking lot, Earnhardt turned and quietly offered his hand. I returned the gesture, offered as thanks for helping him get through one of the more difficult of the usual headaches of dealing with the media.

Typically for ol' Ironhead, it had taken some jousting to get him going. The deep well of molten competitiveness never stopped simmering in him. But if you didn't mind pushing him—or being pushed back—you were more likely to be friends with Earnhardt. For all his verbal hazing of "Wonder Boy" Jeff Gordon, for example, Earnhardt actually liked the young upstart Indiana driver, because Gordon had the talent and the guts to race Earnhardt the same way "The Intimidator" raced him.

It seemed not only Gordon but poor ol' Mister Magoo would find Victory Lane at the Daytona 500 before Earnhardt. But he finally won it in 1998. By the start of Speed Weeks in 2001, he had also won a record fourth IROC championship as well, but a record-breaking eighth championship in NASCAR's newly re-named Nextel Cup continued to elude him after a runner-up finish to Bobby Labonte in 2000.

On the Friday morning three days before the ill-fated Daytona 500 in 2001, I tried to catch up with Earnhardt, among others, in my usual rounds in the garage in search of quotes for a story, in this case on NASCAR's new aero rules package for the 500. Not seeing Dale, I figured I'd catch up with him after the IROC race that afternoon. As it turned out, I had trouble getting anywhere close to Earnhardt, because there had been an incident between former Indy 500 winner Eddie Cheever and "The Intimidator" during the all-star race.

So, the first time I got close to Earnhardt during NASCAR Speed Weeks that year, he was walking down the pit lane surrounded three-deep by a moving gaggle of media trying to get his version of what had happened in the incident with Cheever, who had hit the wall and then hit Earnhardt.

In the main event on Sunday, it would be Earnhardt hitting the wall on the last lap.

Not far from the age of 50 myself, I had looked forward to seeing if Earnhardt could win his eighth title (but had picked Tony Stewart in the preseason). Whatever happened, I tacitly had figured I'd be seeing him around the racetrack as a car owner after he had retired, just like A.J. Foyt and Richard Petty, among others.

None of this supposes Earnhardt and I were best friends. A journalist, ultimately, is an interlocutor for the personalities behind what happens on the track, where fans can see for themselves what makes their favorite drivers so attractive and, on occasion, so heroic—or not. The job does allow you to get much closer to the human side of the men in the steel chariots. But as long as they know you're going to write both sides of the story and not just their side, including any bone-headed mistakes or ill-gotten comments made in anger, the idea of becoming close friends is, well, a different story. About the best that can happen is a driver trying to be friendly out of a modicum of respect and to be sure at least somebody's printing his side of the story.

What made him cool was his confidence in breaking the usual rules. He maintained a loyalty and a friendly bond that went beyond the standard effort to charm enough journalists to at least psychologically believe some of the guys in the press box might see things his way. It came to Earnhardt naturally to actually be a friend, not just act friendly, to do such things as make peanut butter and jelly sandwiches for guests in his motor home. That's why Dale had such a broad and deep personal universe when it came to friendships—despite a driving style and hardheadedness that led to enemies, particularly in the media, and so many boos from the grandstands. From Earnhardt's perspective, being the biggest star in American racing gave him a better chance to be not just The Man, but a bigger man.

In some ways fans, who are free to invest so much in their heroes, may feel their loss when a driver dies far more acutely than a journalist who has to find a way to get to know everybody and still keep his distance—to report on such things as just how Cheever got sideways during that IROC race. Or just how a legendary driver makes a mistake and gets killed.

Maybe it's because we were the same age and the arc of our careers roughly coincided. Mostly, it was Earnhardt's loyalty and effort to be friendly that did it after I got to know him and he realized I wasn't one of those who thought he was washed up after the 1996 and 1997 seasons, including his mysterious asleep-at-the-wheel episode in Darlington. Certainly, his one-of-a-kind, celebrity status was a factor on my part. Against my own intuition and professional experience, which after several fatal accidents blared warnings against getting too friendly with any driver, I had gotten closer to Earnhardt than I ever expected.

Sure, his own Ironheaded ways got him killed. Sure, everybody knew working with him would be like getting hit in the head with a shovel sooner or later if you unexpectedly hit the wrong trip wire in his closely guarded personal territory. But what does one expect from a guy with an eighth-grade education who took on the world and won according to his mill town family's creed? It was this unwillingness to bend or yield that made him a working-class hero, or in the words of Whitlock, "the last cowboy."

As usual, the Monday after the 2001 Daytona 500, I headed north from Daytona Beach on I-95, this time wondering why I was seeing so much rain on a sunny day?

22

No. 3 Car Investigation

AFTER EARNHARDT'S DEATH, CONTROversy ensued about how a seemingly routine crash could have killed NASCAR's greatest driver. Initially, the sanctioning body offered few details about the crash, until it discovered a torn seat belt in Earnhardt's No. 3 Chevy.

Rescue crews had placed a tarp over the car at the crash scene once the driver's body had been removed and a day later transported the impounded car by truck to an undisclosed location in North Carolina. According to NASCAR public relations representative John Griffin, who offered the information on background, a separated left side lap belt had been discovered on Tuesday once an inspection took place. The sanctioning body announced its discovery and displayed the torn belt three days later in front of the large media contingent gathered at the North Carolina Motor Speedway for the second race of the season and the first since Earnhardt's death.

When contacted by the media, Dr. Steve Bohannon, the medical director of the Daytona track, suggested that the separated belt was a cause of Earnhardt's death. The controversy quickly mushroomed in the ongoing absence of any direct communication from NASCAR on what had happened during the crash. By this point, an autopsy had disclosed Earnhardt's death resulted from a basal skull fracture. Some media began reporting that NASCAR blamed the broken belt for Earnhardt's death, although no direct comment had been made by the sanctioning body. Fans began to suggest the torn belt could have been cut after the fact in order for NASCAR to cover up what had happened to its greatest star in a seemingly typical crash.

John Melvin, the longtime safety advocate who had become a consultant after leaving GM, found himself a man in the middle with the media, starting with the ongoing debate about whether the HANS would have saved Earnhardt before the question of the torn belt arose.

Because of Melvin's long-running efforts to introduce awareness about cockpit safety in CART, then the IRL and NASCAR, he had become a go-to guy for journalists. He developed working relationships with media members as part of his effort to educate the racing community on the subject of safety. The first call made by several journalists after the announcement of the torn belt went to Melvin. What did he think about the belt problem?

Writing for *On Track*, this writer called Melvin, who said he didn't think the belt played a significant part in the fatal outcome. "We used to purposely fray one of the lap belts when we were running sled tests," he said. "We found that the belt broke at the same time the tension in the neck of the dummy was at its peak and the dummy's neck had already sustained enough tension to create a fatal injury." In other words, the same peak loading that created enough neck tension to cause a basal skull fracture was enough to simultaneously break a compromised lap belt. By then, under this scenario, the damage to the driver had already occurred.

Melvin's observations dovetailed with a report filed by Dr. Barry Myers. A Duke University professor, Myers was appointed by a court after a dispute over access by the *Orlando Sentinel* to the autopsy photos, sealed in a legal action brought by Earnhardt's widow Teresa. Myers stopped short of concluding a HANS would have saved Earnhardt.

Myers' four-page report filed in early April discounted the lap belt issue, but also suggested that the broken belt may have allowed Earnhardt's chin to hit the steering wheel. Although he concluded head whip killed Earnhardt, Myers, citing abrasions on the chin in the autopsy, acknowledged the chin hitting the steering wheel as a possible cause of the skull fracture.

By this time, NASCAR had hired the Powell Tate agency in Washington, D.C., to guide its response to the media about Earnhardt's crash. Before the independent report of Myers was released, NASCAR President Helton had already made a separate announcement that same morning about the sanctioning body's investigation underway with its own experts.

In late April, controversy heated up further when Tommy Propst, a veteran Emergency Medical Technician, publicly stated that the belt had *not* been separated when he responded to the crash of Earnhardt's car, which implied that it was cut later. Further fanning the story, an ongoing dispute erupted between Bill Simpson, founder of Simpson Safety Products and manufacturer of Earnhardt's belts, and NASCAR. The sanctioning body's lack of comment led Simpson to constantly rail that NASCAR made him look like a fall guy.

NASCAR began its own investigation by hiring two sets of industry experts who were out of the eye of the media. Dean Sicking, Ph.D., and John Reid, Ph.D., professors at the University of Nebraska, were hired to work in the area of barrier impact, accident reconstruction and computer modeling. James Benedict, an M.D. and Ph.D., and James Raddin, M.D., of the Biodynamic Research Corporation, were hired as biomechanical and engineering experts with expertise in automobile crashes. According to the *Sentinel* in a later report, the company of the latter two had billed an average of $13 million per year to automotive manufacturers from 1991 to 1995 for consulting services, including work as expert defense witnesses in legal proceedings.

NASCAR officials began holding secret meetings with its crash investigation experts at a location arranged by Powell Tate in Washington, D.C., which eventually would lead to a voluminous report and announcement in August. The Powell Tate firm had been established by Jody Powell, the former White House press secretary for President Jimmy Carter, and Sheila Tate, press secretary to former First Lady Nancy Reagan. The relationship with NASCAR was directed by the firm's Ramsey Poston, a specialist in strategic and crisis communication with four years of experience, along with the guiding hand of Powell, once a student at the U.S. Air Force Academy who had some background in technical matters.

Poston recalled that during the initial meeting between members of the agency and key officials at NASCAR that Powell spoke directly to NASCAR Chairman France Jr. about his irritation over an ongoing media storm and his reluctance to engage journalists. "Look," said Powell, "I have learned over time that bitching about the media feels good in the short term… but in the long term being pissed off is not a plan." France Jr. recognized good advice and signaled as much by laughing along with others at the meeting.

The public relations firm "learned about biomechanical kinetics, G-forces, Delta V, energy dissipation, the rate of deceleration," said Poston in his account that appeared in the book *Chicken Soup for the Soul: NASCAR*. Powell, he said, "had a good grasp of the physics and explained them to me, sometimes on the back of a cocktail napkin and with the help of a cocktail."

Poston, who was eventually hired by NASCAR to direct its media operations, relied heavily on the expertise and background knowledge of Jim Hunter, a confidante of France Jr. who had directed NASCAR's communications before being named president of Darlington Raceway. As the president of Darlington, Hunter no longer had a direct role with the media on

No. 3 Car Investigation

behalf of NASCAR, enabling him to work behind the scenes on the so-called No. 3 Car project.

With Hunter back on the job unofficially, and with an eye on secrecy, NASCAR also bypassed its media staff in Daytona by relying on an assistant to France Jr. and a former newspaper man Herb Branham to help coordinate NASCAR's participation, which relied heavily on Helton and Winston Cup Director Gary Nelson, the two men in charge of implementing any changes growing out of the investigation. To work with the outside experts, the NASCAR personnel regularly flew one of the company's planes to meetings at an office on the top floor of a Washington, D.C., building with a clear view of the White House.

Looking back, Nelson pointed out that the context of the Earnhardt investigation turned everything else from previous NASCAR history on its head. Prior to that, NASCAR simply didn't consider advice that came from "outside the fence" of the NASCAR garage. Nelson admitted he didn't always understand what outsiders were talking about and sometimes turned to Steve Peterson, an engineer working in the garage as the technical director for NASCAR under Nelson.

"Everything was happening inside that garage. That was our perception of the day," said Nelson of the years prior to 2001. "John Melvin would come around from the outside and talk to us and, I had one guy who befriended him, Steve Peterson. Steve would spend more time with him and talk to John, frankly more than Steve talked to most people. Steve would come around and try to translate what John was saying to guys like me."

During the investigation, Nelson got inundated by requests from the team of Sicking and Reid plus Raddin and Benedict for data and information. As the meetings continued, Nelson became hungry for answers, particularly when it came to the stiffness of the cars as it related to the G-forces drivers were subjected to in crashes.

Many within the stock car racing industry had come to the conclusion that the stiffer the chassis, the harder the crashes—a sort of urban legend among

A computer-generated simulation plus actual crash testing helped NASCAR's experts recreate Earnhardt crash.
(*Official Accident Report — No. 3 Car*)

stock car racers. But as safety engineer Tom Gideon's later research would show, the peak moment of energy transfer in a crash was influenced far more by speed than the construction of the car. Instead, the stiffness of the chassis indirectly influenced crash outcomes by introducing higher cornering speeds. The overall speeds were always high at Daytona and Talladega, but were kept in check by restrictor plates. The three fatalities in 2000 had occurred on intermediate size speedways of 1.0 or 1.5 miles, precisely where cornering speeds were continuing to increase most every season due to chassis improvements and unchecked horsepower.

Despite the obvious issue of speed, the stock car racing industry was awash in speculation that stiffer cars were killer cars.

H.A. "Humpy" Wheeler, the Charlotte track promoter, introduced the concept of the "Humpy Bumper" for the Winston Cup cars, a front end designed to absorb more energy. Leading crew chiefs in the sport also firmly believed that something had to be done with the front end, a story often picked up by the media.

Larry McReynolds, who had moved from his role as a crew chief for Richard Childress Racing into a role as TV commentator in 2001, summed up the attitudes of those in the sport at the time of Earnhardt's crash. McReynolds worked as the crew chief for Ernie Irvan when the driver suffered a basal skull fracture in Michigan in 1994 and directed Earnhardt's long-awaited Daytona 500 victory in 1998.

"I know for a fact as we were moving into the era of bump drafting, we were really starting to stiffen up the front end of our race cars a lot," said McReynolds. "Obviously, from an impact standpoint, the worst place you can stiffen a car is at the front end. If you're going to hit the wall, the front end is what you're going to hit it with. There's sometimes you'll hit it with the back end. There are some cases where you hit it with the side. But seven, eight times out of ten you're going to hit with the nose. I've got to say that when I watched Dale hit that wall—we weren't doing anything different at Richard Childress Racing and it wasn't like we were on an island by ourselves. But one of the first things that crossed my mind was knowing how stiff we were making the front ends of these race cars."

During the investigation, participants within the industry as well as outsiders privately contacted Nelson, who became overwhelmed with suggestions that landed on his desk in Daytona daily. He decided to insist on some answers from the hired experts. "At one of these meetings, I said, 'Look guys, I've got a desk full of ideas. The industry is demanding that we do something. I want to do something, but I've got limited time and limited resources. What do I need to work on first?'

"It was a two-day meeting," continued Nelson. "Those guys said, 'Let us discuss this.' And they went away. And they came back the next day. They said, "Take your resources and allocate them this way. Sixty percent of your safety gains will come from restraining the driver in the car as tightly as possible. Thirty percent of your gains will come from a cushion when they hit the wall, or barrier. And ten percent will come from the rest of the car.'"

That answer put the issue of chassis stiffness on the back burner until the Car of Tomorrow project, which eventually arrived in 2007. While NASCAR would increase its contributions to the "soft walls" project started by the Indianapolis Motor Speedway with Sicking, the outcome that eventually became the SAFER barrier remained a work in progress.

Driver restraints were the key safety factor in crashes by a considerable magnitude compared with "soft walls" or the stiffness of chassis. Two specific questions remained: what were the circumstances of the separated belt and would a HANS would have made a difference? Helton did not attend all the meetings, but occasionally flew from Daytona to Washington for briefings. During one of these visits, Helton asked Raddin if he believed the HANS would have saved Earnhardt. According to one of those present, he responded, "Yes." Given the number of NASCAR officials who had been friends with Earnhardt, including Helton, a poignant and long silence followed.

Raddin's public response when asked by a journalist at the August announcement of the findings of the special investigation would be far less conclusive.

The presentation of the *Official Accident Report – No. 3 Car* at the Hyatt Regency in Atlanta on August 21 after months of tight-lipped responses from NASCAR made up in volume what it lacked in conclusive opinions offered to about 200 print journalists and several television crews. The report, presented in two books, was long, especially on technology. "On the big screen flashed phrases like 'velocity vector' and 'trajectory angle' to an audience of poor souls who entered journalism precisely because they couldn't handle high school physics," wrote Steve Hummer of *The Atlanta Journal-Constitution*. In a more serious jab at the volume of information presented without much in the way of conclusive results, *Orlando Sentinel* columnist David Whitley wrote, "At least we can rule out the CIA or

No. 3 Car Investigation

Castro in the Daytona crash. Almost everything else is still in play."

Given Powell Tate's involvement, it seemed intentional that after six months of detailed investigation an avalanche of information, including the secretly printed two-volume book set given to the media, led to nothing conclusive about how Earnhardt died—at least in public. "I think you can't identify a single factor to say it's this and not that," said Raddin from the stage. On the subject of the HANS Device and whether it would have helped, he said, "We're not clear that if such a system had been in use here what the outcome would have been."

Two very specific and important conclusions were reached and made public. The evidence demonstrated—including a special investigation by additional experts—beyond any doubt that Earnhardt's left lap belt was not cut after the accident as suggested by Tommy Propst, the Emergency Medical Technician who had been a lone wolf in his accusation. Instead, the report demonstrated that Earnhardt's improper mounting of his lap belts resulted in "dumping," or the catching of the belt in the adjuster under heavy loading. The result was the torn belt NASCAR had first presented to the media at the North Carolina Motor Speedway five days after the fatal crash.

Another undisputed finding concerned the enormous impact of the No. 3 car's meeting with the wall. Using a large screen with graphics, Sicking explained why the force of impact had been so great due to Earnhardt's Chevy being turned by contact with the Pontiac of Schrader and how the forces of energy worked in such an impact. His report relied on extensive data gathered from the site of the crash and the car itself. It also used video coverage, GPS tracking and then re-created the crash with a full-scale Cup car. A computer model reinforced the conclusions of the exhaustive investigation.

The report of Sicking and Reid, introduced by Sicking on the Hyatt Rengency's stage, stated that the impact with Schrader resulted in a 9 to 11 mph increase in velocity, or speed, of the Earnhardt car—each car being designated by number. After the black Chevy hit the wall at approximately 160 mph at the angle introduced by contact with Schrader's car, the investigation concluded the 80 milliseconds of deceleration led to a deceleration speed, or Delta V, of between 42 to 44 mph.

The combination of the heading angle, or angle of the car as it hit the wall, the trajectory angle, or the direction of the car's center of gravity due to ongoing inertia, were critical elements. These elements described the velocity vector. The car hit the wall head on at the same time its momentum tried to carry it down the track. Combining this type of meeting with the wall with the lack of any subsequent rotation of the car and the 42-44 mph deceleration "made this a very severe impact," reported Sicking and Reid.

It moved the engine back three inches and bent the transmission housing.

Raddin reported on just how Earnhardt died in an atmosphere similar to a jury trial with two sides presenting different views of the facts. In this case, one set of facts had already been presented by Myers four months earlier as a result of the legal case brought by the *Orlando Sentinel* and Raddin presented an opposing viewpoint. Seated in a theatre-type arrangement, the assembled media made up the jury.

Where Myers' report had concluded that head whip caused the basal skull fracture, Raddin presented data that led to the conclusion he died from a blow to the rear of the head.

Using kinetics, Raddin focused on how the contact with Schrader's car had repositioned Earnhardt's body shortly before the wall impact and how the torn belt resulting from the contact with the wall resulted in the left side of his body moving forward without the restraint of the harness, enabling the back of his head to hit the steering wheel. "The head swung forward in an arcing motion in a manner that caused it to strike the steering wheel more radially on the left side of the head, in an unprotected region in the location of the left-side contusion described in the autopsy report." The detailed explanation of the driver's kinetics in the cockpit included how the helmet slipped up on the driver's head as a result of both the contact with Schrader and the belt breaking, exposing the lower left portion of the skull at the back.

Using a sled test and an anthropomorphic device, or crash test dummy, Raddin and his team had recreated the body movements described in his written account found in the *Official Accident Report*.

When contacted by reporters on the day NASCAR had made its presentation to the media, Myers said he stood by his conclusion. Myers had discounted the blow to the left occipital bone at the back of the head that resulted in a bruise, in part because the ring fracture of the opening at the base of the skull was larger toward the front of the head rather than the back.

A ring fracture is a medical term used for a basal skull fracture. The relatively large opening at the base of the skull, the foramen magnum, is found near the center of the head and is surrounded by the occipital bone, which extends from the back of the head to the middle, creating more or less a floor with the foramen magnum opening almost in the middle. The C1 vertebra, also known as the Atlas, is comprised of bone that is circular and fits into the foramen magnum opening. Along with the spinal nerves, blood vessels that go to the brain pass through the open center section of the C1 vertebra before entering the brain through the foramen magnum.

A ring fracture occurs when there is enough tension or shear force in the neck to break the connection between the Atlas and the skull bone at the foramen magnum opening. A fracture forms surrounding the opening, creating a ring. Nobody disputes that a ring fracture and the subsequent damage to arteries and blood vessels killed Earnhardt. The photographs of the interior of the cockpit made it hard to miss the blood. The debate focused on how the fracture occurred.

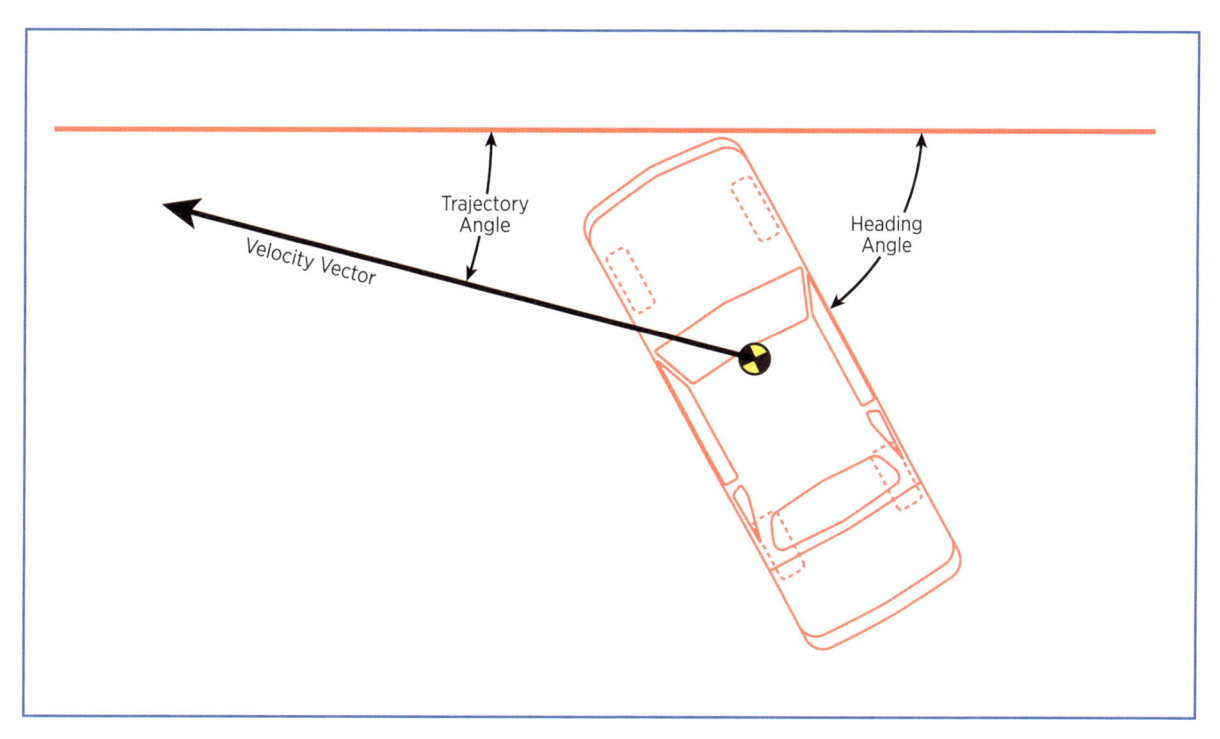

The combination of the heading angle and trajectory angle led to a severe impact. (Adapted from *Official Accident Report — No. 3 Car*)

No. 3 Car Investigation

Part of the debate resulted from the medical community's lack of complete information about head whip leading to a ring fracture. CART's medical expert Terry Trammell observed that his medical training had not included the possibility of head whip leading to a basal skull fracture and instead he was taught a basal skull fracture occurred from a blow to the head such as in a fall, or from an object hitting the head or the head hitting an object. Invariably, when coroners reported on deaths of a race car driver from ring fractures, the reason given was "blunt force injuries," the cause of death initially given in the case of Earnhardt by Dr. Thomas A. Parsons of the Office of the Medical Examiner for Volusia and Seminole Counties.

Although Raddin did not directly address in great detail the nature of the ring fracture in his presentation in Atlanta, in the written portion of the *Official Accident Report* he disputed Myers' conclusion that the ring fracture being most pronounced toward the front confirmed head whip as the cause. Raddin's report stated a blow to the occipital portion, or back, of the skull could indeed produce the pattern discovered in the autopsy report. The production of ring fractures "is not sufficiently understood," stated Raddin's Injury Causation Analysis. It concluded a blow at the back of the head could produce the most severe damage in the ring fracture toward the front of the skull. "The impact produced stresses in the skull, which probably caused the fracture to initiate at some point remote from the contact and then propagate toward that contact, eventually closing the ring."

In either death scenario, neck tension was the over-riding issue. Myers' conclusion of head whip—also supported by Melvin and his colleague Tom Gideon at GM's safety project—meant a HANS no doubt would have made a difference, although Myers' report stopped short of explicitly saying so. Myers also put forward the second option of the chin hitting the steering wheel, which can also be fatal when enough neck tension is present.

The four-point summation at the opening of NASCAR's report explicitly stated that head whip did not cause the basal skull fracture. But the report acknowledged "it is possible that neck tension and torsion at the time of the blow to the head contributed to the basilar skull fracture." There was a second reference to neck tension found on page 55 of the Injury Causation Analysis, which also suggested why Raddin might privately offer an opinion about the effectiveness of the HANS. "Mr. Earnhardt's death," the report stated, "likely resulted from an impact to the occipital scalp in the presence of neck tension producing a fatal ring fracture."

If all agreed that less neck tension might have produced a better outcome, the broken belt posed an unanswered question and an element of doubt. Perhaps the HANS Device would work in the case of a broken belt, or at least help. On the other hand, the device worked by transferring forces in the head and neck to the torso through the yoke held in place by a driver's harness. Nobody—Raddin, the industry safety experts,

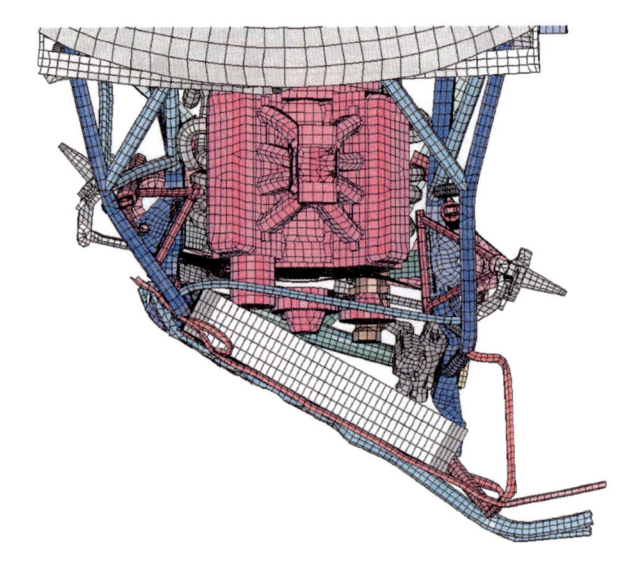

This image used in computer simulation was modeled from the actual wreckage at the front end of No. 3 Chevy.
(*Official Accident Report — No. 3 Car*)

or the makers of the HANS itself—could be certain if the HANS would work in an accident where the safety harness had a failure.

Even HANS Performance Products co-founder Jim Downing, who attended NASCAR's presentation of the *Official Accident Report* in Atlanta, remained uncertain when it came to the broken belt. Although he, too, believed the HANS would have saved Earnhardt even under the NASCAR report's assessment of what had happened.

"The left lap belt obviously held through much of the accident, energy was dissipated," said Downing in an interview with Deb Williams that appeared in the Aug. 30, 2001 issue of *Winston Cup Scene*. "If he'd had that HANS Device on it would have stopped a fair amount of the twist, taken a bunch out of the neck load, and may have pushed him below that threshold where he didn't die. But it's speculation."

Eventually, John Melvin became part of the solution. He was hired by NASCAR to work with Peterson to improve safety in the NASCAR cockpits. He declined public comment on the *Official Accident Report*, released shortly after he was hired and which he had no hand in. According to Hubbard, Melvin, who died in 2014, privately continued to believe head whip resulted in death and that the basal skull fracture and breaking of the belt happened simultaneously.

The process of hiring Melvin indicated that NASCAR Chairman Bill France Jr. accepted the private conclusion of hired experts that the HANS Device would have saved Earnhardt. In the immediate aftermath of the fatal crash, Melvin believed NASCAR had put him on an "enemies list," especially after the separated belt announcement. "My end of the deal was when the press started calling right after the separated belt was announced," said Melvin. "I gave what I thought was an honest evaluation. I didn't know the details, but I said the HANS would have helped. NASCAR hated that. I was on their enemies list I believe."

In August, a sudden change occurred in NASCAR's attitude toward Melvin, which he concluded resulted from his work over the years with Steve Peterson, NASCAR's technical director. NASCAR requested a meeting between Melvin and Chairman France Jr. in Daytona. "The meeting with Mr. France was very brief," said Melvin. "He was at the other end of the table. He said, 'So, Dr. Melvin, do you think a HANS would have saved Dale Earnhardt?' I said, 'Yes sir.' That was it. Then they hired me and we started talking about what do we do?"

Whatever the differences of opinion on the cause of the injury, the sheer weight of NASCAR's public presentation left the media without firm footing when it came to Earnhardt's death—or the certainty of the HANS Device as a solution. NASCAR's official expert report and differing account from that of Myers meant that saying the HANS Device would have saved Earnhardt from head whip became more a matter of speculation. For NASCAR, this also meant better liability protection against any potential lawsuit for *not* mandating the HANS.

The presentation took the wind out of the sails when it came to the media continuing to pound NASCAR on the issue of safety and the HANS Device. On the other hand, on the day of the presentation NASCAR committed to using data recorders on all cars and revamped its safety response systems at tracks to incorporate medical personnel familiar with all drivers' medical histories, two issues that reporters had focused on when comparing NASCAR to CART.

23

NASCAR Mandates HANS

BEFORE DELIVERING THE *OFFICIAL ACCIdent Report – No. 3 Car* in August, NASCAR already had plans in the works to mandate head restraints before the next visit to the Talladega Superspeedway in late October. Led by NASCAR President Mike Helton, NASCAR came to its own conclusions and what actions were needed. If 60 percent of the safety during crashes involved driver restraint and keeping the driver tightly in the seat, six-point harnesses and proper seats had to be installed in all of the competitors' cars. The HANS could reduce neck tension below fatal levels—but that outcome could be jeopardized absent proper seats and harnesses.

Earnhardt may have survived many a harrowing and severe accident with belts that were mounted incorrectly, but in this case his configuration—the lap belt being mounted on the floor approximately eight inches behind where recommended—helped to break the left side lap belt and also allowed his body to be repositioned away from the seat.

The *Official Accident Report* also made clear Earnhardt's shoulder harness had been mounted low behind the seat instead of directly at the shoulders, creating more length and stretching of the belts during an impact. His crotch belt came over the front of the seat instead of through the slot manufactured into the seat and closer to the crotch. These were all factors in the kinetics, or movement, of his body. It very likely led to what is called dynamic overshoot, adding increased head movement and thus neck tension before the belt failure.

The seat in the No. 3 car had an extension next to the driver's ribs for support, but virtually no support in the shoulder area. The lack of shoulder support became another negative factor when it came to the movement of the driver during the crash. The seven-time champion, who evidently believed belts that had some "give" or stretch in them were safer, was not the only one who had his own ideas about how seat belts should be installed and what kind of seat made him feel safe. Because NASCAR left these decisions up to drivers, many had suspect configurations in their cockpits at the time of Earnhardt's crash. On the other hand, the "dumping" of a belt, said NASCAR officials, had not previously been seen, indicative of the severity of this particular crash. That severity, meanwhile, confirmed NASCAR may have succeeded in keeping overall speeds at Daytona and Talladega in check with restrictor plates by continuing to reduce the amount of air available to engines. But restrictor plates did not have direct influence on cornering speeds, which continued to increase at the two NASCAR behemoths.

Technical Director Steve Peterson had already been leading the effort to make changes in the NASCAR garage before the *Official Accident Report* was ever finished. Afterward, he had the assistance of Melvin, keenly aware of the need for six-point harnesses to keep the pelvis in place instead of a single crotch belt in the five-point harness, the crotch belt being limited to keeping the harness centered on the body under loading as well as preventing a driver from submarining under the steering wheel. As for lap belts, they would have to be installed with mounting points directly below and slightly behind the driver's waist, according to manufacturer instructions, to prevent "dumping." Harnesses would have to be installed at shoulder height.

Head surrounds or side nets in case of side impacts were also needed, since the new model HANS Device focused on frontal impacts. Only after NASCAR had confirmed that its teams had installed properly mounted belts, head surrounds and side nets could a head and neck restraint be relied on to do its job. The formal process of educating the teams about cockpit specifications began in a meeting with drivers and other key team personnel at a country club in Davidson, North Carolina, just outside of Charlotte on the morning of the *Official Accident Report* presentation made at the Hyatt Regency in Atlanta to the media.

The sanctioning body, dependent on media coverage of its sport to generate billions in TV revenue and sponsorship dollars, had to take control of its own destiny when it came to safety, just as the FIA had done after the death of Senna. It could ill afford any further lack of credibility on safety, much less more deaths of major stars on live television in front of a viewership of as many as 17 million.

To implement its new cockpit safety procedures, NASCAR relied on Technical Director Steve Peterson. "Steve was essential to the implementation of the safety advancements of NASCAR once he was given the permission to go ahead and do that," said Hubbard. "He was the cornerstone of safety implementation in NASCAR. Steve was a hero in his ability to understand and then advocate for safety in NASCAR in this transition from recommending to requiring. He went about his business quietly and was a very important person in terms of the renaissance of racing safety in NASCAR."

Several months before NASCAR's head restraint mandate went into effect, Jeff Gordon had voluntarily worn a HANS that he believed saved his life in Charlotte in May of 2001 in a crash during the All-Star race. He used it only after Peterson made sure he had

Engineer Gideon began at General Motors before moving to NASCAR Research & Development. (Photo by MGA Research Corporation)

NASCAR Mandates HANS

The HANS that Gordon credited with saving his life at the Las Vegas Motor Speedway.
(Photo by Jim Goodroe)

the HANS properly installed in conjunction with the seat and harness.

In 2008, Peterson passed away and Gordon attended his memorial service, one of the few drivers present.

"After his untimely death, there was a memorial service for Steve," recalled Hubbard, "a gathering in Indianapolis. All the members of the safety community attended. All the drivers were invited. Jeff Gordon was the only driver I recall who showed up. Jeff and Steve had worked together in the Hendrick Motorsports organization in order to improve safety, in implementing the HANS Device, developing a seat with John Melvin's guidance. They also worked on restraint mounting points, recommendations in getting the restraints mounted to the drivers as closely as possible. And, so the belts were the best that could be had at the time. So, Jeff was sort of the poster person of racing safety."

The memorial service for Peterson took place in a room in the Pagoda of the Indianapolis Motor Speedway. "When I was standing in line to sign the book they had, I noticed that Jeff Gordon was right behind me," said Hubbard. "I shook his hand and said hello. The first thing he said to me was, 'You've saved my life twice already.' He was very grateful and was referring to a second major accident he'd had earlier that year in Las Vegas where he'd hit a wall head-on that didn't have a SAFER barrier. We ended up talking about New York City. I thought it was particularly significant that Jeff Gordon was there.

"Steve's ashes were eventually sprinkled in a ceremony at a little local dirt track in southwestern Michigan," continued Hubbard. "We gathered at Harford Speedway with John Melvin, Tom Gideon, me and Steve's family and friends, Steve's children. There was maybe 15 people there. As people do at memorial services, we said our good-byes with testimonials for

Steve and what he meant to us. His ashes were sprinkled by his brother from a vintage race car all around this little track."

In addition to investing in the "soft walls" that became the SAFER barrier, NASCAR would spend an estimated $10 million to build its new Research and Development Center in Concord, North Carolina, where a full-time staff under one roof could focus on safety—a markedly different approach than the FIA's reliance on a variety of privately-owned technical centers for safety development. And, a very different approach from the initial plan to simply remodel the Busch Series shops of Dale Jarrett after the three deaths in 2000.

The new push on safety led to state-of-the-art computer modeling; investigations of any and all crashes in its traveling series; overseeing the development of a new carbon fiber seat with better leg protection and head surrounds; the creation of the Car of Tomorrow chassis with better driver protection and crushable structures.

One more fatal stock car accident occurred in 2001. Blaise Alexander's car got turned into the wall at the Charlotte track during an ARCA race in early October and he died from a basal skull fracture, yet another confirmation that speeds on the sport's fastest tracks were were high enough to require a head restraint. Stories in a variety of media outlets subsequently concluded that Alexander's accident forced NASCAR's hand on mandates.

But NASCAR was already committed to a mandate and became the first to mandate head restraints for every race in its premier series, which included the Busch and the Truck Series, when the announcement was made in mid-October. NASCAR President Helton had set a deadline of the fall race at Talladega for the implementation of head restraints; the formal announcement of the mandate came two days prior to the event at the Alabama track.

The key issue had been properly installed harnesses, proper seats, head surrounds or side nets in all cars more so than the fatal crash of Alexander, which may have helped further persuade some of NASCAR's drivers to accept a mandate. As importantly, without the new standards for seats and restraints, the credibility of the HANS itself might be put at risk if it failed due to other problems in the cockpit. The issue of legal liability cast a long shadow in this scenario since NASCAR was being proactive.

The deadline of the mid-October Talladega race gave NASCAR enough time to prepare all its teams for the mandate in its three major series. The track itself was problematic, too. In addition to the high cornering speeds at Talladega, multi-car wrecks induced by restrictor plate racing's inevitable large packs of drafting cars posed the possibility of another Earnhardt-type incident.

A promising 25-year-old driver from Montoursville, Pennsylvania, Alexander had won three ARCA races and was leading in Charlotte at the time of his crash. He had committed to the A-B-C route (ARCA Series, Busch Series and Winston Cup) to get to the top of the stock car racing ladder when he tragically ran out of luck.

The driver of the other car in the Alexander incident was the same driver who had become the first family member to win a race after the death of his famous father. Kerry Earnhardt had won an ARCA event at the Michigan track in June of 2001 prior to his half-brother Dale Earnhardt Jr. winning the Cup race at Daytona in July.

In the ARCA race in Charlotte that fall, after contesting Alexander for the lead, the car of Earnhardt's first-born son wound up on its roof down on the apron and briefly caught fire. Fortunately, Kerry Earnhardt, without a head restraint, soon crawled out of the overturned, smoking car and sat down on the infield retaining wall to catch his breath. ARCA declared the race over due to the tragic circumstances and so few laps remaining, making Earnhardt the winner.

NASCAR had a flaw in its plan to introduce head and neck restraints at Talladega in October. Once again,

NASCAR Mandates HANS

the issue of legal liability raised its head. The sanctioning body felt it had to mandate the Hutchens device, which eventually failed to meet industry standards established by the SFI Foundation, to accommodate those drivers who continued to adamantly refuse to wear the HANS. This strategy also gave drivers a choice, which could help mute liability issues. It had been created, manufactured and introduced by a restraint engineer, Trevor Ashline, who had previously worked at Autoliv North America.

Ashline quickly dubbed his new device as the "Hutchens" after the engineer on the Richard Childress Racing team, Bobby Hutchens. The Childress engineer had nothing to do with the product itself, but had helped try to persuade Earnhardt to use it. A series of straps around the chest, waist and legs at the crotch comprised the "Hutchens", which attached to the helmet in the same location as the HANS tethers.

Autoliv provided product testing to the automotive industry and had a facility in Auburn Hills, Michigan, as well as Windsor, Ontario. The company had begun working on developing a relationship with NASCAR in 2001, an effort led by Marketing Manager Chipp Jackson, perhaps best known for the double-p in his first name. At the outset of the 2001 season, Autoliv became an associate sponsor for the Harry Melling-owned team and driver Stacy Compton. Jackson had introduced the company to reporters during the pre-season media tour in Charlotte. The company would eventually host sled testing conducted by the investigation team behind the *Official Accident Report – No. 3 Car*.

Ashline, who called his company Safety Solutions, had approached the Childress team with the hopes of resolving NASCAR's headache about the seven-time champion's stance against the HANS and head restraints. Although Childress teammate Mike Skinner elected to use the Hutchens along with Melling Racing's Compton, again Earnhardt showed no interested.

This decision by Earnhardt might have been for the best, because the Hutchens likely would not have saved him and as a result might have given the concept of head and neck restraints a serious setback. Where the HANS provided a means for the loads in a crash to move from the helmeted forehead through the tethers and the carbon fiber device to the shoulders and torso, the Hutchens provided only relatively mild resistance through straps and a negligible transfer of energy in the absence of the carbon fiber yoke and collar. (In 1979, stock car driver George White of Alabama had introduced a similar strap-like device, which also failed to recognize the need to transfer energy from the head and neck.)

While wearing a Hutchens at the Richmond International Speedway in the fall of 2002, driver Sterling Marlin suffered a broken neck. Leading the points standings at the time, the injury sidelined Marlin after a later exam discovered the injury. Marlin subsequently switched to a HANS Device.

In July of the same year, driver John Baker was killed by a basal skull fracture after a head-on collision with the wall in a Featherlite Southwest Series race while wearing a Hutchens in the NASCAR-sanctioned event at the Irwindale Speedway in California.

The Hutchens and its strap approach proved unable to reduce neck tension and shear forces below the minimum standards once testing was established in 2003 by SFI Foundation, Inc., the testing laboratory used by sanctioning bodies and safety equipment manufacturers. NASCAR dropped the Hutchens from its list of eligible head restraints in 2005 due to the failure to pass certification.

Ashline would eventually develop the carbon fiber Hybrid Pro that successfully passed SFI testing and gained FIA as well as NASCAR approval. The Hybrid Pro would prove attractive to some smaller drivers. Because it attached to the shoulders with its own chest straps as well as being held in place by a car's safety harness, the Hybrid Pro also appealed to some rally competitors, who often got out of their cars and worked on them during events.

24

SAFER Barrier Arrives

THE SAFER BARRIER BECAME ONE OF THE most significant developments already underway before Dale Earnhardt's fatal accident. Providing a more visceral view of safety in action during a major crash, the barrier often gets credit for preventing serious injury or death in dramatic incidents. More accurately, the barrier became a key element in a broader system of safety.

The arrival of the barriers did not change the original assessment made during NASCAR's investigation of Earnhardt's accident that the biggest safety gains were to be found in cockpit restraints. That crucial recognition means the vast majority of race car drivers in America, who compete on circuits without SAFER barriers, can still control their own destiny. Despite the usual presence of concrete walls, drivers can achieve a high level of safety with proper restraint systems that are well within their budgets and technical expertise.

The SAFER barrier can make the difference between life and death—as evidenced by Sebastien Bourdais' horrific crash during Indy 500 qualifying in 2017. But these barriers sometimes receive too much credit for elimination of fatalities in NASCAR or the prevention of deaths in the Indy Racing League. An important element in major league racing's safety system—one beloved by drivers due to less painful impacts when hitting walls—the barrier does not necessarily prevent basal skull fractures, according to a scientific paper authored by Tom Gideon, John Melvin and two engineers from Delphi Automotive Systems.

A team of engineers led by Dean Sicking designed the Steel And Foam Energy Reduction, or SAFER, system at the Midwest Roadside Safety Facility in Lincoln, Nebraska. A joint undertaking between the engineers based at the University of Nebraska and the Indianapolis Motor Speedway, NASCAR joined the project after the disastrous 2000 and 2001 seasons. Initially installed in the corners of IRL and NASCAR oval tracks starting in 2002, the new-style barriers helped sustain the ongoing safety campaigns in major American series. Like the HANS Device, the SAFER barrier comprised an entirely new racing invention, one dedicated solely to the sport's safety and not borrowed from an outside source.

Where they are available, the SAFER barriers make crashes more survivable during deceleration. This includes helping the cockpit safety cocoon and restraints remain intact as well as helping reduce loads on the driver. In terms of milliseconds, the slightly longer duration of a crash induced by the consistent crush rate of the SAFER barrier reduces the G-forces. Compared with traditional concrete walls, this consistent crush rate helps reduce the spike of energy being transferred to the occupant, particularly in the area of the head and neck.

The paper "ATD Neck Tension Comparisons for Various Sled Pulses" underscored the benefit of a crushable structure. Gideon, Melvin, et al, measured head/neck tension in test dummies under different crash pulses, which simulated different barrier characteristics. The tests confirmed that a more favorable "crush characteristic" in a vehicle and barrier resulted in lower neck tension. But the tension forces "are not likely to be lowered to an extent that precludes the need for

SAFER Barrier Arrives

The Indy qualifying crash of Bourdais's car into the SAFER barrier at a speed of 227 mph registered 108 Gs. (Photo by Mike Levitt)

head/neck restraint."

Would a SAFER barrier have saved Dale Earnhardt? Given the role played by neck tension according to the *Official Accident Report* by NASCAR, that seems unlikely, especially in the absence of a HANS Device. The paper by Gideon and Melvin, et al, concluded any crash with a Delta V higher than 40 mph, such as Earnhardt's, could lead to a basal skull fracture without a certified head and neck restraint, even in the presence of a SAFER barrier. In a *USA Today* article written by Mike Hembree, inventor Sicking drew no firm conclusions about the barrier and the seven-time champion's death. "I can't say that it would have prevented it, but it surely wouldn't have made it worse."

The SAFER barrier consists of eight-inch by eight-inch rectangular steel tubes welded together and strapped to existing concrete retaining walls. Bundles of polystyrene foam are placed between the barrier and wall. In addition to lowering the amount of G-loading in a crash, the barriers, built in 10-foot segments, generally do not need extensive repair after getting hit and do not send cars rebounding into oncoming cars. The barriers are, in racing parlance, "soft walls." "There's no question it reduces the G-load on the car," said Gideon, the engineer and safety expert who worked the GM Motorsports Safety Technology Research Program before moving to NASCAR R&D.

In very high-speed crashes—the airplane-type crash into a solid wall that killed Greg Moore, for example—the SAFER barrier can be critical to survival. In the 2017 crash of Bourdais at the Indianapolis Motor Speedway, it contributed to a far better outcome than would have been possible without a SAFER barrier.

Bourdais's car hit the Turn 2 SAFER barrier at 227 mph with an impact measured at 108 Gs. Through consistent crush characteristics, the SAFER barrier helped prevent catastrophic blunt trauma injuries. Dr. Steve Olvey, the longtime medical director for CART, cited the SAFER barrier, cockpit padding, the strength of the chassis used in the IRL, and the HANS as the source of a welcome outcome to Bourdais's crash.

"Bourdais's crash was survivable due to several things," said Olvey, "the main one being the SAFER barrier. Both the HANS and the head surround also played major roles in reducing the loads experienced by the driver's head and neck. The Indy cars have a very strong tub with carefully placed energy-absorbing materials."

This accident demonstrated one of the most important roles of the SAFER barrier: protecting against the deformation of the key elements in the safety cocoon of the cockpit. That might prevent the harness, seat, head surrounds and HANS Device from doing their job when a very high Delta V is encountered.

"What happens with real high Gs is you start to put (sustained) loads on some of the stuff, whether it be the seats or restraints, that are now high enough that the restraints may not survive," said Gideon. "If they break, all the restraint business is over. You always want

The SAFER barrier, his car's safety elements and the HANS saved Bourdais from critical or fatal injury. (AP Photo)

to reduce the Gs because the Delta V always plays a part in these crashes."

Some of the best evidence of the effectiveness of the cockpit restraints has occurred in high-speed NASCAR crashes where drivers' cars found sections of walls not yet fronted by the SAFER barrier on straightaways or walls at the interior of circuits. Just before the arrival of NASCAR's safety-conscious Car of Tomorrow and its major upgrades for driver protection, for example, Kyle Busch had a horrendous crash at the Talladega Superspeedway in the spring of 2007. But the safety cocoon created by NASCAR up to the time of Busch's incident held up well.

At the end of the 4,000-foot back straight, Busch's car got turned sideways and hit the outside concrete barrier (where SAFER barriers had yet to be installed) almost head-on after flipping over. His Hendrick Motorsports Chevy then slid down the track on its roof before hitting the grass adjacent to the apron. The car barrel-rolled seven times in rapid succession and came to a stop after briefly catching fire. Busch quickly emerged with his helmet and HANS Device on and walked straight to an awaiting ambulance unassisted.

An examination by personnel at NASCAR R&D discovered a crack in Busch's HANS Device, which was returned to HANS Performance Products in Atlanta for examination. The conclusion: The crack in the carbon fiber confirmed the device had done its job, absorbing the energy transferred to the driver's head and neck during the course of the violent crash without deforming to the point it did not work despite an extended series of rolls.

One of NASCAR's new generation of brilliant, tough-minded and sometimes outspoken stars continued his career without interruption.

Busch's crash at Daytona in 2015, where he found an unprotected barrier in the infield at Daytona with his Xfinity Series car, turned out differently. He didn't walk away. The head-on collision broke his foot and leg, but there were no other serious injuries. Remarkably, Busch returned that same season to win the 2015 season Sprint Cup championship. Without the restraint systems of the NASCAR-required seat, which helped keep his lower limbs in place, and the HANS Device, more than Busch's career may have been in jeopardy, not just a first championship.

No crash in NASCAR brought more energy transfer than the 2010 crash of Elliott Sadler's car into an Armco barrier fronting a dirt bank at the Pocono International Raceway, a segment of the track without a SAFER barrier. Sadler, according to an ESPN.com story by David Newton, was told by NASCAR officials that the G-force recorded was the highest for any crash since the sanctioning body began using the data boxes on cars in 2002.

The engine from Sadler's Ford was torn off its motor mounts and sat farther up the track from the remains of Sadler's Car of Tomorrow chassis. The driver credited the COT chassis, a carbon fiber seat that met NASCAR's requirements, and the HANS for his ability to walk away after regaining his breath. "I'm very thankful for that," said Sadler. "I think ten years ago in the aluminum seat and no HANS and having that same wreck we'd be maybe talking about something different now."

In 2012, when Danica Patrick made her Cup Series debut as a full-time Cup driver at Daytona in a qualifying race, her impact with the barrier at the exit of Turn 2 registered, according to a NASCAR official, at 80 Gs due to the front end of her Chevy slicing through the foam portion of the SAFER barrier. But in-car footage showed only a slight movement of Patrick's head to the right during the milliseconds of impact due to the HANS. "It felt pretty big," said Patrick of the right front corner impact. "I don't know what it looked like."

The crash looked big, too. The video replay showed the rear wheels of her Chevy lifting off the ground. The impact completely demolished the front end of her car.

Denny Hamlin, who broke his back in 2013 at the Auto Club Speedway in a head-on collision with an inside retaining wall without any SAFER barrier, became yet another example of how the required seat by NASCAR and the cockpit restraints helped transfer a tremendous load and reduced the chances of injury. Hamlin suffered a compression fracture in his lower back in the crash, but the restraint system, including the HANS, prevented any other injuries.

Perhaps no driver visually demonstrated the benefit of the HANS better than Michael McDowell. In 2010, he hit the SAFER barrier at the Texas Motor Speedway in Turn 1 at approximately 185 mph, then slid down the track and hit the wall a second time before his Toyota flipped eight times. McDowell walked away and later did media interviews with a cap pulled low over his forehead.

He had suffered a significant "HANS bruise"—indicative of the device doing its job in a crash where the SAFER barrier could not sufficiently reduce G-forces below an injurious level. "I did have a bruise all the way across my forehead where your hat line would be," recalled McDowell, "a bruise from the HANS working, stopping the acceleration of my head going forward. For a few days, it looked like somebody beat me up pretty bad."

25

F1 Mandates HANS

IN THE CLOSING STAGES OF THE 2003 BRAZILian Grand Prix, Fernando Alonso could not avoid seeing the double yellow flags waving at each of the marshal stands, which signaled trouble on the track. But the Spaniard kept pushing. Running third on the Interlagos circuit, where rain had played havoc and caused crashes throughout the race, the 21-year-old sensation held third place aboard his Renault and decided to ignore the yellow flags.

His ill-fated attempt to gain ground despite the double yellow flags flying led to Alonso hitting an errant wheel from the accident of Mark Webber. "I thought the accident had happened behind me, because I was close to the end of the lap," said Alonso. He would indeed finish third, but under very unusual circumstances. Officials ended the race after a red flag occasioned by Alonso's accident, resulting in the Spaniard securing his podium finish while riding in an ambulance.

It was the third race since the HANS Device had finally been mandated in Formula 1, three seasons after being ratified by the sport's Safety Commission. This mandate turned out to be very fortunate for Alonso.

Webber's heavy crash had occurred in the final, high-speed bend just before the entrance to the pit road. At the outer edge of a debris field, Alonso's Renault hit one of the wheels torn from Webber's Jaguar. The high-arched nose of the Renault had its right front wheel nearly ripped off, making Alonso a passenger unable to steer or brake. In a full, frontal impact, the car walloped the barriers on the left, which jutted out just before the entrance to pit road. The Renault then careened across the track into the outside wall. Alonso climbed from the car and gingerly laid himself down by the wall.

Alonso may have survived without a HANS Device by virtue of hitting his helmeted head on the steering wheel or against the surrounding cockpit. But the enormity of the incident suggested otherwise.

Dr. Dino Altmann, the physician who treated Alonso, said the driver would have been seriously hurt without the HANS Device. "I believe we would have had a couple of heavily injured drivers that Sunday without HANS," said Altmann, referring to an earlier "vector type" crash involving Jenson Button at Turn 3. The following day, Alonso pronounced himself fit for the upcoming race at Imola and praised the HANS for contributing to a good outcome.

The Brazilian Grand Prix had been preceded by nine months of resistance to the HANS from the F1 drivers, during which almost half of the series' 20 drivers spoke unfavorably of the FIA's mandate calling for a head and neck restraint. But in the case of Alonso, the effectiveness of the HANS in helping a driver leave a wrecked car with minor injuries after a major impact became self-evident. Alonso's accident also underscored the fact the HANS, in his case made by his Renault team, stood up under multiple impacts, and that this passive device did not cause unexpected injuries.

Getting drivers and teams to accept the HANS became a final piece of the complete overhaul of safety in F1 conducted by President Max Mosley that began with the creation of the Expert Advisory Group chaired

Jordan's Giancarlo Fisichella in an FIA-spec HANS. Lack of contour in legs, 40-degree collar presented problems.
(Photo by James Penrose)

by Professor Sidney Watkins after the black weekend at Imola in 1994.

"When the Watkins group was first set up," wrote Mosley in an article that appeared in the 2011 issue of *IQ* magazine, "I suggested it study the work being done by governments on road safety. With tens of thousands of deaths being recorded on public roads in Western Europe each year, it seemed obvious that massive amounts of research would be backing up efforts to reduce casualties and improve safety.

"To our astonishment," continued Mosley's article, "we found very little was being done. Crash testing according to then-current European Union requirements (unchanged since 1974) was primitive; a car could pass despite abysmal performance in a real-life accident. Worse, the relatively modest proposals for improvement, particularly from researchers in the UK and Sweden, were being systematically diluted in Brussels by car industry lobbyists. Safety added costs and the car industry believed it didn't sell cars."

Mosley saw an opportunity. If the FIA could establish better construction standards for road cars and then point to F1 as a source for the funding and technology, the type of political criticism that had raged after Ayrton Senna's death could be entirely blunted. Given that F1 produced the largest amount of income by far among the FIA's many world championships, this safety push could help build a political fence around the sport going forward. Pushing road car construction standards and improved conditions for safe travel in general meant the FIA officials would also constantly be in contact with politicians around the world, another means of buffering any future criticism of professional racing.

Mosley was taking the FIA back to its roots as an international federation of car clubs that promoted best practices in automotive transportation and a wide variety of universal standards, such as tire sizing. The FIA's new initiative to evaluate the structural integrity of road cars created a comprehensive set of standards for car construction called the European New Car Assessment Program (known as NCAP). Although not legally binding, these standards put pressure on manufacturers to improve practices in new car construction by grading their vehicles using a star system (five stars being the best). Despite initial protest from the automotive industry and infighting, with help from key executives like Louis Schweitzer, then chairman of Renault, the NCAP standards were eventually accepted as legitimate by European automakers. They replaced a patchwork of testing programs and complemented the improvements in highway automobile construction that had previously been called for by the European Parliament.

By generating technology and standards for safety, the FIA had an answer to those who might declare F1 and motor racing in general to be useless, too dangerous or lacking in moral value or purpose. The FIA could suggest, with some real evidence, that thousands of people a year were being saved from serious injury or death due to the NCAP standards for car construction.

Next, a sudden jump in load requirements for F1 cars starting on Jan. 1, 2001, demonstrated how technology in F1 could lead to improvement in automotive construction and safety. The new standards for F1 chassis were extraordinary. The lateral load capacity requirement for the rear roll structure of the F1 cars increased fourfold, from 1.2 tons to 5 tons. The loads that would be tested on a longitudinal basis went from 4.5 tons to 6 tons and from 6 to 9 tons when it came to vertical load tests.

By dramatically increasing the structural integrity of the cars, these new standards would place fresh emphasis on the protection in the cockpit area, considered the most important line of defense for driver safety.

The HANS Device played a significant role in this safety push. The extraordinary strength and load bearing capacity of the new generation of F1 chassis were not enough. Cockpit restraints were crucial to preventing head and neck injuries to drivers.

Initially, the FIA left the challenge of getting the HANS into cockpits in the hands of the ten F1 teams and their 20 drivers racing in 2001. The teams made stabs at creating a head restraint according to the specification paper issued by the FIA, but few made building their own version of a HANS that worked in terms of comfort for their drivers a priority. Drivers, who performed at incredibly high levels of competency under great pressure in terms of money and prestige, were more than willing to accept the risk of racing without the strange new device. As CART's Steve Olvey pointed out, like any high-performance athletes they were highly sensitive to changes in their established routines.

In his book *Aussie Grit*, F1 driver Mark Webber describes a litany of steps he would go through prior to the start of each Grand Prix race, including always

Penrose, holding the helmet and HANS of Montoya, helped ease tensions in F1 about the mandate.
(Photo by Anti Puskala)

'Prof' Watkins stands proudly with first two drivers to wear a HANS, Sauber's Massa (left) and Heidfeld.
(Photo by James Bearne for LAT Images)

getting into the car from the left; checking the belts first, then going for a pee before climbing back in.

By the time of the start, Webber wrote, there's not much opportunity for a driver to feel comfortable. "You are strapped into a space barely big enough to contain you in the first place. You can scarcely move except for your feet, arms, hands. The headrest comes in pretty snugly around you; down goes the visor, the radio sits about three millimeters off your lips, earplugs in, drink tube coming in beside the radio… and the sensation of enclosure is heightened even more. With that comes stress and elevated heart rate, which goes up because of the pressure on your ribcage; you can't breathe normally as you would when standing or running or riding a bike, you're in quite a different position."

Frustrated by the teams' and drivers' unwillingness to take up the HANS, Watkins turned to the Open Cockpit Research Group he had formed, which included experts from around the world. In 2002, one year before Alonso's accident, Watkins invited Terry Trammell, a member of the group and one of CART's medical experts most familiar with the HANS, to support the push for mandatory use of the HANS by having him make a presentation to all drivers at the Interlagos circuit in Brazil about the device and how it worked. Given that this would help save future two-time champion Alonso from critical injury—or worse—at the same circuit the following season, Trammell's visit proved prophetic.

Reinforcing the FIA's own research with the real-world experience of Indy car racing by the presentation in Brazil, Trammell's talk included the video he called "Olive Verte," or green olive. Using an olive on a toothpick, it demonstrated how the head kept moving at high velocity when a harnessed driver and race car came to a sudden stop.

Teams were given enough time to test and develop their own devices, but little had come of it by the end of 2002, although seven teams had each built their own versions of the HANS under an agreement made between HANS Performance Products and the FIA. In September of 2002 at Monza, Felipe Massa and Nick Heidfeld each wore head and neck restraints built by Sauber. A beaming Watkins was photographed standing beside the two drivers with their HANS Devices sitting on their shoulders while in the garage at Monza. Massa became the first F1 driver to wear a HANS in a race, but Heidfeld declined to compete with it.

Jenson Button, driving for Renault that year, became one of many drivers who had a garden variety of complaints when experimenting with the HANS. "I can do about one lap with it and my arms ache," he

146

Crash! How the HANS Helped Save Racing

said. "It is very strange. Whatever we have tried with it, it has been the same."

Others, such as Jacques Villeneuve, seemed spooked by the device. Villeneuve vigorously attacked the HANS after a heavy crash in practice for the Japanese Grand Prix in October of 2002, declaring himself glad he didn't have one on. "My body would have moved and the HANS device would have stayed where it was," he said. "It would have dug into my neck. It could break your backbone. I think there are some situations where you could get hurt by the HANS."

For the most part, F1 drivers had legitimate complaints. The HANS had been developed in CART by the method of a "plug" tailor-made and sculpted for each driver and then used to make a mold at HANS Performance Products, which custom-built the device. Limited by distance and long-established cultural barriers such as teams making every piece used on their cars, HPP had little access to F1 teams.

In CART, drivers were finding successful fits with devices that had a range of the degrees of collar angle at the back. The "plug" method also helped Jerry "Rabbit" Lambert, who was making the devices at Downing Atlanta, to further improve the always tricky element of getting a hard carbon fiber part to be comfortable across the shoulders, chest and collarbones. Lambert ingeniously figured out how to make a generic form from the variety of custom-fitted HANS Devices made for CART drivers, one that would comfortably fit a wide variety of body types using pads, which had always been part of the fitting and comfort scheme.

This resulted in the Model III, a generic version of the device that offered a better universal fit. The Model III, which was designated as "RP" for its use by reclining drivers, came with 20-degree, 30-degree or 40-degree angles on the collar—to be used according to the size and build of the driver. Meanwhile, the FIA's specifications given to F1 teams based on the Model II to build their own bespoke versions called for only a 40-degree angle and legs that were noticeably lacking in contour.

FIA President Mosley kept abreast of events taking place in motor racing around the world, particularly in CART, which had been a potential rival to the F1 World Championship. After CART teams had begun using the HANS Device for all races in 2002, Mosley recognized that they could be adapted for F1. "Our position is very simple," said Mosley, referring to the season-opening Australian Grand Prix of 2003. "You don't have to wear a HANS Device. But you won't leave the pit lane in Melbourne unless you do."

During the 2003 season's first joint F1 test session at Barcelona, Watkins got in touch with Jim Downing and insisted that he go to Spain to help quell any remaining rebellion against head restraints. "I was at the Autosport International show in England," said Downing. "Sid Watkins found me and said that I had to get on the plane to Barcelona and help the drivers. So that's what I did."

Downing had with him some of the Model III HANS that had been developed in CART, including devices with 20-degree and 30-degree angles intended for drivers who raced in a reclining position and meant for display at the Autosport show. He was met at the Barcelona airport by James Penrose, a representative for Arai helmets whom Watkins had asked on short notice to help with the process of getting drivers comfortable with the HANS. Because fitting drivers with helmets often required hands-on assistance from a factory rep, Penrose knew the drivers and was accustomed to the demands of making sure they were comfortable by listening to their worries, pinpointing areas of discomfort and resolving issues.

Penrose soon got down to the basis of the problem drivers and teams had been experiencing in the two years since the announcement that the HANS would be required. The majority of the teams had manufactured their own devices, including Williams, Ferrari, McLaren, Jordan, Jaguar, Renault and Sauber. But only two teams, Renault and Sauber, had made the effort to get their devices homologated by the FIA according to its testing specifications. As it turned out, their designs provided proper fit for their drivers and were used for several seasons, because the teams had made a concerted effort to make the device comfortable for their drivers.

Most devices, it seemed, were being designed according to the FIA's technical specs without deviation. Many teams, including Ferrari, ended up with devices with 40-degree collars, where less angle at the back would have been preferable. Confusion about the rear collar angle and the need for contour in the legs resulted in legitimate concerns about the comfort of the HANS and how it affected driving. Villeneuve, for one, had a short neck, which required the right collar angle for him to wear the device comfortably.

Penrose described the dilemma for many of the drivers. "Sit yourself slouched low on a sofa, hold your arms out horizontally in front of you as though on a steering wheel and press your chin down on your chest," he said. "Then pull your chin back as far as you can, tight to your chest, and—keeping your chin there—see how much you can see over where the steering wheel would be. Hold yourself for a few minutes there and see how bloody uncomfortable it is. That is a description of using a 40-degree head restraint where you really need a 30-degree."

At his initial test as a HANS representative in Barcelona, Penrose first went to the Williams team's garage. "Williams had been trying all sorts of 'homemade by Williams' HANS constructions," he said. "As I went into the garage an enraged Juan Pablo Montoya screamed, 'I'm not using that fucking thing again!' and threw it across the garage, into the wall." Montoya had driven in CART through the year 2000 when teams and drivers were preparing for the mandate on ovals in 2001. But he had switched to F1 and Williams for the 2001 season. His subsequent experience with the HANS at Williams apparently did not turn out successfully.

A quick study with tutelage from Downing on how to get a HANS to fit comfortably, Penrose later returned to the Williams garage. "I'd known JPM for some time," said Penrose of the driver who had competed in the FIA's F3000 series before migrating to CART. "So, I left him alone a while. Later, things were a bit calmer and I asked him to use a standard HANS from the U.S. I adjusted the tethers, adjusted the padding and his seat belts angles and so forth.

"He went out on a long run—maybe 30 laps, came in, got out of the car and started talking to his race engineer. He still had the HANS on so I tapped him on the shoulder and said 'Was this thing OK this time?' he looked mystified and suddenly realized he'd had it on."

For the second test at Barcelona in the final week of February, it was Hubbard who met Penrose in Barcelona, bringing with him 20-degree, 30-degree and 40-degree Model III devices for those drivers unable to get comfortable due to their physique, seating position or cockpit arrangement. He also brought inflatable pads.

"Schumacher had tried the Ferrari-built device at first," said Hubbard. "It was the wrong shape for the human body. It was a toss-up whether the 30-degree or 40-degree would work better for him. I had also made up some air pressure devices for use as a cushion underneath the legs of the HANS. It was an air bladder with an adjustable valve and pressure could be changed using a coffee stirring stick. The air bladder would lift the device off the shoulders."

"I put a Model 30 with an air pad on Schumacher," continued Hubbard. "The device needed to be put on so that it didn't touch anything that would push it out of position. It needed some wiggle room in the cockpit.

"Michael did ten laps and came back to the garage. I kind of tricked him and didn't seek him out. But after a while, he was sitting in the car and I caught his eye. He said, 'HANS? Oh yes, feels pretty good.' When he said that, it was a home run. He had worn it for ten laps and didn't even notice it."

Penrose said that once comfortable, the defending World Champion Schumacher individually called other drivers to inform them of his experience. "At the end of the day he said, 'OK, it's OK, it works, thank you' and got out his mobile phone. There and then he called all his driver friends in F1 and said, 'The HANS is OK, it works, get on with it and work with James.' Call after call after call." (How sadly ironic that Schumacher would suffer a critical head injury while skiing during his retirement.)

Villeneuve practically seethed when Hubbard approached him in the garage at Barcelona with devices in hand. "Jacques was in a baggy driving suit like he always wore," said Hubbard. "He started coming at me. He was not looking forward to competing with the HANS on, he told me. I was there to help. So, I told him, 'I don't want to argue with you. I'm here to help.' I got him set up pretty quickly and there weren't any more problems."

Although six different models of the HANS had to be made and homologated prior to the opening round—an effort coordinated by Penrose through HANS Performance Products—the 2003 season began with every driver wearing a HANS Device on the starting grid at Melbourne. But after crashing his Ferrari midway in the race, Barrichello blamed the HANS. "It was really hurting me and I lost concentration," he said. "Even if I had not gone off, I would have struggled to get to the end of the race." The air cushion supporting the carbon fiber legs had deflated, putting painful pressure on Barrichello's collarbone. (Penrose had offered the Ferrari team use of inflatable pads with stronger material that he had manufactured on his own in Italy, but initially he got turned down.)

Barrichello raced without a HANS after getting a medical dispensation for the season's second round in Malaysia, much to Watkins' consternation and dismay. Worse, Justin Wilson, driving for Jaguar, made a trip to the hospital after the Malaysian race due to arms battered throughout the race when his shoulder belts slipped off the HANS, leaving him to be tossed around the cockpit, which banged his shoulders and arms enough to have him in acute pain after the race.

With an eye toward mandating the HANS in other FIA-sanctioned world championships, the FIA had required HANS to establish licensees who could construct the HANS and sell them directly to customers under a royalty agreement with HPP. The two companies selected by Hubbard and Downing were safety equipment manufacturers: Stand 21, located in France; and Schroth, which manufactured its harnesses and other safety equipment in Germany.

Schroth, among others, had already manufactured dual "over under" shoulder belts for the HANS that Hubbard and John Melvin had suggested to the company. "The double harness belt came out of a discussion between John and me about the function of the belts," said Hubbard. "David Coulthard, when he got his HANS, said he wanted his belts level with his shoulders. Before that, he wore them a little below the shoulder level. Adding the HANS added another inch vertically or so and it didn't hold him down in the seat well enough and he couldn't work the pedals. So, we kept the body harness mounting point slightly below the shoulders in the back. That was the belt that cinched the driver into place. Then a second belt from the same mounting point came on top of that to hold the HANS in place. This method worked fine."

The "over under" shoulder harness, already in use by Coulthard, resolved the issues for Barrichello and Wilson. For his part, Mosley made it clear prior to the season's third race in Brazil that no driver would be granted a medical dispensation.

The HANS-equipped Barrichello—now using sturdier pads—was leading aboard his Ferrari in the closing stages in Brazil before a fuel issue surfaced. His performance confirmed that a properly fitted HANS did not interfere with performance. But Alonso's crash became far more persuasive than any argument doctors, engineers and rule makers could make about the HANS.

None other than Montoya cast a decisive vote on the HANS a short while after the Brazilian race. During his CART days, Montoya had told team owner Chip Ganassi that he was worried he would survive a crash as a cripple due to the HANS, and would not be able to continue racing. He preferred death to that outcome. But he came to a different conclusion once in F1.

Two weeks after the Brazilian Grand Prix, he

F1 Mandates HANS

Kubica's double impact during the Canadian Grand Prix in 2007 gave his Sauber chassis and HANS a major test. (Photos by Peter Nygaard)

had a major crash into tire barriers at Becketts while testing the Williams-BMW at the Silverstone circuit. The Williams had spun quickly, then skimmed across a gravel trap and hit the tire barrier head-on with enough force to trap the car underneath it. Both of the front wheels and suspensions were torn off, but thanks to the FIA-mandated strength of the chassis the nose remained intact. Once extracted after ten minutes, Montoya walked away with a slight limp. "The HANS helped," said Montoya, which marked the final turning of the tide when it came to public discussion by drivers of the new device.

It was in 2004 that Felipe Massa's high-speed impact with a tire barrier during the Canadian Grand Prix again confirmed the value of the HANS and Sauber's own head restraint design. After a suspension failure in his Sauber-Petronas, the Brazilian went straight off entering the Hairpin and hit the tire barriers with an impact that measured 113 Gs.

"If he hadn't been wearing a HANS and had all the latest gear in place, he'd have probably hit the steering wheel very substantially," said Mosley. "The impact would have been in excess of what we believe to be the limit for injury, in fact. So, we think he might have been badly hurt or possibly worse." Massa walked away with a minor elbow injury.

At the end of the 2004 season, Watkins retired from his position as the safety and medical delegate for F1, succeeded by Dr. Gary Hartstein. Before departing his race weekend duties Watkins, who would continue as the president of the FIA Institute for Motor Sport Safety and Sustainability, saw firsthand his push for the HANS prove to be crucial for driver safety in incidents, including a 76 G impact by Ralf Schumacher in his Williams-BMW at Indianapolis following a spin on the track's oval segment.

It was at the Circuit Gilles Villeneuve in Montreal in 2007 where the HANS got its ultimate test in F1 and, according to experts at the scene, saved the life of Robert Kubica. Driving a Sauber-BMW and coming into the hairpin section, the Polish driver's front wing contacted the rear wheel of Jarno Trulli, sending the Sauber out of control and off the track. The excursion lifted the front wheels of the Sauber, which hit an unprotected concrete barrier head-on at 145 mph. The car barrel-rolled across to the opposite side, hitting the concrete barrier there at the rear, which nearly brought Kubica up and out of the cockpit. The car came to rest on its side with no wheels or suspension fully attached. The driver walked away with minor injuries and only a slight concussion kept him out of the following U.S. Grand Prix.

Replying to the media after the incident, Peter Wright, the president of the FIA Safety Commission, said a variety of factors influenced the safe outcome, starting with the improved strength of F1 monocoques. "If you asked me to list the factors that had a direct influence on Robert's accident," he told Automotive, the FIA-published magazine, "I'd say the following: the extremely strong survival cell, the restraint system, the front and side impact structures, the high cockpit sides with padded head rest, the new high-spec carbon helmet and the HANS device."

Watkins observed the incident and thought the driver would at least be unconscious. He heard a different story from the medical crew who responded to the incident. "He was cracking Polish jokes as they were lifting him out," the crew informed the Professor, who himself enjoyed humor as often as possible. Watkins, among many others, acknowledged the HANS saved the life of the driver in a subsequent issue of *IQ*, the FIA Institute's quarterly magazine.

Once Mercedes-Benz had completed its research led by Hubert Gramling in 1998, the presence of HANS in F1 came down to the persistent work of Mosley, Watkins and Wright against the usual tide of antagonism toward new approaches to safety and legitimate complaints occasioned by the missteps when it came to the importance of individually fitting the HANS. Without the HANS, drivers would have continued to unnecessarily risk critical or fatal head and neck injuries, despite all the other progress made in F1 safety.

26

Weekend Warriors: Living Dangerously

IN THE DECADE AFTER THE MAJOR SANCtioning bodies began mandating head and neck restraints, a sharp contrast developed between the upper reaches of professional motor racing and the broad middle of the sport where weekend warriors competed. Head and neck restraints were far less likely to be mandated when it came to weekend warriors, particularly in the U.S. when compared with international racing.

In the decade after Dale Earnhardt's death, a study conducted by the *Charlotte Observer* showed an increase in deaths among drivers on short tracks and drag strips in the U.S. at the same time the major leagues were becoming safer. A study conducted by Simpson Performance Products concluded that 34 of those deaths on short tracks and drag strips may have been prevented by the use of a head and neck restraint.

Three major problems arose when it came to persuading weekend warriors to use head restraints on short tracks and drag strips. Drivers worried about the cost of devices—despite relatively large outlays of cash for racing vehicles, tires, engines and transport vehicles. Many believed drivers only needed a head restraint for events where speeds are extraordinary such as on super speedways or in drag races featuring the high-end professional classes. Or, just the faster classes on short tracks.

A third, familiar problem arose. In addition to balking at costs and a belief they didn't really need one, many weekend warriors didn't like the idea of changing their cockpits and routines to accommodate a head restraint.

Sanctioning bodies, meanwhile, were sensitive to drivers' refusal to wear head restraints—because in the minor leagues of racing a driver could always elect to move to another series or track. Car counts often ruled the decisions of sanctioning bodies and race track promoters more than safety. As a result, sanctioning bodies used recommendations and looked for volunteer usage. The issue of liability hovered in the background as always.

When it came to isolated fatal incidents on dusty dirt tracks and little-known ovals or drag strips, the media pressure on minor league events went missing when compared with coverage of major series. Yet, the regularity of deadly incidents at these tracks, including young teenagers, confirmed weekend warriors were fast enough to need improved safety.

By contrast, fatal crashes after the tipping point of Earnhardt's death were notably reduced between 2001 and 2018 for the world's major series. In America, this included the Indy Racing League, CART (later renamed Champ Car in 2004 before it merged with the IRL in 2008), and NASCAR's three major traveling series.

With four fatal crashes, Indy cars and their open cockpits remained an outlier. Tony Renna was killed at

Indianapolis when his car got above the wall and hit the catch fence in a testing accident in 2003. Paul Dana died in a crash at the Homestead-Miami Speedway in 2006. Also killed in a car that hit the fencing above the wall like Renna, Dan Wheldon died at the Las Vegas Motor Speedway in 2011. Justin Wilson was killed when debris from another car struck him in his open cockpit during the IRL event at Pocono in 2015.

F1 witnessed two deaths, including the crash of Maria de Villota, who died of a head injury in 2013 after her car and helmet hit a truck parked near the pits at an airfield being used for testing in 2012. Jules Bianchi's car went off track and underneath a trackside safety vehicle during the Japanese Grand Prix in 2014. He succumbed to his head injury the following year. (In a third fatal accident in an FIA series related to open cockpits, Henry Surtees was killed when hit by a tire and wheel from another competitor's car in a Formula 2 race in 2009.)

NASCAR had no fatalities in its three major professional traveling series from 2001 through the 2018 seasons.

In addition to personal regard for the drivers, commercial success—which made the major series vulnerable to corporate partners, TV partners and the political realm—helped forge the unprecedented new appreciation for safety in the major leagues. Vigilance by sanctioning bodies in the U.S. in terms of circuits and tracks, the SAFER barrier, car construction and driver safety equipment resulted in an admirable record on safety, although a move to install protective windscreens on IRL cars to prevent head injuries continued to meet resistance after Wilson's death. Meanwhile, F1 introduced halos for its open cockpits in 2018 in the wake of the deaths of de Villota, Bianchi and Surtees as well as earlier incidents involving debris.

In addition to the age-old tactic of keeping top-end and cornering speeds in check, the same new technology accessed to make cars perform better also helped improve safety in the major leagues.

Material technology alone accounted for major changes. The FIA's leveraging of the minimum strength for chassis, the HANS Device and a new full-body seat that went into use in NASCAR's Cup series all depended on the effective use of carbon fiber. Padding introduced in cockpits absorbed energy far more efficiently. The construction of barrier systems for FIA events and the SAFER barrier introduced on American ovals as well as selected locations on road circuits meant applying rational approaches to absorbing energy during crashes with existing materials such as rubber, plastic, tires, foam and steel.

Digital technology also came into play. For 2018, NASCAR installed miniature cameras in the cockpits of its Cup series cars, activated in a crash just like data recorders. The object: observe all the details of a driver's movement in a cockpit during an incident.

For a number of years, it almost became standard procedure to talk about the value of head restraints in the upper echelons. In F1, Heiki Kovalainen symbolized the new generation of drivers and attitudes after a 125-mph crash into a barrier when his McLaren suffered a front wheel failure at the Circuit de Catalunya in Barcelona in 2008. "When you stop that suddenly," he said, "your head still wants to carry on moving forward. Without the support and protection of the HANS, you're going to damage your spine and neck. There's potential for huge injury. So, I'm glad I had my HANS."

The HANS proved decisive in other forms of international racing. Mike Rockenfeller literally drove his Audi R18 prototype through the barrier at the Le Mans circuit during the night in 2011 after an incident with a GT competitor's Ferrrari at one of the fastest points on the circuit. Rockenfeller got out and walked away from a completely destroyed Audi chassis—in fact safety crews initially could not locate him in the darkness. "The safety standards are simply enormous and have saved my life," he said. "I've never had such an accident in my life and hope that I'll never have such an experience again." Absent the strength of the car and the properly installed restraint system in the cockpit of his Audi, including the seat, harness, head surround and

Weekend Warriors: Living Dangerously

HANS Device, Rockenfeller may not have had another opportunity to race.

Le Mans later became the scene of a death from a neck injury despite a driver wearing a HANS Device. In 2013, Danish driver Allan Simonsen died from a broken C1 vertebra after his Aston Martin hit a barrier that was backed by a large tree at the entrance to the public road portion of the track. His car underwent consecutive right front corner, right rear corner impacts into Armco that remained rigid due to the tree behind it. The dual impacts and sudden stop resulted in a deadly vector of energy.

While there was no official information available from the organizing Automobile Club de L'Ouest, the following year officials forbade teams from using any kind of flexible cords in conjunction with shoulder harnesses to enable quicker driver exchanges during the endurance race featuring three competitors per car. Evidently, the shoulder harness allowed Simonsen to slip out of it during the crash and his helmeted head missed the seat's head surround.

Indy car racing offered the best view of the performance of the HANS due to the presence of full-time safety crews. The ongoing efforts continued to generate a valuable database from crashes followed by scientific papers. The International Council of Motorsports Sciences, which Steve Olvey and Terry Trammell helped organize along with McGill University's Dan Marisi and Jacques Dallaire, continued to be a primary source of safety information for the industry and participants.

Despite so much awareness about safety in the upper reaches of motor racing, in the ten years after Earnhardt's death, short track racers and drag racers in the U.S. experienced a different fate as reported by the *Charlotte Observer*. The *Observer* conducted two 10-year studies, one before the fatal crash at Daytona and one afterward for the years 2001 to 2011. How does one

With weekend warriors in mind, HPP cut the price in half for its head restraint with the injection-molded Sport Series.
(Photo by HANS Performance Products)

explain the over-all increase in fatalities in American motor racing in the ten years after Earnhardt's death than in the ten years before it?

The deaths increased significantly. According to the *Observer's* study, from 1991 to 2001 driver deaths from crashes in the U.S. numbered 144. During the ten-year period after Earnhardt's death, the total rose to 171, an *increase* of 27 driver fatalities due to racing accidents.

Of the fatalities from crashes in all forms of racing in the U.S. in the second ten-year period, 126, or 73 percent, resulted from crashes on small ovals and drag strips commonly used by part-time sportsman drivers as well as professionals. This was a dramatic increase of 27 percent when compared with the 99 drivers who suffered fatal injuries in crashes on these types of tracks in the ten years before Earnhardt died.

Weekend warriors, as evidenced by the statistics, faced two safety problems. The technology available, including off-the-shelf "crate engines" that delivered better horsepower, continued to improve and so did speeds. The knowledge about what made cars faster in the major leagues of NASCAR, drag racing and open-wheel cars inevitably trickled down to the minor leagues of racing. In addition to crate engines, the knowledge of how to make a chassis stiffer or more rigid were primary sources of better cornering—or straight-line speed for drag racers. But the corresponding safety of the cars did not necessarily keep up with the increases in speed and performance. And, there were no SAFER barriers in the minor leagues.

Even without SAFER barriers, drivers had a practical choice when it came to head and neck restraints. But given the increase in deaths on short tracks and drag strips, it became evident that weekend warriors—like the professionals before them—resisted the use of certified head restraints that might have saved their lives.

In 2012, Simpson Performance Products released a white paper entitled "Death at the Track," based on the *Observer* study. It found that a significant number of deaths could have been prevented by the proper use of a certified head restraint. Part of that report, written for Simpson Performance Products by this author, is reprinted here:

> "In reviewing the crashes in this ten-year period, we estimate as many as 27 percent of the deaths on drag strips and small ovals, or a total of 34 fatalities, could have been prevented by the use of certified Head and Neck Restraints.
>
> "To reach this conclusion, we used the anecdotal reporting, which included police, coroner and medical examiner reports listed in the Observer's study. We focused on descriptions of the accidents where the cause was reported as a broken neck or head injury. Further, we used the criteria of an initial frontal or offset impact as the critical element in the crash.
>
> "In addition, where the *Observer's* descriptions were limited to such descriptions as 'hit wall' or 'head injury,' where possible we documented the precise nature of the injury and cause of death by contacting the county coroner or the presiding medical examiner."
>
> "Although we make no claims to scientific reconstruction of these accidents, we think it's fair to use the cause of death in the case of head and neck injuries to apply our experience and conclude where a certified Head and Neck Restraint likely would have prevented the fatal injury when used in a vehicle with a proper chassis, seat, helmet, head surround or side nets and safety harness."

STATISTICS WERE NOT NECESSARY TO persuade weekend warriors about the risks they were taking. Participants often knew a driver could be killed despite the relatively lower speeds compared with major league events. Many of these hardy souls acknowledged as much in their own comments about their love of the sport and dedication to it. Drivers sometimes articulated the possibility of being killed as worth the risk. Defying the odds by beating an entire field of cars while liter-

Weekend Warriors: Living Dangerously

Proper cockpit safety equipment such as window, side nets and enclosed seats with head surrounds are available to all weekend warriors. (Photo by Jay Braxton)

ally risking one's own mortality remained part of the fundamental appeal.

Sports Illustrated writer Lars Anderson wrote a feature on racing safety that appeared in May of 2014 looking back on the particularly unlucky fate of two friends who raced Dwarf cars on the Fernley Speedway, a dirt oval in Nevada. Leroy Kay and Dave Richardson had confided to friends that they would rather die in a race car than quit and both ended up getting killed because of head and neck injuries in the same incident.

Kay had confided to his girlfriend, "If I have to die, I sure hope it's in a race car and not some drawn-out thing in a hospital." Richardson had expressed a similar sentiment to a friend. "I'll die on the track before I quit racing."

The Dwarf cars that became popular vehicles for fans and competitors on dirt tracks in the western U.S. were capable of a top speed of 130 miles per hour in the best circumstances due to their small size and light weight. On a Saturday night in May of 2013, Kay and Richardson were involved in a late-race accident where their cars collided. They were pronounced dead at the track from blunt head trauma by medical personnel after a helicopter from a Reno hospital arrived.

It turned out that Richardson owned a HANS Device, but did not wear it the night of his accident, because he considered it too restrictive and said he couldn't see while wearing it. His wife Kari regretted that decision, according to the story by Anderson. "I can't help but think the HANS could have saved his life," she said. "They should be mandatory at these races." Her next comment summed up one of the key benefits of head restraints—the value to other family members. "I have good days and bad. Saturdays are the worst. Those were his racing days. I'll never get over this."

The *Sports Illustrated* story, among other accounts, confirmed an ongoing pattern when it came to head injuries in situations where the use of head and neck restraints remained voluntary and some drivers wore them and others declined—even when they owned one. The age-old problem initially faced in CART, NASCAR and F1 was replayed. The devices were not always easy to fit, took some getting used to initially, and in the absence of peers using one or a mandate, some drivers declined to take the necessary steps to wearing a head and neck restraint, whether a HANS or others on the market.

Three years prior to the double-fatality at the Fernley track in Nevada, a similar story unfolded in a different form of racing at the Nelson Ledges Road Course in Garrettsville, Ohio, where John Metzger was killed by a frontal crash. Driving a C Sports Racing prototype, a regular class in Sports Car Club of America racing, he had a frontal impact that severely damaged the chassis. The cause of death: a basal skull fracture. A family member later acknowledged that Metzger had a HANS Device sitting in his truck the day of the accident. (In 2012, the SCCA mandated SFI specification 38.1 head and neck restraints for competitors in all of its road racing classes.)

By contrast, less than a month after Metzger's crash, veteran road racer and HANS user Greg Pickett limped away from a crash in his sports prototype at the Mid-Ohio Sports Car Circuit, about 100 miles from the Nelson Ledges course. "The HANS probably saved my life," said Pickett, who suffered a compression fracture to one of his lower lumbar vertebra and broken ribs at the American Le Mans Series event, where the sanctioning body required an SFI specification 38.1 head and neck restraint. Pickett's crash occurred at the precise location where Patrick Jacquemart's fatal accident had taken place 29 years earlier, which had prompted Downing to ask the significant question about head and neck injuries.

Two years after Pickett's crash, Downing himself crashed at Mid-Ohio in his C Sports Racer on the same straight leading to this corner due to a rear wing failure. His car flipped and dug into rain-soaked grass alongside the track. The roll hoop collapsed, but Downing escaped more serious head and neck injuries due to the helmet being compressed onto his HANS Device and the load being reduced by the transfer of energy to his shoulders and torso. He spent several weeks in a back brace, but had no other injuries beyond a bruised back. Three decades after deciding he wanted better head and neck protection, Downing got saved from more serious, perhaps critical or deadly injury, by his own idea.

In the same year as the fatalities in Fernley, another set of accidents took place in Nevada at the Las Vegas Motor Speedway in a National Hot Rod Association race with a different type of outcome. Scott Hedlund, a Comp Eliminator driver who wore a HANS Device, survived a 160-mph crash that nearly destroyed his Chevy Cobalt. In a sad contrast, Derek Sanchez hit the wall at the same drag strip on the same weekend in his '33 Ford and suffered a head injury. The 47-year-old Yuma, Ariz. driver died in a Las Vegas area hospital several days later without regaining consciousness. His brother confirmed the Super Gas driver had suffered a basal skull fracture and had not been wearing a head restraint.

A corrugated box salesman from Anaheim Hills, California, Hedlund returned to work following his crash and contemplated repairs to his Chevy Cobalt that would allow him to return to drag racing later that summer. "I truly believe the HANS Device saved my life by saving my neck and head," said Hedlund, whose car abruptly turned left at the finish line. "I went in at a diagonal angle and I was conscious the whole time," he continued. "Everything went into super slow-mo. I remember my head being pushed forward. I could feel the HANS stopping my head from going forward."

There may be no form of racing as exhilarating as sprint car racing—or as dangerous. The cars reach high speeds on relatively short dirt tracks with lightweight frames and engines that can exceed 700 horsepower. The wings used by some sprint car series provide downforce and more speed, but also raise the cars' center of gravity, making them less stable. The oversized, exposed wheels and tires also make sprint cars and midgets, their smaller cousins, vulnerable to flips in wheel-to-wheel contact. All of these factors create thrilling races by determined and skilled drivers that help support a vibrant short track culture across America. This includes massive turnouts for major events like The Chili Bowl in Tulsa, Oklahoma, the Knoxville Nationals at the Knoxville Raceway in Iowa, and the Four Crown Nationals at Ohio's Eldora Speedway.

Despite the danger, no category in American racers resisted the use of head and neck restraints more than sprint car drivers during the timeframe covered by the *Observer's* report. A Darwinian outlook—one that a man like Eddie Rickenbacker might admire—and the ultimate thrill of survival seemed to have as much to do with the exhilaration for sprint car drivers and fans as the speed and competition. It all harkened back to the words of announcer Ken Squier and the old-school racer's creed: "Here were men who believed so wholly in what they did and were so committed to what they did that they were willing to take the risks… They were people who were committed and trying to do something better than others could."

After well-known driver Jason Leffler died in a sprint car race on a New Jersey track in 2013, *The New York Times* sought out Donny Schatz, a perennial series champion in the World of Outlaws, the most prominent sprint car circuit in the U.S. "It's like a bad addiction," he said of sprint car racing. "It's something you grow to love and learn to enjoy." Leffler wore a Hybrid Pro head restraint, but issues with the head surround left him with a fatal neck injury. The fatality of the popular driver reminded all that cockpit restraints must work as a system and be properly fitted for the individual driver using them. Leffler, who drove an unfamiliar car, did not get the protection he needed from the cockpit surround after a 90-degree side impact.

The loss of Leffler despite wearing a head restraint further slowed safety advocates already having difficulty persuading sprint car drivers that head restraints could save lives. The year before Leffler's crash, Schatz, along with other multiple champions Danny Lasoski and Steve Kinser, persuaded officials at the World of Outlaws to back down from a proposed head restraint mandate. The situation exemplified the Wild West aspect of sprint car racing, where the relatively high number of sanctioning bodies make promoters wary of displeasing team owners and drivers, because they might pull up stakes and move to another series. (For his part, Schatz later decided to start using a head restraint.)

This resistance played out when the United States Auto Club, the largest sanctioning group when it comes to sprint cars and midget cars, rescinded its mandate for SFI Spec. 38.1 head and neck restraints in 2010 after three years. In a severe financial recession, the rule change helped sustain car counts for USAC and draw in some entrants who had moved to other sanctioning groups.

Doug Auld, a racer-turned-journalist, exemplified the attitude toward head restraints by lobbying against the rule requiring a SFI spec. 38.1 device, helping to end the USAC mandate. He cited the different nature of accidents in sprint cars versus stock cars—rolls and end-over-end crashes—the different straight up seating positions and the role of shoulder harnesses. "If the shoulder restraint was to work its way off the HANS, what happens?" he wrote in an editorial in *Sprint Car & Midget* that called for individual choice over mandates.

Auld could cite all the differences in sprint car racing compared to NASCAR, where more than 3,000 incidents had been tracked by NASCAR R&D without any belt slippage. Ultimately, his resistance to head restraints represented a carbon copy of complaints made in virtually every other form of racing around the world: "We are different," goes this attitude. "Mandates won't work here." In addition, various other myths about the HANS were sustained in chat rooms and forums such as broken collar bones resulting from the device's legs crossing over the chest. In fact, such fractures result from shoulder impacts from the side.

In addition to Leffler's fatal crash, two other deadly accidents began to change attitudes in open wheel short track racing. Josh Burton, aged 22 when he was killed in 2013, and long-time pro Bryan Clauson, who died four years later, were killed by penetration of their driver compartments from outside components. These accidents hastened an emphasis on full containment seats, a cutting edge for change in attitudes about safety in sprint cars and on short tracks in general.

Anecdotal evidence from dealers in the field indicates an increasing percentage of drivers in a variety of different sanctioning groups for sprint cars and midgets are voluntarily using SFI Spec. 38.1 head and neck restraints, a positive change from the time when USAC first dropped its mandate and an indication of change among younger sprint car drivers.

Beyond education by companies selling safety equipment, this cultural shift in American racing can also be attributed, in part, to the Safe Is Fast online program founded in 2011 by the prestigious and long-tenured Road Racing Drivers Club. Dedicated to educating young drivers, through 2018 the website for Safe Is Fast brought in 137,396 unique users. YouTube has generated 1.2 million tutorial page views and the Facebook page for Safe Is Fast averages six million downloads of its tutorials per year.

Motorsports Safety Education Foundation, founded in memory of driver Sean Edwards, one of those killed in 2013, is another organization seeking to promote better safety education online through expert advice from racing professionals.

Despite changes in drivers' attitudes, American sanctioning bodies have lagged behind their international counterparts when it comes to mandating head restraints, because of the FIA's commitment to acting on behalf of safety in the automotive industry. In 2009, six years after head restraints became mandatory in F1, the FIA began requiring all participants in its multitude of international championships to use an FIA-approved head and neck restraint. It also mandated head restraints for all international series listed on its calendar.

The FIA's general assembly is comprised of one national sporting association from each member country and these organizations tend to follow the lead of the FIA on safety, particularly in Europe. In "cradle of racing" countries such as Britain, France, Italy, Belgium, the Netherlands and Germany, nearly all participants in national racing outside of slaloms, autocross, historic events or highway "regulation" rallies have been required to wear certified head restraints.

The member countries of the FIA also have tended to be more responsive when safety becomes an issue. The year 2013 was particularly deadly worldwide when it came to racing accidents. At least 26 died in reported crashes, which included the fatal incidents of Simonsen at Le Mans, Leffler in New Jersey as well as Richardson and Kay in Nevada, Sanchez in Las Vegas and Burton in Indiana.

In Australia, one circuit driver and one rally driver were killed, while two other rally drivers died in accidents in Tasmania and New Zealand. In two of these rally accidents, the other occupants who were wearing HANS Devices survived. The following year, the Confederation for Australian Motorsport announced FIA-approved head restraint mandates starting in 2015 for all national and state races on circuits or rally events.

In Germany, where four rally drivers were killed in 2013, mandates for head restraints were extended to all national level rallies. In Britain, where one circuit racer and one rally driver were killed, the Motor Sports Association (MSA) began to move on implementing head restraints for all circuit and rally drivers at the national and club level—meaning more than 23,000 licensed drivers were affected by the change. The MSA's annual report in 2017 indicated it did not lose any participation in terms of the number of licensed drivers racing under its rules.

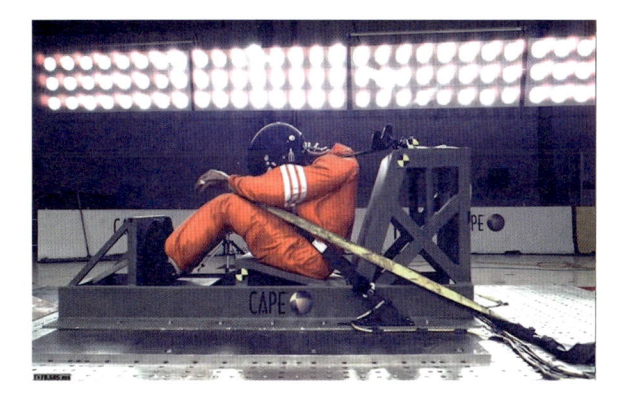

Photos from the sled test at CAPE in 2012 demonstrate results of 'without HANS' (top) and 'with HANS.'
(Photos by Center for Advanced Product Evaluation)

The responses by sanctioning bodies to safety issues has been dramatically different in the U.S.

In addition to Sanchez, drag racers Lawren Jones (who suffered head injury while not wearing a restraint) and Tubby Wells, a bracket racer at a non-sanctioned track in Alabama, whose injuries were not known, were killed in 2013. In the four following seasons, the website DragStripDeaths.webs.com reported 15 additional fatal accidents for drag racers competing in cars, including the highly successful Ronnie "The King" Davis.

Weekend Warriors: Living Dangerously

But no changes resulted when it came to head restraint rules for weekend drag racers—despite the fact the number of deaths confirmed drivers were going fast enough to need one. The NHRA maintained its head restraint requirements for all drivers exceeding 200 mph or traveling a quarter mile in 7.49 seconds or less, which left out at least 15,000 bracket racers in the organization claiming 40,000 licensed drivers. The International Hot Rod Association had no head restraint mandates for bracket racers at its sanctioned events in 2017.

On short tracks in 2013, hall of fame sprint car driver Kramer Williamson was killed by blunt head trauma in addition to the crashes of Kay and Richardson, but no significant change in head restraint rules resulted in the multitude of sprint car or dirt track sanctioning bodies in the ensuing seasons.

NASCAR, the first to mandate head and neck restraints for an entire series, took a different approach when it came to short tracks. In 2017, NASCAR sanctioned 64 short tracks in the U.S. and left the decision about head restraints up to the individual tracks. Its guidelines for the Whelen All-American Series, which crowns a national champion each year by using statistical analysis of results, recommended a head restraint. But drivers can wear a so-called neck brace—a stiff wrap-around collar that sells for $40 and offers little neck protection in a crash—if they chose not to wear a head restraint.

In a familiar theme of avoiding liability, NASCAR officials point out that the role of its sanction at the short track level does not include making the rules and is more of a marketing relationship.

The International Motor Competition Association (IMCA), which sanctions short track classes for five different types of cars on tracks across the country, had the same approach as NASCAR when it came to neck collars in lieu of head restraints.

At the end of 2017, there were at least 756 short tracks in the U.S. where an estimated 130,000 drivers competed according to modeling from season-ending points standings. In a random sampling of one track from each of the 50 states, only eight tracks required head restraints—and usually only for the fastest class.

These rules stood in sharp contrast to a demonstration in 2012 by Simpson Performance Products during the annual Performance Racing Industry show for racing manufacturers held in Indianapolis. The demonstration at the Center for Advance Product Evaluation (CAPE) consisted of back-to-back sled tests of a Hybrid III dummy with and without a HANS Device. The sled tests confirmed that injuries exceeding the limits for neck tension established by SFI's Specification 38.1 could occur at a speed as low as 40 mph and that a HANS could prevent such injuries.

The test also demonstrated the age-old adage about coming to an abrupt stop causes injuries, not necessarily top speed. Indirectly, the test confirmed that a crash with a Delta V of 40 mph—such as a car going 120 mph suddenly reduced to 80 mph by a collision into a wall—could transfer enough force to a driver to be fatal. Crashes of this description are not unusual scenarios for weekend warriors.

"When drivers die on short tracks or drag strips, especially with weekend warriors involved, other than local stories it doesn't get the kind of media coverage that takes place among major series," said Jim Downing, the featured speaker at the CAPE demonstration. "But we've identified the same type of head and neck injuries that killed drivers on superspeedways are also killing them at lower speeds. A head and neck restraint can prevent these unnecessary racing deaths."

That message continues to go unheeded by many in the minor leagues of U.S. racing—including weekend warriors, short track and drag strip promoters, and sanctioning bodies. A certified head restraint is comparable to a seat belt in terms of necessity. *Car and Driver* magazine called the HANS the greatest safety invention since the seat belt. But until sanctioning bodies choose to mandate head and neck restraints for all their competitors, drivers will continue to avoid using them and predictably that decision will result in critical and fatal injuries.

27

HANS Performance Products

IN 1988, A SINGLE-STORY BRICK BUILDING—formerly an electrical appliance assembly plant—began serving as the home for Downing/Atlanta owner Jim Downing and his various enterprises. Located in the hamlet of Chamblee, cheek-by-jowl to the city limits of Atlanta, two delivery bay ramps provided easy access to the extensive work areas, converted into a vast indoor garage and fabrication shop by Downing. Behind the office space at the building's front, race cars and road vehicles regularly came and went, all part of Downing's eclectic array of businesses.

The move from nearby Standard Drive comprised a large expansion in terms of space and operations for Downing's racing team. The enterprising race car driver and businessman had come a long way from the rented space near the Georgia Tech campus where he built his first race car from salvage while a student.

Downing's new headquarters enabled him to pursue the business of designing, building and selling sports prototypes branded as Kudzu for competition in IMSA and the FIA's Group C2 category. At the rear of the Downing/Atlanta building, a separate high-ceilinged room held the composite shop directed by Jerry "Rabbit" Lambert, where body parts were fabricated for the Kudzu chassis as well as for other racing customers. Downing's Mazda rotary race engines were built by Rick Engman at another nearby Downing enterprise known as Mazmart that sold used Mazda street car parts.

The Kudzu prototypes were named, with a nod and a wink, after the noxious weed of Japanese origin that Downing's father had helped introduce to the Southeast.

They became quite successful in the hands of Downing as well as other competitors. This included class victories at major endurance events at Daytona and Sebring as well as a victory in the LMP2 class in 1996 at the prestigious Le Mans 24-hour, where Downing became the only American to co-drive a prototype of his own construction to victory.

Downing operated various other businesses from his Chamblee location, including vintage street car sales; used race car sales and restoration; heavy equipment salvage; and a supercharging business for street cars.

The size and scope of the building on Peachtree Rd. enabled Downing to launch another new business—one dedicated to the manufacture and sale of the HANS head and neck restraints. After racing safety companies showed no interest in the business of head restraints, Hubbard/Downing, Inc. was formed in 1990 and began doing business as HANS Performance Products. Until acquired by Simpson Performance Products in September of 2012, the company and its dedicated staff sold as many as 175,000 devices worldwide, including sales by licensed companies in Europe.

At the time of its origin, HPP was faced with many challenges, including the paltry sales of the Model I throughout the 1990s. The transition to the frontal head restraint developed in conjunction with Mercedes-Benz in 1996 and 1997 was then followed by the sudden upsurge in demand for the downsized second generation of HANS Devices after the death of Dale Earnhardt in 2001. The volume of business eventually required outsourcing. Reducing the cost and

Crash! How the HANS Helped Save Racing

HANS Performance Products

Downing/Atlanta in Chamblee, Georgia served as headquarters for HANS Performance Products. (Photo by HANS Performance Products)

weight of the HANS became an ongoing priority, as did responding to driver critiques.

The task of privately testing devices at outside facilities in order to certify new HANS Devices also fell to HPP. This included sled testing for SFI certification at various facilities around the country and staying abreast of tests conducted by NASCAR and the FIA. After demonstrating the need and creating a market for head and neck restraints, a watchful eye had to be kept on those who would introduce head restraints in violation of the patents held by Hubbard.

For its first decade of operation, HPP's day-to-day operations consisted of Downing and composite shop manager Lambert, who produced the bulky Model I devices in response to individual demand. Once HPP began producing the sleeker, standardized second-generation devices in 2000, following the lessons learned in the introduction of the HANS to CART, additional personnel were added to increase the inventory of devices. Encouraged by prospects for the frontal head restraints derived from the Model II, these new generation devices were to be sold through traditional channels of sales and marketing instead of the small batch method used for the Model I. Events in February of 2001 blindsided this fledgling operation.

The day after Earnhardt's death at Daytona, Downing arrived to a scene very different from the usual Monday morning routine. The extensive front lawn was filled with TV media trucks and their satellite dishes. Downing would spend much of this day fielding questions from the media in person at his shops and by phone. During the same period when Hubbard took 85 calls at his home in East Lansing, Downing did not keep a log and soon lost track.

The HANS had first gained regular coverage in newspapers that staffed the NASCAR circuit during the dreadful summer of 2000, but after Earnhardt's death the interest in racing's first head restraint reached critical mass with stories appearing coast-to-coast.

Shortly after the fateful crash, *The Los Angeles Times* ran a story quoting Ken Adams, an office worker at Downing/Atlanta who helped look after the HANS business. The reporter asked how many devices could be built on short notice and who had called to order them? Penske Racing's driver Rusty Wallace, a former NASCAR Winston Cup champion, was among those placing orders, replied Adams, and defending NASCAR Busch Series champion Jeff Green another. The company had been producing only three devices a week the previous year, but the production would be stepped up to five a day. (Additional workers were hired to start laying up the carbon fiber and Kevlar in the composite shop at the rear of the building usually reserved for fabricating race car bodywork and wings.)

"I've never seen a day like this in my life," said Downing during a phone call to a writer from the *Poughkeepsie Journal* in New York.

In the 11 years of operation prior to 2000, an estimated 280 of the Model I devices had been sold to customers. Including production of the universally shaped, new generation of devices that began in June of 2000, the company had sold a total of 350 devices. HPP received almost that many orders for new devices in just one week following Earnhardt's death.

Race car drivers of all backgrounds finally recognized the vulnerability of their heads and necks. "If it could happen to Earnhardt," went their line of thinking, "it could happen to me."

Newspapers and their broadsheet pages were full of stories on the fatal Daytona crash from every conceivable angle. Even the Monday, Feb. 19 editions of papers that did not ordinarily devote detailed coverage to NASCAR had multiple accounts about the entire day at Daytona and its aftermath. Stories on the cause of death by a basal skull fracture shared space with accounts of mourning by fans and fellow drivers and men such as Ned Yost, at the time the third base coach for the Atlanta Braves and one of Earnhardt's regular hunting buddies. There was debate about the wreck itself, how it happened and why it was so injurious. The gruesome rescue scenario was recounted as well as individual tributes to Earnhardt by writers. Future champion Kevin Harvick being named the replacement driver at Richard Childress Racing was almost a footnote.

One of the most prescient stories appeared two days after the crash in *The New York Times*, which carried a graphic of the Model IV device, the type used by five drivers in the Daytona 500. Robert Lipsyte, who covered selected NASCAR races for the paper, wrote a lengthy story that ran 28 column inches—about 1,500 words—on the state of safety in NASCAR following four deaths in less than a year. He closed with a long summation that began, "Could Big E have been saved?" He wrote about Earnhardt's refusal to wear a full-face helmet, much less the HANS. He covered the debate about the device and some of the doubts voiced about it after the Daytona crash.

"Still," he wrote, "this could be NASCAR's opportunity to mandate such protection. In that way, Dale may yet talk to us."

No statement could have been more accurate. As events played out, NASCAR became the first sanctioning body to mandate head restraints for all races in its major series, before CART took such action for its entire schedule. But the influence of Earnhardt's death went far beyond these series. Sanctioning bodies in other forms of U.S. racing eventually mandated the HANS as well. Many drivers made individual choices.

Butch Leitzinger, who drove for the Dyson Racing sports prototype team based in Poughkeepsie, also received a call from the *Poughkeepsie Journal*.

"A lot more attention needs to be paid to the HANS," said Leitzinger, who had just turned 32 and had been racing since his teenage years. "I think there is a future for it. Ten years ago, some of the drivers weren't even wearing gloves (for fire protection). Drivers are much more safety conscious and after this (crash), it will be another step up in everyone's interest in safety."

Hundreds of drivers saw no need to wait for a mandate and ordered their device direct from the HANS manufacturer in Chamblee. In the days and weeks after Earnhardt's death, the halls of the offices and shipping area at the front of the Downing/Atlanta building were lined with helmets owned by drivers who wanted a HANS installed, which required clips in the helmet for the tethers. The helmets had attached paperwork with the date the driver needed it returned in time for competition. The shelves first established for the helmets awaiting devices were quickly filled, so helmets had to be put on the floor in hallways and the office entrance area.

Just as Downing had skillfully managed to keep the HPP business running for 11 years despite slow sales, he became equally adept once the deluge arrived.

The switch in focus to a volume production business model had begun in the summer of 2000 with universal fits for the HANS that could be adjusted by the use of pads. Initially, the company made a distinction for drivers in reclining seats (Model III) and then those using upright seats such as stock cars (Model IV). The devices came with collar angles of 10, 20, 30 and 40 degrees. As a result of sled testing, technical papers and safety conferences, the racing departments at GM and Ford had started buying the new Model II HANS Devices in 1998 to give to drivers they had under contract in professional series such as NASCAR and the NHRA. In addition to encouraging the use of the HANS, which remained a driver choice, this income helped Downing to start growing the business prior to the onslaught that began in February of 2001.

Once Lambert had established a universal shape to the device, standard sizes followed for the fit at the shoulders and neck (small, medium, large, and extra-large, plus extra small for youngsters). To accommodate larger volume, outside suppliers were established, supplementing the devices being built in-house.

In 2003, Downing hired international business expert and racing enthusiast Mark A. Stiles as the CEO of the company, succeeding the chief administrator Vince Tidwell. Stiles' tenure would run until 2010. His assignment included the sale of the HPP company itself. When a sale didn't take place (in part due to the Great Recession), Stiles eventually departed. A seven-year veteran at HPP, Gary Milgrom took over the day-to-day operation of the company until the sale to Simpson Performance Products in 2012.

"I brought Mark in because he was a friend," said Downing. "I had gotten to know him indirectly through his other work, behind the scenes work identifying companies in the U.S. for possible purchase by companies in Britain. I hired him and he did a great job for us for many years.

"Mark was instrumental in dealing with Mercedes after the creation of the Model II to a very positive effect for us. He got the office organized and made it a lot more formal than I had done up to that point. He did us a lot of good. He contributed to several of the patents for the auxiliary equipment such as the post anchors on the helmets and tethers, patents that were in his name as well as some of the other people who worked here."

As the CEO, Stiles developed sales and in-house fulfillment staffs and worked with outside U.S. suppliers such as Applied Composite Engineering and HiPer Technology to build devices.

Crucial to the success of HPP was working with SFI Foundation, Inc., the private testing laboratories, when it came to certifying the HANS. SFI first began developing what became known as Specification 38.1 in 2003 once it had been recognized by sanctioning bodies that standards were needed to ensure a head restraint's ability to keep drivers' heads and necks below an injurious threshold during crashes.

U.S. sanctioning bodies relied on SFI testing as a buffer to liability lawsuits as well as to eliminate head restraint inventions that did not work. The FIA, which only required tests for the robustness of head restraints and left liability up to the manufacturer, also relied on these standards indirectly by only testing devices that had been certified by SFI. NASCAR, meanwhile, started with the SFI results, then performed its own in-house tests before granting acceptance to a head restraint.

Stiles helped oversee the relationships with sanctioning bodies and with the two vendors in Europe—Schroth Safety Products in Germany and Stand 21 in France. In order to mandate the HANS, the FIA required Hubbard/Downing, Inc. to establish licensing agreements for the production of the HANS. For the FIA, this avoided reliance on a sole supplier, encouraged price competition and ensured ready availability in Europe.

The cost of the carbon fiber Pro model of the HANS dropped to $1,200 from the original pricing of more than $2,000 for a custom fit version during the days of outfitting CART drivers. (The original, custom-built Model I device had usually sold for more than $2,000; the cash flow generated from these sales helped keep HPP afloat through its lean years.) Eventually, Stand 21 became the source for all the Pro models sold by HPP, manufacturing them in France before shipment to the U.S. for finishing. A hollow core in the legs reduced weight without losing the strength needed to pass HPP's self-imposed "pull test" of resistance to at least 1,500 pounds of force before breaking. (The FIA's approval procedures included pull tests as well.)

HPP introduced the Sports Series in 2008, an injection-molded device designed for weekend warriors weighing more but costing half the amount of the HANS Pro. To help reduce weight in the Sports Series devices, production began in 2010 of the Sports Series

HANS Performance Products

The lab at HPP featured equipment to test the HANS for durability standards. (Photo by HANS Performance Products)

II, a carbon fiber/fiberglass injection-molded device made with nylon fibers known as polyamides. To further reduce problems for drivers exiting vehicles and to reduce weight, rounded corners on all models of the HANS began to be introduced in 2010.

HPP sold devices through wholesale distribution. The company certified sales staff at dealers through training sessions. These dealer representatives were instrumental in instructing drivers on the installation of the HANS in combination with proper seats, head surrounds and belt mountings. The instructions to drivers included reassuring them that tethers long enough to enable full movement of the head were also sufficient for restraining the head in a crash. The dynamics of the HANS initially sliding back on the shoulders until the friction rubber caught on the belts while the helmet moves forward and down on the forehead sometimes remained difficult for drivers to fathom. They often thought the device worked only by holding the head back, without realizing the transfer of energy played the key role during one dynamic moment lasting only milliseconds.

Although little movement of a driver's head is needed to view other cars or the mirrors, in 2009 a sliding tether system was introduced to further enhance head movement. A single tether attached on either side of the helmet slid back-and-forth at the rear of the device through a groove and was held in place by plastic retainers. Previously, two individual tethers

HANS Performance Products

were attached separately to either side of the device to connect the HANS to the helmet anchors.

The strength and reliability of ancillary parts such as helmet clips, soon followed by post anchors, were critical to maintaining the reliability of the device and it fell to HPP to maintain quality control on these manufactured pieces.

One of the thorniest issues for Downing and Hubbard concerned protecting the patents on the HANS.

From the outset, Hubbard recognized the importance of a patent. He had spent his own time and used his intellectual skills as well as taking out a $10,000 loan to keep the project going and finding grants to support the initial sled testing. If Hubbard entered the marketplace with a totally new concept that worked according to its stated goals, it had to be protected with a patent and a trademark.

Once persuaded by his own work and peer review that the HANS would work, Hubbard began pursuing a patent in 1984, five years prior to the first sled test. He contacted Dr. John Cantlin, who managed intellectual property for Michigan State. "We reviewed relevant MSU intellectual property policies," recalled Hubbard. "We agreed that MSU did not wish to have an interest in HANS because there was no apparent immediate market for it to justify MSU payment for the patenting and other legal expenses. Also, I had not used MSU resources and the patent would be based on work that I had done while in crash injury biomechanics prior to my work at MSU. Dr. Cantlin suggested that I set up a Subchapter S corporation to hold my intellectual property. He also recommended that I contact Ian McLeod, a local patent attorney and somewhat of a car nut."

Working with McLeod, Hubbard was awarded an initial patent in 1987 (No. 4,638,510) titled, "Neck Protection Device with Occupant of a High Performance Vehicle." He later received a second patent for "Improvement on a Head and Neck Support for Racing" in 2000, which succeeded the Model I patent

Crew members at HPP at time of sale to Simpson. From left, Paul Humphreys, Jim Goodroe, Jay Braxton, Gary Milgrom, Dave Warner, Richard Libera, Holly Woodward, Trish England.
(Photo by Gary Milgrom)

after the development of the Model II frontal head and neck restraint, which had two attachment tethers at the rear on the narrower collar instead of the three found on the original wraparound collar.

Having an entirely new invention helped the process but obtaining a patent did not ensure the HANS would perform as intended, even after sled testing. The acceptance of the HANS would still depend on driver comfort while using it—both physical and psychological—as well as performance in racing crashes. As Hubbard often said, "We didn't really know if the drivers were going to accept the device or not."

Once turning the corner after gaining acceptance in the racing marketplace, the patents assured Hubbard/Downing, Inc. of sustaining the business along with opportunities to improve the device and make it more appealing in terms of cost and comfort.

"The cornerstone of a patent is the claims," said Hubbard. "All else in a patent explains, illustrates, and supports the claims. While drawings are helpful in explaining it, the words primarily define the scope of the patent. Drafting the claims determines the breadth of their field of application. This requires careful collaboration between the patent lawyer and the patent applicant."

The combination of proven performance and the patent helped Hubbard eventually become involved in the Orion space project designed to send astronauts to Mars. To better ensure a return of astronauts from deep space to the earth's atmosphere, the National Aeronautics and Space Administration entered into a consulting contract with Hubbard. Having lost the Space Shuttle Columbia in 2003 during a turbulent re-entry, NASA began studying ways to enable astronauts to continue their mission despite unexpected turbulence that could lead to head or neck injuries.

The astronaut version of a head and neck restraint started with a collaboration first undertaken in 2008 at the Texas Motor Speedway, where officials from NASA's Johnson Space Center and Hubbard met with NASCAR officials to discuss the use of the sanctioning body's data base for assessing crash injury dynamics. NASCAR subsequently provided data taken from recorders in race vehicles, which helped NASA develop injury criteria for astronauts using computer modeling.

After starting work in 2007, the first series of sled tests with a dummy using a device designed by Hubbard for an astronaut occurred in 2010 at Wright Patterson Air Force Base. Directed by Dustin Gohmert of the Crew and Thermal Systems Division of NASA, the test employed a prototype HANS-type restraint comprised of a round collar and yoke made from carbon fiber. The helmet and neck ring of the space suit were fitted to the round collar and yoke, a single unit to be held in place by an astronaut's shoulder belts.

"The issue is to understand crew safety well enough to optimize crash injury reduction with the many, many other considerations such as weight and the unique environment of space and other threats to crew safety like emergency egress," said Hubbard following the test and NASA's media release. (As of 2019, no definitive decision had been taken by NASA on astronauts using a HANS.)

In the racing marketplace, the devices of rival manufacturers had to meet the standards established by SFI starting in 2004 to gain acceptance—without violating the HANS patent. In particular, the high mounting point of the tethers on the HANS, which helped make the transfer of energy from the helmeted head to the torso through the hard collar and yoke so effective, was most important to the claims of the patent along with the device's general shape.

Hubbard/Downing, Inc. went to court twice to protect its patent, winning each time against Kevin Heath Enterprises, a company launched by South African Kevin Heath.

In 2010, Hubbard/Downing, Inc. won its suit against the DefNder G70 device, only distinguishable from the HANS by its relatively low-cost manufacturing method. (But, as with all competitors, the G70 was priced similarly to the HANS.)

In the settlement, company owner Heath agreed to cease marketing the DefNder G70 and agreed not to return to the market with a device that resembled the G70. HPP successfully sued Heath a second time when he returned to the market a short while later with the NecksGen head restraint, judged to be similar to its predecessor.

Competitors eventually were able to design and introduce head restraints that met the SFI standard of protection by being able to successfully resist neck tension and shear forces up to 4,000 Newtons. They did not violate the HANS patent in large part by using lower mounting points for tethers. While sanctioning bodies welcomed the alternatives with an eye on spreading liability through a choice for drivers, the HANS continued to produce significantly better testing numbers for the critical neck tension and shear due to higher tether attachments at the carbon collar.

Manufacturers seeking to jump into the head restraint market to compete with HPP sometimes exploited a lack of knowledge about how head restraints worked for the sake of sales.

Where the original HANS Model I had accounted for side head movement with its built-in surround and three tethers—including one mounted on each side— the subsequent frontal head restraint HANS models

HANS Performance Products

sacrificed 90-degree side protection in the name of downsizing the device and allowing it to fit in all types of cockpits.

The staff at HPP and its dealers knew that frontal head restraints did not offer protection in side impacts of 90 degrees and avoided such claims, instead encouraging the use of head surrounds or nets. Competing head restraint companies sometimes sought to distinguish themselves by claiming their devices provided better side impact protection than the HANS, which sometimes led drivers to believe a competitor's device alone could provide side protection without the use of side nets or head surrounds. This unfortunate—and possibly deadly—misconception showed up regularly in online forums and chat rooms, posted by racers who didn't fully understand how head restraints worked or the need for head surrounds or side nets.

SFI testing did not directly address the side impact issue. In addition to straight-ahead impacts, the sled testing by SFI required offset impacts at a 30-degree angle.

It was clear to safety experts such as Tom Gideon, John Melvin and Paul Begeman that safe outcomes in side impacts beyond 45 degrees depended on head surrounds or side nets to curb the excursion of a driver's head. (Single seater cars with reclining drivers, meanwhile, required high cockpit sides and proper padding.) The introduction to a paper on side nets co-authored in 2004 by Gideon, Melvin and Begeman ("Race Car Nets for the Control of Neck Forces in Side Impacts") stated their outlook. "In side impacts from 45 degrees to 90 degrees head restraints do not provide protection due to the geometry of the restraint tethers." In other words, all head restraints needed surrounds or side nets if a driver's head was to be protected in side impacts.

Long before the SFI regulations were established for frontal head restraints, HPP and testing organizations regularly put videos of its sled tests online, which demonstrated the outstanding performance of the HANS Device. Eventually, this included a sled test video released in December of 2012 following a live

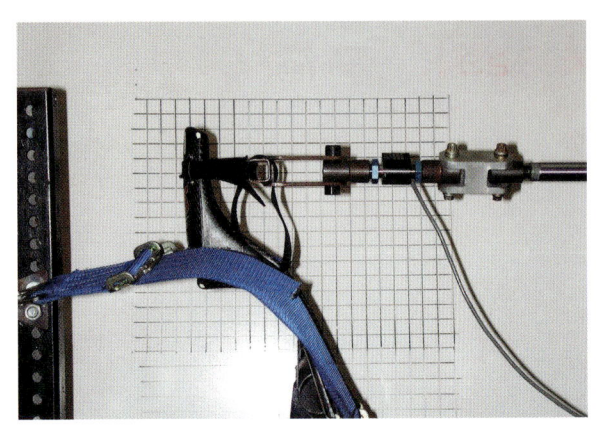

HPP built its own pull rig to assess strength of devices before they were independently certified elsewhere.
(Photo by HANS Performance Products)

demonstration at the Center for Advanced Product Evaluation facility near Indianapolis. The live test, hosted by Downing, took place in front of industry experts assembled for the annual PRI trade show for racing equipment.

The videos were shot with high-speed cameras capable of recording action in milliseconds and were usually shown in two segments. In the straight-ahead impacts where the test dummy has no HANS Device, the dummy's head catapults forward with the chin eventually snapping down to the chest. The same speed pulse on the same sled with a HANS in place demonstrates the virtual elimination of head excursion, a visual way to confirm the reduction in forces on the head and neck during a crash.

Downing and Hubbard surmised that competing head restraint companies did not show videos to avoid the issue of head excursion visibly taking place despite certification from SFI. This was a problem inherent with not having high mounting points for the tethers on a tall collar like the HANS and instead mounting the tethers closer to the shoulders, which allowed head excursion even if neck tension and shear were kept within SFI guidelines. Certainly, no rival manufacturer ever backed up side impact claims with a public video.

28

Saving the Day

IN LATE OCTOBER OF 2000, BOB HUBBARD stood alone by the pit wall at the California Speedway, about to witness history of his own making.

The HANS Device would be put to its first major racing test by the fastest field to ever take a green flag in automotive racing history. In qualifying for the 500-mile CART season finale, the median speed for the 26 starters stood at an amazing 234.521 mph and Gil de Ferran won the pole with a closed-course record of 241.428 mph.

During practice leading up to the qualifying, several drivers eclipsed 240 mph average lap times, including Michael Andretti and Juan Pablo Montoya. The latter recorded the fastest lap during practice at 242.253 mph, a riveting speed to be racing side-by-side and nose-to-tail. Speed differentials on the 2.0-mile oval were sometimes enough that Max Papis destroyed his primary entry for the Bobby Rahal team during practice when he literally ran over a slower Roberto Moreno. Wearing the HANS, Papis emerged with only a minor knee injury.

Once race day arrived, Hubbard stood by the pit wall as teams hovered around the Lola and Reynard chassis, preparing their drivers for the daunting task of racing on the 2.0-mile oval. In the same grid scene a year earlier, Greg Moore had been handed his trademark red gloves only to lose his life a short while later.

The exit of Turn 2 where Moore had lost his life due to an uneven, grassy runoff area had been paved over to make it safer and the wall configuration had been changed. But the CART teams had returned to the track running faster than the year before. Competition between the team owners who ran the series and among engine manufacturers meant any efforts to reduce speeds in the name of safety by reducing horsepower were nullified.

In light of the risk, the HANS Device, which had been mandated for use on ovals by CART starting with the 2000 season finale, received an ultimate first test.

To avoid the hubbub on the grid, Hubbard had taken up a position on the pit wall towards Turn 4. "Most of the people were working far to my left near the start/finish line," recalled Hubbard. "There were just a few people near me. I felt helpless and alone. I had no active role in the scene around me, yet I was deeply engaged.

"A reporter who was nearby asked, 'Dr. Hubbard, you must be really happy about this'. I waited a few moments to understand how I really felt and said back, 'Quite frankly, this scares the hell out of me.'

"This was the first race where my HANS was mandated for use in a major race. While I had been working for several years in conceiving and developing the device, at this time I felt helpless to control what might happen next. I questioned myself. 'Had I thought of all the possible problems that could injure drivers—even after years of testing in a lab, worrying, commiserating with Jim Downing and others who had encouraged me like John Melvin?'

"Encourage was the right word," continued Hubbard. "Trusted coworkers gave me the courage to move ahead into the unknown. This moment at the

Saving the Day

California Speedway was pivotal. There was a past of frustration and disappointment and a future of acceptance and success. The past went back almost 20 years and the future was going to be changed forever."

Without the development and mandating of the HANS in CART, the world of motor racing safety might have looked dramatically different going forward. The subsequent development undertaken for the individual CART drivers to get the proper fit for the HANS led to a universal shape that would make it accessible to any racer. This effort would become a clarion call for NASCAR and F1. In each of those series, the HANS models pioneered in CART would become the catalyst for change in the face of doubts about how such a strange-looking device could ever be compatible with racing at 200 mph.

On that sunny day in California, Hubbard could not anticipate three and a half months later, on the other side of the continent in Daytona Beach, the death of Dale Earnhardt would accelerate dramatically the demand for his new device. The same future held the use of more than 275,000 HANS Devices around the world.

"After the initial testing that was so successful in 1989, we felt morally obligated to make and sell the device even though there wasn't really any market for it and the device was fairly big and cumbersome at the time," said Hubbard. "Jim Downing and I felt like we needed to move ahead with this. We were actually coming back from Road America in Elkhart Lake in the summer of 1990 and I had approached a couple of racing safety equipment companies. They weren't interested in making a device because there was no market. It wasn't a commercially viable enterprise. So, Jim and I decided during that trip to start a company.

"It was very frustrating in the early 1990s, because we would watch the racing reports of the weekends and there were people being killed on a fairly regular basis. I couldn't see why people didn't realize this was a big issue, a big problem. People just weren't aware of it and they weren't upset about it. The best explanation I can understand is that people who race are people that

Fittingly, it was Fittipaldi on top step at Fontana in 2000, the first race where HANS was required by CART. (Photo by Mike Levitt)

decide to accept the risk or they are willing to ignore the risk. They're self-selecting to not be too concerned about it. That mindset was very common and it still continues.

"I had to realize that the people I was associating with, many of them engineers, also worried about injury in racing. They had special knowledge that really helped them understand that it was a big problem and it was a solvable problem. That had not been the typical mindset in the racing culture at the time. It was extremely frustrating to me. But what could I do about it except to keep chipping away?"

All the chipping away eventually led to the day in Fontana when Hubbard came to a jolting realization that his dream for safer racing was about to be realized. At the finish, despite a multitude of blown engines that crashed or sidelined all but six cars, no driver was seriously injured.

Fittingly, in every sense of the word, Christian Fittipaldi, the driver who had done the most work to develop the HANS Device, won the race and stood on the top step of the podium that day. Since then, hundreds of racers have been able to continue their lives and racing despite serious crashes, thanks to the sport's first head and neck restraint.

Awards

Robert Hubbard, Jim Downing and the HANS Device

1997   HANS Device wins George P. Snively Award from the Sports Car Club of America for "Outstanding contributions to safety in motorsports."

2000   HANS Device wins SEMA Motorsports Engineering Award.

2001   HANS Device wins Lewis Schwitzer Award at the Indy 500.

2001   HANS Device wins CART Champion Drivers Award.

2003   HANS Device wins the Grand Prix F1 Special Safety Award.

2007   Robert Hubbard, Jim Downing win Pioneering and Innovation Award from *Autosport* Magazine.

2011   Robert Hubbard wins President's Award from the Michigan Automobile Racing Fan Club.

2016   Robert Hubbard, Jim Downing and Hubert Gramling win the John Melvin Motorsports Safety Award presented by SAE International.

In 2007, Jim Downing and Bob Hubbard received the Pioneer and Innovation Award at the *Autosport* Awards, held at London's Grosvenor House Hotel, where Steve Rider was the presenter. (LAT Images)

Halls of Fame

2012   Jim Downing — Sebring International Raceway

2013   Robert Hubbard, Jim Downing — Sports Car Club of America

2015   Jim Downing — Georgia Racing Hall of Fame

Crash! How the HANS Helped Save Racing

Acknowledgements

IN ADDITION TO LENGTHY CONVERSAtions with Bob Hubbard and Jim Downing, the bulk of the book's research was done through interviews with participants in auto racing's safety revolution and others who helped tell the story. Without their contributions of time and insight, a full history of auto racing safety as viewed in the context of the HANS story would not have been possible.

Thanks to Matt Amato, Brett Bodine, Ann Bradshaw, Christian Fittipaldi, Tom Gideon, Hubert Gramling, Mike Helton, Jerry "Rabbit" Lambert, Larry McReynolds, the late John Melvin, Gary Nelson, Steve Olvey, Max Papis, the late Steve Peterson, Kirk Russell and Terry Trammell.

The Official Accident Report – No. 3 Car produced by NASCAR also proved invaluable.

For the sake of continuity, I elected to write about each sanctioning body's role from start to finish where possible, occasionally causing an overlap in terms of a time line. Because some readers may be more interested in engineering and invention than racing, I've done my best to provide fundamental racing references where needed for a more universal approach.

One important note: there is more than one accepted spelling for the word describing a fracture at the base of the skull; both are used by medical practitioners. This book uses basal, because it was in common usage when the HANS Device first arrived.

The visual presentation of this story comes down to the work of Damion Chew. Many thanks to him for outstanding work and patience.

Due to her editing skills and knowledge of racing, Lori Lovely did an excellent job of reviewing the manuscript. A special thanks to Connie Downing and JoAnn Hubbard for their proofreading and Gary Milgrom for his photo research. If I've missed anybody who is not mentioned here or in the text, my apologies. It's been a long, complicated and worthwhile story. I am grateful for all the assistance received.

Bibliography

Branham, Herb, *Big Bill, The Life and Times of NASCAR Founder Bill France Sr.,* Penguin Random House, New York, 2015

Busbee, Jay, *Earnhardt Nation,* HarperCollins, New York, 2016.

Canfield, Jack, etc., *Chicken Soup for the Soul NASCAR,* Simon & Schuster, New York, 2010.

Chapin, Kim, *Fast As White Lightning,* The Dial Press, New York, 1981.

Cimarosti, Adriano, *The Complete History of Grand Prix Motor Racing,* Aurum Press, Ltd., London, 1997.

Daley, Robert, *Cars at Speed,* Collier-Macmillan, Toronto, 1962.

Daley, Robert, *The Cruel Sport*, Bonanza Books, New York, 1963.

Fox, Charles, *The Great Racing Cars & Drivers,* Grosset & Dunlap, New York, 1972.

Garner, Art, *Black Noon,* Thomas Dunne Books, New York, 2014.

Green, David; Ingram, Jonathan; Pearce, Al, *Unseen Earnhardt,* MBI Publishing Co., St. Paul, 2002.

Hallman, Randall, *Grand National Stock Car Racing,* Fast Company Ltd., Richmond, Va., 1982

Henican, Ellis; Waltrip, Michael, *In the Blink of an Eye. Dale, Daytona And the Day That Changed Everything,* Hyperion, New York, 2011.

Ingram, Jonathan, *Dale Earnhardt, The Life Story of a NASCAR Legend,* Carlton Books Ltd., London, 2001.

Ingram, Jonathan, *NASCAR in Photographs,* Carlton Books, Ltd., London, 2004.

Lewis, W. David, *Eddie Rickenbacker, An American Hero in the Twentieth Century,* The Johns Hopkins University Press, Baltimore, 2005.

Lindamood, Jean, *Road Trips, Head Trips, and Other Car-Crazed Writings,* The Atlantic Monthly Press, 1996.

Melvin, John W; Russell, J. Kirk, *Developments in Modern Racecar Driver Crash Protection and Safety,* SAE International, Warrendale, PA, 2014.

Mosley, Max, *Formula One and Beyond,* Simon & Schuster, London, 2015.

Neely, William, *Tire Wars, Racing with Goodyear,* AZTEX Corporation, Tucson, AZ, 1993

Olvey, Steve, *Rapid Response,* Haynes Publishing, Somerset, UK, 2006.

Riley, Bob with Jonathan Ingram, *The Art of Race Car Design,* Icon Publishing Ltd., Worcestershire, UK, 2016

Roach, Mary, *Stiff, The Curious Lives of Human Cadavers,* W.W. Norton & Company, New York, 2003.

Roebuck, Nigel, *Chasing the Title,* Haynes Publishing, Somerset, UK, 1999.

Taylor, Rich, *INDY 75 Years of Racing's Greatest Spectacle,* St. Martin's Press, New York, 1991.

Watkins, Sidney, *Life at the Limit – Triumph and Tragedy in Formula One,* Pan Macmillan Ltd., London, 1997.

Webber, Mark, *Aussie Grit,* Pan Macmillan Australia Pty Ltd., Sydney, 2015.

Scientific Papers

Gideon, T., Melvin, J., Begeman, P. *"Race Car Nets for the Control of Neck Forces in Side Impacts,"* SAE paper no. 2004-01-3513, 2004.

Gideon, T., Melvin, J., Streetz, L., and Willhite, S., *"ATD Neck Tension Comparisons for Various Sled Pulses,"* SAE Technical Paper Paper 2002-01-3324, 2002.

Gramling, H., Hodgman P., and Hubbard, R., *"Development of the HANS Head and Neck Support for Formula One,"* presented at and in the Proceedings of the Motor Sports Engineering Conference and Exposition, Soc. of Auto. Engin., Dec., 1998, SAE paper no. 983060, 1998.

Gramling, H., and Hubbard, R., *"Development of an Airbag System for FIA Formula One and Comparison to the HANS Head and Neck Support,"* presented at and in the Proceedings of the Motor Sports Engineering Conference and Exposition, Soc. of Auto. Engin., Nov., 2000, SAE paper no. 2000-01-3543, 2000.

Hubbard, R., and Begeman, P., *"Biomechanical Performance of a New Head and Neck Support,"* presented at and in the Proceedings of the 1990 Stapp Car Crash Conference, Society of Automotive Engineers, SAE paper no. 902312, 1990.

Hubbard, R., Begeman, P. and Downing, J., *"Biomechanical Evaluation and Driver Experience with the Head and Neck Support,"* presented at and in the Proceedings of the Motor Sports Engineering Conference and Exposition, Soc. of Auto. Engin., Dec., 1994, SAE paper no. 942466, 1994.

Mellor, A., *"Integration of HANS Device within Formula One,"* SAE Technical Paper 2002-01-3351, 2002.

Melvin, J., Little, W., Jedrzejczak, E., and Pierce, J., *"Race Car Restraint System Frontal Crash Performance Testing,"* presented at and in the Proceedings of the Motor Sports Engineering Conference and Exposition, Soc. of Auto. Engin. (P-287), Dec. 5-8, 1994, SAE paper no. 942482, 1994.

Trammell, T., *"Neck Injury in Open Wheel Racing,"* presented at the joint safety meeting of the Federation Internationale de l' Automobile and the International Council of Motorsport Sciences, London, Dec. 1999.

Wilcox, A., *"Studying Friction for HANS® Device Function,"* SAE Technical Paper 2006-01-3632, 2006.

Index

Entries in bold indicate image or caption

Air bags   *65–69*
Alesi, Jean   *55, 56*
Alonso, Fernando   *143, 146, 149*
Amato, Matt   *52, 172*
American Automobile Association (AAA) Contest Board   *36, 37*
American Automobile Association (AAA) National Championship   *36, 37, 41*
Anderson, Andy   *69, 70*
Anderson, Lars   *156*
Andretti, John   *120, 121*
Andretti, Mario   *47, 94*
Andretti, Michael   *77, 83, 86, 87, 88, 169*
Assael, Shaun   *77*
Automobile Club de L'Ouest (ACO)   *154*
Autosport (Downing business)   *10*
Autosport International   *147*
Autosport (magazine)   *ix, 61, 64, 121, 122, 171*
Baker, John   *138*
Barnhart, Brian   *97*
Barrichello, Rubens   *54, 55, 57, 149*
Begeman, Paul   *25, 68, 168, 174*
Benedict, James   *127, 128*
Benson, Andrew   *61*
Bianchi, Jules   *153*
Bock, Henry   *88, **96**, 98*
Bodine, Brett   *12, **103**, 104, 106, 108, 172*
Bohannon, Steve   *126*
Bourdais, Sebastien   *139, **140**, 141*
Bradshaw, Ann   *57, 172*
Brayton, Lee   *94*
Brayton, Scott   *viii, 21, 93–96, **95***
Bright, John   *81*
Brooklands   *34, 35*
Burman, Bob   *36, 41*

Burton, Jeff   *108*
Burton, Josh   *158, 159*
Busbee, Jay   *110, 173*
Busch, Kyle   *141, 142*
Button, Jenson   *143, 146*
Caracciola, Rudolph   *37*
Casey, Phil   *97*
Championship Auto Racing Teams (CART)   *viii, 41, 63, 66, **72**, 75, 76–86, 87–97, 106–109, 112, 113, 119, 126, 132, 133, 140, 145–147, 149, 152, 156, 162–164, 169–171*
Chapman, Colin   ***48**, 53*
Cheever, Eddie   *118, 125*
Chevrolet, Gaston   *31, 35, 41*
Childress, Richard   *114*
   Racing Team   *3, 115–117, 129, 138, 163*
Clark, Jim   *42, 46, **48**, 49, 52, 53, 60*
Conover, Steve   *11, 28*
Coulthard, David   *75, 149*
Dallaire, Jacques   *154*
Dallenbach, Wally: Sr.   *76, 82*
Daytona 500   *1, 3, 12, 13, 47, 100, 105, **107**, 109–111, 113, 114–118, 120, 121, 123–125, 129, 163*
Daytona International Speedway   *ix, 1, 12, 13, 41, 44, 47*
"Death on the Boards"   *31*
Demmer, Bill   *26*
Demmer, John   *26*
Downing/Atlanta   *4, 11, 26, 90, **92**, 161–163, 172*
Downing, Jim   *ix, 2, 3, 4, 6–11, 13, 15, 16, 17, 26–28, 30, 31, 42, 64, 69, 74, 82, 87, 89, 90, 103, 106, 108, 133, 147–149, 157, 160, 161, 162–165, 169, 170, 171*
Downing, JoAnn   *10, 14, 16, 172*
Earnhardt, Dale   *viii, 1, **2**, 3, 4, 12, 30, 41, 50,* cont.

Crash! How the HANS Helped Save Racing

89, 96, 102, 104, 105, 109, 114, 120, 133, 139, 140, 152, 161, 170, 173
Earnhardt, Dale, Jr.   *114, 117–119, 137*
Earnhardt, Kerry   *137*
Earnhardt, Teresa   *119, 120, 122*
Ecclestone, Bernie   *50, 52,* **60***, 62, 84*
Edwards, Sean   *158*
Engman, Rick   *11, 161*
Expert Advisory Group   *62, 63–66, 143*
Fédération Internationale de l'Automobile (FIA)   *5, 10, 37, 44, 48, 49, 51, 59–64, 66, 69–71, 74, 75, 86, 106, 113, 135, 137, 138, 143–151, 153, 161, 162, 164, 174*
  Air bag concept   *65, 67*
  FIA-spec HANS   **144**
  Traction control   *55, 56, 58*
Fittipaldi, Christian   *77, 83, 86, 87, 88, 89, 90,* **170***, 172*
Fittipaldi, Emerson   *86, 87*
Fontana, Noberto   *88*
France, Bill, Jr.   *112, 122, 133*
France, Bill, Sr.   *173*
Franchitti, Dario   *76–79,* **85***, 88, 90, 109, 112*
Franchitti, George   *76*
Ganassi, Chip   *80, 84, 119, 149*
Garone, Joe   *108*
General Motors Research Laboratories   *15*
George, Tony   *77*
Gideon, Tom   *99, 100, 106, 128, 132,* **135***, 136, 139, 140, 168, 172, 174*
GM Motorsports Safety Technology Research Program   *63, 66, 85, 96, 106, 108, 109, 140*
Goodwin, Barry   *80*
Gordon, Jeff   *3, 110, 115, 121, 123, 124, 135, 136*
Gramling, Hubert   *67–71, 73, 74, 82, 86, 151, 171, 172, 174*
Gugelmin, Mauricio   *91, 92, 97*
Haas, Carl   *82, 83, 86*
Hakkinen, Mika   *58, 63, 64, 66, 67, 75, 95*

Hallberry, Andy   *79*
Hamlin, Denny   *142*
Hamlin, Kevin   *118, 119*
HANS Model I   *11, 26, 65, 67, 83, 86, 102, 167*
HANS Model II   **71***,* **72***, 75, 82, 86, 87, 88, 90, 147, 163, 164, 166*
HANS Model III   **75***, 90, 103, 147, 148*
HANS Model IV   *106, 107, 163*
HANS Performance Products   *3, 30, 64, 68, 70, 74, 90, 103, 107, 133, 141, 146, 149, 161,* **162**
HANS Sport Series   **154**
Haug, Norbert   *62, 70*
Head Injury Criteria   *73*
Head, Patrick   *58*
Hearn, Richie   *24, 76, 81, 98*
Heath, Kevin   *167*
Hedlund, Scott   *157*
Heidfeld, Nick   **146**
Helton, Mike   *4,* **117***, 134, 137*
Highway Safety Research Institute   *15*
Hill, Phil   *7, 40, 41*
Hinton, Ed   *105, 108*
Horn, Ted   *38*
Horton, Jeff   *98*
Hubbard, Bill   *15*
Hubbard, Bob   *ix, 3, 4, 10, 12, 13, 17, 63, 69, 169, 171, 172*
Huffman, Patti   *101*
Hummer, Steve   *129*
Hutchens, Bobby   *138*
Hutchens Device   *97*
Hybrid III crash test dummy   *86*
Indianapolis Motor Speedway   *3, 4, 35, 37, 77, 93, 103, 107, 129, 136, 139, 140*
Indy 500   *viii, 7, 18, 21, 31, 35, 36, 42, 43, 46, 47, 52, 53, 66, 76–78, 88, 92, 93, 97, 98, 109, 117, 124, 139, 171*
Indy Racing League   *viii, 77, 78, 87, 89, 91, 92, 93, 94, 95, 96–98, 101, 108, 126, 139, 140, 152, 153*

176   *Crash!* How the HANS Helped Save Racing

International Council of Motorsports Sciences   *154*
International Motor Sports Association (IMSA)   *5, 6, 10, 11, 16, 28, 63, 77, 82, 83, 85, 161*
Irwin, Kenny   *4, 101–103, 105, 106*
Jacquemart, Patrick   *6, 11, 16, 17, 21, 22, 157*
Johnson, Junior   *111, 115*
Kanaan, Tony   *76–79, 89*
Kay, Leroy   *156, 159, 160*
Kendall, Tom   *63*
King, Albert   *25*
Kubica, Robert   **150**, *151*
Kudzu chassis   **8**, *11, 161*
Lambert, Jerry "Rabbit"   *74, 87, 90,* **92**, *147, 161, 162, 164, 172*
Lamy, Pedro   *54, 58, 62*
Leffler, Jason   *157, 159*
Lehto, J.J.   *54, 55, 58*
Le Mans   *33*
  24 Hours of   **8**, *10, 11, 15, 74, 97, 153, 161*
  death at   *154, 159*
  Tragedy, 1955   *viii, 41, 59*
Linas-Montlhéry, Autodrome de   *34*
Lockhart, Frank   **35**, *36, 37, 41*
Lund, Dwayne, "Tiny"   *47, 109*
MacDonald, Dave   *42,* **43**, *45*
Marcelo, Jovy   *95, 96*
Marisi, Dan   *154*
Massa, Felipe   **146**, *151*
McDowell, Michael   *142*
McDuffie, J.D.   *96, 102, 113, 119*
McReynolds, Larry   *110, 116, 129, 172*
Mears, Rick   *5, 84, 85, 94*
Melvin, John   *12,* **13**, *15, 21, 25, 27, 29, 63, 66, 68, 69, 72, 74, 82, 85, 96, 99, 103, 107, 108, 126, 128, 132–135, 139, 140, 149, 168, 169, 171, 172, 174*
Metzger, John   *156*
Mid-Ohio Sports Car Course   *6, 89*
Milgrom, Gary   *164, 166*
Mille Miglia   *41, 59, 122*

Miller, Robin   *89*
Minter, Rick   *107*
Montoya, Juan Pablo   *76, 77, 89,* **145**, *148, 149, 169*
Monza, Autodromo Nazionale   *34, 40, 45, 146*
Moore, Greg   *viii, 41, 76, 77–81,* **78**, *140, 169*
Mosley, Max   *49, 58, 59,* **60**, *61, 75, 143, 144, 147, 149, 151, 173*
Mosport Park   *4, 5, 16, 42*
Motorsports Safety Education Foundation   *158*
Murphy, Jimmy   *35, 41*
Nakano, Shinji   *88*
NASCAR   *viii, 1, 2, 4, 8, 12, 13, 19, 21, 44, 45–48, 50, 53, 63, 75, 89, 99, 100, 101, 102,* **103**, *104, 105, 106, 107, 108, 109, 111, 112, 113, 114, 115, 117, 118, 120, 121, 122, 124, 125, 126, 127,* **128**, *129, 130, 131, 132, 133, 134, 135, 137, 138, 139, 140, 141, 142, 152, 153, 155, 156, 158, 160, 162, 163, 164, 167, 170, 172, 173*
NASCAR Research & Development Center   *104, 135, 140, 141, 158*
National Aeronautics and Space Administration (NASA)   *20, 64, 91, 167*
National Motorsports Press Association   *38*
Nelson, Gary   *3,* **103**, *107, 128, 129, 172*
New Car Assessment Program (NCAP)   *144*
Newey, Adrian   *58*
New Hampshire Motor Speedway   *99*
Newman/Haas Racing   *82, 83, 87, 90*
Newman, Paul   *74, 82, 83*
Nürburgring   *34, 37, 41, 48*
Official Accident Report – No. 3 Car   **128**, *129,* **131**, *132, 134, 138, 172*
Olvey, Steve   *66, 81–86, 87–91,* **91**, *98, 112, 140, 145, 154, 172, 173*
Ongais, Danny   *5, 84*
On Track (magazine)   *ix, 93, 126*
Orlando Sentinel   *105, 127, 129, 130*
Papis, Max   *76,* **78**, *79, 89, 90, 169, 172*
Passarini, Maurizio   *58, 59*

Patrick, Danica   *98, 142*
Peach Bowl   *7, 8, 9*
Penrose, James   *78*, **145**, *147, 148*
Penske Racing   *80, 81, 162*
Penske, Roger   *50, 76, 94, 117, 119*
Peterson, Steve   *12, 128, 133, 134, 135, 172*
Petty, Adam   *4, 101*
    death of   *99, 100*
Petty, Kyle   *12, 99–102, 104, 106, 108*
Petty, Richard   *100, 105, 111, 125*
Pickett, Greg   *156*
Pierce, John   *85, 103, 174*
Pilgrim, Andy   *117, 119*
Piquet, Nelson   *63*
Pockrass, Bob   *112*
Pocono International Raceway   *103, 112, 142, 153*
Polyethylene Energy Dissipation System (PEDS)   *102*
Portago, Marquis de   **38**, *39, 40, 41, 59*
Poston, Ramsey   *127*
Powell, Jody   *127*
    Powell Tate (agency)   *127, 130*
Prost, Alain   *51, 52, 55, 56*
Raddin, James, Jr.   *127–132*
Rahal, Bobby   *90, 169*
Ratzenberger, Roland   *ix, 54*, **55**, *57, 59, 62, 63, 65, 67, 80, 96*
Redman, Brian   *5*
Reid, John   *127, 128, 130*
Renault, Louis   *34*
Renault, Marcel   *34*
Rice, Buddy   **96**, *98*
Richardson, Dave   *156, 159, 160*
Rickenbacker, Eddie   *34, 36, 37, 157, 173*
Roberts, Fireball   *44*
Robinson, Bill   *100*
Rodriguez, Gonzalo   *76, 77, 79, 82, 86*
    death of   **80**, *81*
Roebuck, Nigel   *48, 51, 173*
Roper, Dean   *104*

Roper, Tony   *104*
Rosemeyer, Bernd   *37*
Russell, Kirk   *82, 83,* **85**, *86, 89, 90, 172, 173*
Rutherford, Johnny   *5, 42, 43*
Sachs, Eddie   *42, 43, 46*
Sadler, Elliott   *142*
Safe Is Fast   *158*
SAFER barrier   *103, 129, 137, 139,* **140, 141**, *142, 153, 155*
Sanchez, Derek   *157, 159*
Schatz, Donnie   *157*
Schroth Safety Products   *149, 164*
Schumacher, Michael   **14**, *51, 56–58, 62, 98, 148*
Schumacher, Ralf   *58, 151*
Senna, Ayrton   *32,* **51**, *52, 55, 56,* **57***, 58, 59, 60, 67, 78, 79*
    death of   *viii, ix, 41, 49, 50, 53, 54, 59, 63, 64, 106, 135, 144*
Sicking, Dean   *127–131, 139, 140*
Simonsen, Allan
    death of   *154, 159*
Simpson Performance Products   *152, 155, 160, 161, 164*
Society of Automotive Engineers (SAE)   *20, 69, 73, 171, 173, 174*
    Conference, 1998   *71*
Sports Car Club of America (SCCA)   *9, 63, 70, 83, 156*
Sports Illustrated   *ix, 15, 121, 156*
Squier, Ken   *38, 157*
Stand 21   *149, 164*
States, John   *25*
Stewart, Jackie   *44–47,* **47***, 49, 53*
Stiles, Mark   *164*
Texas Motor Speedway   *91, 92, 100, 104, 142, 167*
The New York Times   *41, 157, 163*
Trammell, Terry   *66, 80–82, 84,* **86***, 90, 91, 97–99, 112, 132, 146, 154, 172, 174*

United States Auto Club (USAC)   *46*, *47*, *83*, *101*, *104*, *158*
Vanderbilt Cup   *34*, *37*
Vanderbilt, "Willie"   *34*
Villeneuve, Gilles   *51*
   death of   *49*
Villeneuve, Jacques   **96**, *109*, *147*, *148*, *149*
von Trips, Wolfgang   *40*
Waltrip, Darrell   *112*, *113*
Waltrip, Michael   *114*, *117*, *118*, *119*, *173*
Watkins Glen   *3*, *63*, *83*, *96*, *102*, *105*, *113*, *119*
Watkins, Sidney   *51*, *52*, *54*, *55*, *57*, *60*, *62*, *63*, *64*, *66*, *70*, *144*, **146**, *146–150*, *173*
Wayne State University   *20*, *25*, *29*, *68*, *73*
Weatherly, Joe   *45*, *46*
Wendlinger, Karl   *55*, *60*, *61*
Wheeler, H.A. "Humpy"   *109*, *110*, *122*, *128*
Whiting, Charlie   *62*, *65*, *67*, *68*, *69*, *70*
Whitley, David   *129*
Williams, Deb   *133*
Williams, Robert   *31*, *37*
Wilson, Justin   *149*
   death of   *153*
Winston Cup Scene   *133*
Wright, Peter   *67*, *68*, *69*, *70*, *151*
Zanardi, Alessandro "Alex"   *80*, *85*

hans SAFETY TIMELINE

	EVENTS	TECH	RULES	CRASHES	AWARDS
1981	When Jacquemart killed by basal skull fracture at Mid-Ohio, Downing inspires Hubbard to create head/neck restraint.				
1984		Hubbard completes first HANS Device. Model 1 wrap-around style will feature 'Darth Vader' look in black carbon.			
1986	Downing wears HANS Device for first time in competition in IMSA season finale at Daytona.				
1987		First of HANS patents issued for Model 1.			
1988	Actor Paul Newman becomes second driver to wear HANS Device in competition.				
1989		First successful sled test run by Dr. Paul Begeman at Wayne St. University.			
1990	HANS Performance Products (HPP) formed after safety companies decline production of HANS Device.	Production begins on first HANS Device for sale to competitors.		NASCAR's Grant Adcox killed in Atlanta, Neil Bonnett suffers head injury in Darlington crash.	
1991	HANS Device enters market. Custom, hand-made devices cost $3,000 to $5,000 each.	Hubbard presents paper on HANS to Int'l. Conference of Motorsports Sciences.		McDuffie killed at Watkins Glen by basal skull fracture. Powerboat racer Anderson gives first HANS testimonial.	
1994		Dr. John Melvin presents HANS research paper sponsored by GM to Motorsports Engineering Conference.		Bonnett, Rodney Orr killed at Daytona. F1's Ratzenberger dies from basal skull fracture at Imola; Senna killed next day.	
1996	Hubbard, Downing meet with FIA's C. Whiting, P. Wright and H. Gramling of Mercedes-Benz.			Indy 500 pole winner Scott Brayton killed by basal skull fracture during practice.	
1997	Hubbard/Downing agree with Mercedes-Benz on joint development of head and neck restraint.	Mercedes-Benz link results in second generation Model II. Smaller HANS will lead to use in CART, NASCAR, F1.	FIA begins studies, testing that results in Standard 8858 for frontal head restaints.		HANS wins SCCA's George P. Snively award for "outstanding contributions to safety in motorsports."
1999				CART driver Rodriguez killed by basal skull fracture at Laguna. Moore killed at Fontana.	
2000	Fewer than 300 HANS Devices sold in first decade of production.	Testing in CART results in universal shape for HANS after work by Downing/Atlanta fabricator Jerry Lambert.	CART mandates HANS Device on oval tracks for 2001 season. FIA announces HANS mandate.	NASCAR drivers Petty, Irwin killed by basal skull fractures. Roper dies from neck injury.	HANS wins SEMA Motorsports Engineering Award.

180   *Crash!* How the HANS Helped Save Racing

	EVENTS	TECH	RULES	CRASHES	AWARDS
2001	*Charlotte Observer* study of racing deaths: most occur on short ovals, drag strips.		NASCAR mandates head and neck restraints for Cup drivers in October. Vast majority choose HANS.	Earnhardt killed in Daytona 500 in February. ARCA's Alexander dies from basal skull fracture in Charlotte.	HANS wins Louis Schwitzer Award for innovation and excellence, CART Award for dramatic safety improvement.
2002	Melvin paper on comparison sled test of HANS/no HANS presented at SAE Conference.	Agreement reached with Schroth, Stand 21 to license HANS manufacturing and sales in Europe.		Hearn's wife writes thank you note to HPP after IRL driver survives 139-G impact at Kentucky oval.	
2003	Improved production and sizing techniques lower HANS Device cost to $1,650.	After seat angles, HPP introduces standard shoulder sizing for better fit of all drivers.	FIA mandates HANS for F1 under Standard 8858 three years after initial announcement.		HANS wins F1 Special Safety Award.
2004	SFI's spec 38.1 established for head restraints. Includes neck tension and compression testing.	HANS posts best results in SFI 38.1 testing. Original strap-based Hutchens device fails.	NASCAR rejects all other head restraints, mandates "HANS only" for NASCAR's three major traveling series for 2005.		*Car and Driver* hails HANS as "The best safety device since the seat belt."
2006	New production techniques allow HANS Device Pro cost to be reduced to $995.		NHRA, IHRA announce SFI 38.1 head restraints to be required in 2007 for fastest classes.	NHRA's Ron Krishner survives crash and roll at U.S. Nationals with HANS Device.	
2007	Hubbard begins consulting contract with NASA to design HANS for astronauts.		HANS Device becomes mandatory for all FIA world championships.	FIA credits HANS with helping to save Kubica's life at Canadian Grand Prix.	Hubbard, Downing win Autosport's Pioneering and Innovation Award.
2008	Injection-molded Sport Series HANS introduced for weekend warriors at $695.	Sliding Tether system provides full range of vision for all drivers.		NASCAR's Jeff Gordon walks away from heavy crash in Las Vegas.	
2009	HANS sales exceed 100,000 units worldwide.	Conway's Indy crash confirms HANS Device Extension improves rear collision safety.	FIA mandates Standard 8858 for all events listed on its International Sporting Calendar.		
2010	HPP introduces Sport II made from organic DuPont polymer to reduce weight, improve fit.	NASA's first test of HANS restraint for astronauts at Wright Petterson AFB a success.		NASCAR's Sadler survives huge impact at Pocono. Pickett survives Porsche crash at Mid-Ohio. Both credit HANS.	
2011	*Charlotte Observer* cites increase in racing deaths in 10 years after Earnhardt's crash, mostly on short tracks and drag strips.			Audi's Rockenfeller walks away from head-on crash at Le Mans.	Hubbard wins President's Award from Michigan Automobile Racing Fan Club.
2012	HPP sold to Simpson Performance Products.		New mandates for SFI 38.1 include SCCA club racers, NHRA classes of Top Dragster, Comp and Top Sportsman.		Downing elected to Sebring Hall of Fame.

Crash! How the HANS Helped Save Racing